THE DEPARTMENT CHAIR AS
TRANSFORMATIVE DIVERSITY LEADER

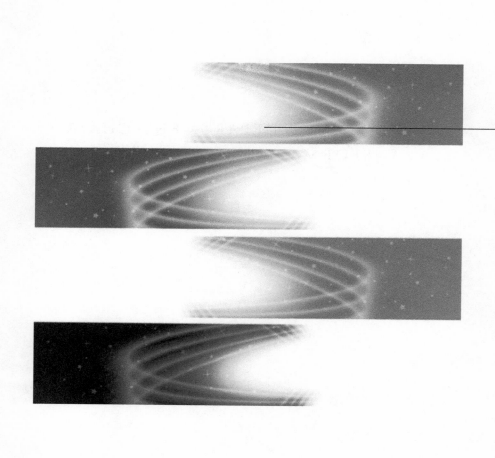

THE DEPARTMENT CHAIR AS TRANSFORMATIVE DIVERSITY LEADER

Building Inclusive Learning Environments in Higher Education

Edna Chun and Alvin Evans

Foreword by

Walter H. Gmelch

STERLING, VIRGINIA

COPYRIGHT © 2015 BY STYLUS
PUBLISHING, LLC.

Published by Stylus Publishing, LLC
22883 Quicksilver Drive
Sterling, Virginia 20166-2102

Library of Congress Control Number: 2014952708

13-digit ISBN: 978-1-62036-237-2 (cloth)
13-digit ISBN: 978-1-62036-238-9 (paperback)
13-digit ISBN: 978-1-62036-239-6 (library networkable e-edition)
13-digit ISBN: 978-1-62036-240-2 (consumer e-edition)

Printed in the United States of America

All first editions printed on acid-free paper
that meets the American National Standards Institute
Z39-48 Standard.

Bulk Purchases

Quantity discounts are available for use in workshops and for
staff development.
Call 1-800-232-0223

First Edition, 2015

10

We dedicate this book to our children—Alexander David Chun, Shomari Evans, Jabari Evans, Kalil Evans, and Rashida VanLeer—who are the inspiration for the study and for continuing the struggle toward the attainment of truly inclusive educational institutions.

CONTENTS

ILLUSTRATIONS

Tables

Figures

Exercise

"The academic chair stands at the crossroads of diversity transformation in higher education today." The authors, Edna Chun and Alvin Evans, begin this text with this passage. Throughout the book they astutely provide direction, strategies, and means by which academic leaders can navigate the road to transform their departments and achieve inclusive excellence.

This term, *inclusive excellence*, represents a powerful rubric and conceptual framework the authors use to advance diversity in institutions of higher education. They open and conclude their book with the challenge of not only transforming academic departments but also focusing on student intellectual and social development and competencies needed to function in a global society.

The literature on academic leadership and diversity is silent. Although a proliferation of new books has been published on the challenges and skills needed to effectively lead a department, none of these books have directly addressed the issue of building an inclusive department and advancing diversity. This book moves well beyond the usual book on diversity or department chair development. It blends the two into a powerful and authoritative resource guide for academic leaders: (a) a conceptual framework for understanding the importance and challenge of diversity, and (b) practical strategies gleaned from their qualitative research with department chairs. It is a compendium of important insights and essential information for championing the cause of diversity and effective leadership.

As the authors point out, "One of the primary problems for department chairs seeking to implement new diversity realities is to move beyond rhetoric to action." This book perfectly blends theory with practice: the theoretical underpinnings leaders need to understand the challenges of inclusive excellence and the practical advice to foster and develop departmental action plans for diversity. At the end of chapters 2 through 7, the reader is provided a "Concluding Perspectives" section with strategies for action. A wealth of citations and resources are also cataloged and made available for department chairs' personal action plans.

Diversity represents an elusive concept that begs for an academic and operational definition. It represents the blind man and elephant parable; no one quite knows what diversity is and why it is integrally connected with educational mission. Because everyone defines it differently, it is not seen as an imperative. The interviews conducted by the authors, however, illuminate how *diversity* is defined and operationalized within the academic department through the lens of department chairs. Unfortunately, some department chairs do not see the need for diversity or its importance in the core curriculum, in the effectiveness of department chairs, in the hiring of qualified faculty, or in the mentoring of students as they form their identity. It is not enough for department chairs to passively accept diversity; they need to advance and champion it.

As pointed out by Chun and Evans in chapter 8, even for those enlightened department chairs, creating and sustaining change can stall for several reasons: (a) the challenge of implementing a systems-based approach to diversity that transcends hit-or-miss sporadic efforts, (b) the fact that strategic diversity transformation requires systematic and sustained organizational learning processes, and (c) the almost exclusive focus of many faculty and administrators on representational diversity as an end in itself, causing substantial pushback. Let me add a few questions you might ponder when you read this book and assess your ability to create and sustain change:

- Have you, as a department chair or dean, made a clear and compelling case for why you should pursue this agenda (e.g., inclusive excellence)?
- Do you have support of your senior administrators: dean, provost, president?
- Are your faculty change leaders involved, and do they support the agenda and initiative?
- Do you have supportive structures, incentives, and resources to support the change initiative?
- Do you have a clear plan to celebrate your diversity initiative's "small wins" to begin to change your culture?
- Do your department and institution have a climate of goodwill and trust?
- Will you, as an academic leader, stay long enough to sustain the change?

The authors insightfully address the instrumental leadership role of deans and provosts in setting the direction for diversity progress, shaping overall climate, influencing the pace of change, building accountability structures, and creating incentives for positive change. However, the average length of tenure of provosts (five years) and deans (six years) does not bode well for sustained change. These leaders are integral in terms of conveying authentic commitment to diversity and ensuring accountability. Also, department chairs typically come to their position without leadership training, without prior academic leadership experience, without a clear understanding of the chair's critical and complex roles, and without effective succession planning between leaders in transition. The time of amateur administration is over. This book addresses key concepts and strategies imperative for effective departments.

It is difficult for me to envision any authors more qualified than Edna Chun and Alvin Evans to address one of the most important topics in higher education today. Not only do they possess mature thinking and an investigative mind-set, but also their study is richly enhanced by department chair testimonials that provide personal insights and tried-and-true strategies to advance the diversity agenda. I recommend this splendid book without a single reservation to not only department chairs but also deans and provosts who are, or should be, serious about building inclusive excellence in their institutions.

—Walter H. Gmelch,
Former Dean and Professor of Leadership Studies,
University of San Francisco

ACKNOWLEDGMENTS

We would like to express our deep appreciation to John von Knorring, president of Stylus Publishing, for his vision and extraordinary commitment to the realization of diversity and inclusion in higher education. We thank the academic department chairs who shared their perspectives with us in the survey and interviews and whose courage and innovative spirit are reflected in the narratives in this study.

We would like to express our sincere gratitude to Professor Joe Feagin, Ella C. McFadden professor of sociology at Texas A&M University, for his generosity, encouragement, and invaluable suggestions throughout the evolution of the manuscript. We especially thank Dr. Walter H. Gmelch, professor of leadership studies at the University of San Francisco, for his great help and support of this project. In addition, we would like to express our appreciation to Dr. Charles Behling of the University of Michigan's Program on Intergroup Relations (retired) and Professor Earl Smith of Wake Forest University (retired) for sharing their in-depth expertise and insights on the chair role.

We would like to express our appreciation to Bryan Cook, senior vice president for institutional capacity building at the American Dental Educational Association for his generous help. We also thank Kimberly Rosenfeld for her highly skilled and responsive research assistance throughout the course of the project. In addition, we would like to thank Alexander D. Chun for his valuable work in the development of the online survey.

We would like to express special appreciation to our family, mentors, and friends for their continuous support. Alvin Evans would like to thank Ethel and Horace Bush, Patricia and Leon Scott, Karen and Hassan Rogers, Patricia and Donald Marsh, Brian and Lisa Marshall, Victoria Thomas, and Lesley Green. Edna Chun would like to express her appreciation to Trustees Levi Williams Esq. and Georgette Sosa Douglass Esq. for their visionary leadership of diversity at Broward College over the last decade. She would also like to thank Jay Kyung Chun, Alexander D. Chun, David and Laura Tosi Chu, George and Eleanor Chu, Ronnie Rothschild, and Karen Williams.

I

PRELUDE

Successful academic leaders must be able to create and foster partnerships, bringing diverse individuals and interests together around a shared vision and mission based on common values.

—Stanley Ikenberry (2013, p. xix)

The academic chair stands at the crossroads of diversity transformation in higher education today. The role of the academic department chair in creating diverse and inclusive learning environments is arguably the most pivotal position in colleges and universities. As institutions of higher education seek to prepare students for citizenship in a global, knowledge-based society, the department chair is positioned uniquely to impact diversity progress. Chairs represent the nexus or intersection between the faculty and the administration and are at the core of the student academic experience. Research indicates that the department chair makes more than 80% of academic decisions such as those regarding appointments, curricula, tenure and promotion, classroom pedagogy, and student outcomes in consultation with the faculty (Gmelch & Miskin, 2011). Yet the academic leader, and in particular the department chair, is one of the least studied and frequently misunderstood management positions in the United States (Gmelch, 2004).

In the United States, dramatic increases in minority student enrollment coupled with the emergence of a minority majority American nation by 2042 create an urgent mandate for change within the heart of academic institutions. The rapidly accelerating shift in the demographics of the student body challenges the notion that educational institutions do not need to consider diversity in their programs, practices, and pedagogies. Consider these statistics:

- According to a report issued by the Western Interstate Commission for Higher Education (2012), minority students will account for 45% of the nation's public high school graduates by 2020.

1

- Between 1976 and 2010, the percentage of White college students declined from 83% to 61%, whereas the percentage of minorities doubled from 14% to 33% (National Center for Education Statistics, n.d.).
- Latino students are the fastest growing student population and by 2011 had attained a record 16.5% of all college enrollments, paralleling their representation in the U.S. population (Fry & Lopez, 2012).
- The number of Hispanic and Latino students graduating with an associate's or bachelor's degree has increased sevenfold over the past four decades, outpacing the graduation rate of other groups (Fry & Lopez, 2012).

Table 1.1 depicts the increasing percentages of minorities enrolled as undergraduates in the institutional types included in our study between 2001 and 2011.

Minority students now represent approximately one third of the total enrollment in these institutional types. The overall changes by demographic group are vividly depicted in Figure 1.1.

If this enrollment trend continues, perhaps within two decades, more than half of the undergraduate student population will be minority-majority. Few educational administrators are prepared for the sweeping implications of this demographic shift. Rather it may be the expectation that diverse students must assimilate and fit into the existing framework of White-dominated practices, norms, and programs. Given that the policies and practices of most institutions are based on a dominant White culture, we know already that minority students are likely to experience greater cultural dissonance than their White counterparts and may be inclined to seek out ethnic subcultures on their campuses (Jayakumar & Museus, 2012).

Yet despite the rapidly shifting demography in student populations, one of the most striking aspects of leadership in colleges and universities is the relative absence of racial and ethnic diversity in top administrative positions in public and private research universities, as well as in four-year colleges. A pictorial display published in the *Chronicle of Higher Education* of the individuals in the highest levels of university administration in the Ivy League (Brown, Columbia, Cornell, Dartmouth, Harvard, University of Pennsylvania, Princeton, and Yale) reveals that most academic leaders in these prestigious institutions are White and male (Patton, 2013).

In doctorate-granting institutions, provosts or chief academic officers (CAOs) are predominantly White (85%) and male, with women composing only 32% of CAO positions (Eckel, Cook, & King, 2009). A relatively

TABLE 1.1

Percentage Change in Demographics of Undergraduate Enrollment From 2001 to 2011

| | Institution Type | | | | | | |
| | Private | | | Public | | | |
Demographic	Bacc.	Master's	Research/Doctorate	Bacc.	Master's	Research/Doctorate	Total
American Indian or Alaska Native men (n)	60	113	133	35	242	484	1,067
% change	0.0	59.2	64.2	-2.8	-5.1	9.0	
% of total	0.1	0.2	0.1	0.2	0.3	0.2	
American Indian or Alaska Native women (n)	74	89	114	38	254	525	1,094
% change	138.7	50.8	178.0	8.6	33.0	50.4	
% of total	0.2	0.2	0.1	0.2	0.3	0.2	
Asian American/Pacific Islander men (n)	1,039	1,576	8,251	554	4,183	17,618	33,221
% change	21.5	44.6	91.7	45.0	31.9	54.4	
% of total	2.2	2.7	7.1	3.5	4.7	7.3	

(continues)

TABLE 1.1
Percentage Change in Demographics of Undergraduate Enrollment From 2001 to 2011 (Continued)

| | Institution Type | | | | | | |
| | Private | | | Public | | | |
Demographic	Bacc.	Master's	Research/Doctorate	Bacc.	Master's	Research/Doctorate	Total
Asian American/Pacific Islander women (n)	**964**	**1,203**	**5,145**	**329**	**2,606**	**8,699**	**18,946**
% change	91.7	107.4	184.9	79.8	94.6	109.9	
% of total	2.0	2.0	4.4	2.1	2.9	3.6	
Black or African American men (n)	**1,601**	**1,120**	**2,198**	**585**	**3,066**	**4,630**	**13,200**
% change	11.6	43.8	14.4	7.3	11.2	12.5	
% of total	3.4	1.9	1.9	3.7	3.4	1.9	
Black or African American women (n)	**1,894**	**1,460**	**2,447**	**601**	**3,355**	**4,810**	**14,567**
% change	47.7	82.0	61.3	34.2	26.2	28.0	
% of total	4.0	2.5	2.1	3.8	3.8	2.0	

(continues)

Hispanic or Latino men (n)	1,038	1,198	2,685	685	1,934	5,483	13,023
% change	46.4	41.9	72.2	−23.6	36.8	37.5	
% of total	2.2	2.0	2.3	4.4	2.2	2.3	
Hispanic or Latina women (n)	1,136	1,299	2,288	712	1,776	4,464	11,675
% change	65.1	56.1	100.0	−18.8	65.7	54.5	
% of total	2.4	2.2	2.0	4.6	2.0	1.8	
White men (n)	21,215	25,561	50,434	6,199	35,784	103,776	242,969
% change	1.9	16.1	20.3	0.6	−6.1	−0.6	
% of total	44.5	43.2	43.5	39.7	40.1	42.8	
White women (n)	16,529	22,584	29,132	4,991	31,546	67,556	172,338
% change	29.4	44.4	52.4	26.4	20.6	28.5	
% of total	34.7	38.2	25.1	32.0	35.4	27.9	

Source. Data from U.S. Department of Education, 2012, Washington, DC: National Center for Education Statistics, Integrated Postsecondary Education System. Analysis by authors.

Note. Bacc. = Baccalaureate.

Figure 1.1. Graph of demographic change in undergraduate enrollment between 2001 and 2011.

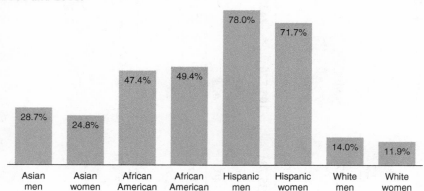

Source. Data from U.S. Department of Education, 2012, Washington, DC: National Center for Education Statistics, Integrated Postsecondary Education System. Analysis by authors.

small number of minorities have attained this academic leadership role: Only 6% are African American, 4% are Hispanic, 2% are Asian American, 1% is American Indian, and 1% reported race/ethnicity as other (Eckel et al., 2009). And between 2008 and 2013, a survey of 149 four-year institutions found that the percentages of Black, Asian, and Hispanic provosts had actually declined (Stripling, 2013). Because the provost role remains the chief pathway to the presidency, with 34% of presidents having previously served as CAOs, this lack of diversity is troubling (see Kiley, 2012, for review).

In fact, Whites hold close to 85% of the top-ranked academic and administrative positions in doctorate-granting institutions, and males hold 66% (King & Gomez, 2008). In the administrative leadership ranks, 90% of chief financial officers are White and 68% are male (National Association of College and University Business Officers, 2010). Furthermore, as Bryan Cook, former director of policy analysis at the American Council of Education, indicated, the lack of racial and ethnic diversity at 149 four-year colleges has persisted for 25 years (Patton, 2013). Cook also observed that institutions rarely replace a minority administrator with another when he or she leaves (Patton, 2013).

Although little research has been conducted on the demographics of deans and department chairs, available studies have suggested that most incumbents in these positions also are White males. For example, a survey of nearly 800 deans at 360 colleges in education, business, nursing, and liberal arts found that 41% were women and 12% were minority, half of whom were African American. Despite the high participation of women in the survey, the normal distribution pattern of deans tends to be approximately 25% female (Wolverton & Gmelch, 2002). The largest representation of minority deans in the study was in education (35%) and liberal arts (31%), with only 13% in business and 2% in nursing (Wolverton & Gmelch, 2002). Of particular relevance to our study is the finding that minority deans experienced greater stress relating to their interactions with the provost and also reported shorter tenure in their positions (Wolverton & Gmelch, 2002).

And to compound the picture, data from the survey we conducted of department chairs for this book indicate that roughly 90% of chairs are White, and the majority of these individuals are male. Narratives of minority, female, and lesbian, gay, bisexual, and transgender (LGBT) chairs in our study reveal that in many institutions, barriers still exist for diverse individuals in these positions seeking to operate on a level playing field within a normative White culture.

The Pivotal Role of Department Chairs in Advancing Diversity

Why is department chair leadership so critical in advancing diversity? As Stanley Ikenberry's quote at the beginning of this chapter suggests, the academic department crystallizes the mission and transmits the fundamental values of colleges and universities. Given its strategic location, the academic department can serve as a fulcrum for diversity change within the institution as a whole. Emanating from the academic core, departmental diversity practices radiate throughout the broader concentric circles composed of the college or professional school, the academic affairs division, and the institution.

First and foremost, the academic department represents a focal point in the student's experience of diversity in the legendary "ivory tower." The department is the main place that defines a student's academic experience (Esterberg & Wooding, 2012). The concrete ways that chairs frame everyday experiences influence student engagement and perceptions of the institution's climate for diversity. Social theorist Joe Feagin emphasized that "concepts delineating and probing racism need to be clear and honed by everyday experience, not framed from an ivory tower" (Feagin, 2010, p. xii). The student's day-to-day experience with diversity in the academic department coalesces in multiple dimensions: interactions with faculty, curricular content, advising, classroom experiences, cocurricular activities, and research opportunities.

The chair sets the tone for a departmental environment that supports student access, identity development, academic orientation, and degree progress and attainment. He or she can champion innovative pedagogies and modes of interaction that create inclusive classroom experiences for diverse students and stimulate learning outcomes that broaden perspectives on difference. In essence, the department chair is a key player who mediates the student's experience of diversity in these contiguous spheres. He or she is a boundary spanner, working between the formal organization and the groups surrounding the organization (Chu, 2006). We shall elaborate further on this boundary-spanning role in chapter 3.

Chairs are also influential in the career progress of diverse faculty and staff. They can be a catalyst for improvement by building a climate that welcomes and respects the contributions of diverse faculty and students (Buller, 2010). For example, chairs can cultivate relationships with diverse feeder groups and academic networks to identify potential candidates for vacant positions, appoint faculty personnel and search committees, and help newly hired diverse candidates to establish themselves and start their research agenda (Silver, 2002). The chair's role in mentoring diverse tenure-track faculty is crucial in terms of providing feedback, sharing unwritten norms and rules, and helping faculty navigate the process of "white water rafting" that characterizes the seven-year tenure process (Evans & Chun, 2007, p. 79).

As tenured faculty, chairs operate with significant autonomy and independence yet must sometimes pursue diversity efforts amid changing academic leadership, without clear support or needed resources. They can lead, stimulate, and even spearhead change efforts, but they still need faculty collaboration to do so. They are called on to mediate and mitigate potential conflicts, mentor junior faculty, and implement curricular change. Wearing many hats, they serve as representatives of faculty interests to upper administration yet must build consensus and collegiality at the departmental level.

Despite the chair's broad portfolio of responsibilities, his or her influence and power may be limited in some respects. In a culture of peer collegiality, the chair's chief tactical resources often consist of persuasion and influence rather than hierarchical power. One study of 23 department chairs revealed that the chair's highest priority was to establish and maintain harmonious relations within the department, and the preferred style for attaining this harmony was "appeaser" (Hubbell & Homer, 1997, p. 211). Supporting these findings, a study of 126 faculty in a major southwestern university correlated positive faculty satisfaction with effective collegial techniques rather than authoritarian compliance-gaining techniques (Roach, 1991). Emphasis on legitimate authority and threats and punishment were found detrimental to faculty satisfaction (Roach, 1991). Another study that included five department chairs indicated that none of the chairs found glory in being a chair, and few identified increased income as an incentive (Esterberg & Wooding, 2012). As a result, the role appears to have no sticks and few carrots (Esterberg & Wooding, 2012).

Because of rotating responsibilities and defined terms of service, chairs may be able to implement change efforts only over the short term. Of the roughly 80,000 chairs in the United States, approximately one fourth will need to be replaced each year (Gmelch, Reason, Schuh, & Shelley, 2002). As we will discuss further in chapter 3, the chair's impact is dependent on his or her ability to negotiate change within the complexities of the administrative hierarchy. And the limited compensation provided to chairs in some institutions can deter faculty from continued service in a role that detracts from the time needed for scholarly research.

Critical Need for the Study and Research Design

Discussion of the chair's leadership in diversity in the research literature is remarkably sparse, fragmented, and anecdotal. Almost without exception, existing guides or primers for academic department chairs either only briefly touch on the chair's role in diversity or simply omit it altogether (see, e.g., Buller, 2012; Chu, 2006; Cipriano, 2011; Leaming, 2006; Lucas, 1994; Wheeler et al., 2008). Although many of these resources are focused on providing practical advice to chairs, the lack of attention to diversity as a major component of chair leadership is striking and represents a major gap in the existing literature.

This study was conducted specifically to explore the ways in which the department chair can contribute to diversity progress within the department, school, and college or university and to share successful strategies and approaches developed by chairs. As a result, the goal of this book is twofold: (a) to identify prevalent challenges to inclusion that persist within the everyday life of the academy and (b) to illuminate strategies within the academic department that contribute to diversity transformation and the representational vitality of institutions of higher education.

Our interviews with chairs across the nation suggest that the academic department chair likely will be the engine of change in diversity progress in higher education today. The models, perspectives, and research shared here are designed to enable department chairs, deans, faculty, members of faculty governance bodies, presidents, boards of trustees, executive officers, diversity leaders and practitioners, HR professionals, researchers, and governance task forces to

- assess the current level of progress in diversity attainment within academic departments and disciplines,
- address common procedural and behavioral barriers to diversity within the day-to-day departmental environment,

- evaluate environmental factors both external and internal to the department that can hinder or accentuate diversity progress, and
- determine appropriate pathways for the advancement of diverse and talented faculty in light of the predominant underrepresentation of women and minority chairs, deans, and provosts.

At the conclusion of each chapter, we offer specific examples of action-oriented strategies and approaches that will assist chairs in building more inclusive learning and working environments.

Research Focus

Although definitions of *diversity* vary considerably, our primary focus is on the dimensions of race/ethnicity, gender, and sexual orientation based on the salience of these attributes in historical patterns of discrimination in the United States. The physical identifiability of race and gender are intertwined with long-standing patterns of discrimination (Aguirre & Turner, 1998). And individuals with invisible stigma such as LGBT employees face the dilemma of whether to disclose their identity, causing psychological conflict and stress. Furthermore, the intersectionality of the attributes of race, gender, and sexual orientation can create multiple jeopardies for affected individuals in the workplace (see Chun & Evans, 2012, for review). Nonetheless, a broader picture of diversity does include an array of characteristics that have been termed *secondary dimensions* and represent socially acquired characteristics such as class, geographic location, educational background, and marital status (see, e.g., Hubbard, 2004; Roberson, 2006). For the most part, we use the terms *dominant* and *nondominant* in this study rather than *majority* or *minority* to expand the discussion beyond race and gender and include those groups who have traditionally had less power in organizational settings, such as LGBT individuals and individuals with disabilities (Ragins, 2007).

A particular area of focus in our research is on the differential experiences faced by chairs who are members of nondominant groups in their efforts to promote diversity and the resulting intergroup power dynamic among senior faculty. Almost no empirical literature gauges the difficulties that department chairs from nondominant groups face when leading a department composed of dominant group members (see, e.g., E. Smith, 1996). We share a number of striking accounts of exclusionary challenges faced by chairs of nondominant groups and the opposition they have faced in largely majority departments. Such accounts underscore the price of exclusion of women and minorities within the leadership ranks of institutions of higher education. Not only do the individuals who are marginalized and oppressed suffer, but the institution also fails to realize the benefit of the knowledge, innovation, and creativity that these leaders bring to their work. And a society that ignores the wealth of human knowledge and creativity "irresponsibly risks its future" (Feagin, 2010, p. 309).

Survey and Interview Process

For purposes of the study, we conducted an online survey with a sample of 98 department chairs from public and private undergraduate colleges, master's-level universities, and research universities in all geographic regions. Because of the somewhat different challenges in the community college environment, these institutions were not included in the study. The narratives of chairs across a broad array of disciplines provide contrast and depth to this portrait. Chairs in disciplines that have a more defined tie to diversity such as sociology, psychology, English, foreign languages and literatures, journalism, educational leadership, and counseling education appear to have had greater opportunity to integrate diversity in their approaches to the curriculum. For an analysis of the survey participants by discipline, geographic region, and institutional type, see Appendix A.

Although the broad spectrum of types of institutions in the survey does present substantial differences in the contextual landscape, our intent is to identify predominant themes and common challenges faced by chairs in creating more diverse teaching, learning, and working environments. As this is the first study of its kind, we felt it was important to synthesize the major issues and opportunities that chairs perceive in operationalizing diversity within the academic department.

Initial contacts inviting chairs to participate were made through a department chair newsletter list, as well as through LinkedIn invitations. The majority of the online survey respondents declined the follow-up interview, perhaps because of time and workload constraints or perhaps because in certain environments implementing diversity initiatives may still be contested terrain. A subset of the participants (10) that at first agreed to the follow-up interview either were not available, did not respond to the e-mail invitation sent to them on two occasions, or indicated that they could not allocate the time needed. Thirty-one chairs participated in telephone interviews that lasted from 30 minutes to over 1 hour and consisted of an open-ended set of questions, as well as several vignettes designed to elicit the observations of the participants.

Our survey sample includes 54 males and 44 females, suggesting that, unlike the provost position, women faculty have begun to make significant inroads into this administrative position. In terms of race, 78 chairs or 80%

of the sample are White, with 11 African Americans, 5 Asians or Asian Americans, and 4 individuals of two or more races. Two of the individuals reporting two or more races indicated that one of the races is Native American. The representation of African Americans, however, includes 3 chairs from historically Black colleges and universities. In terms of ethnicity, only 5 Hispanic/Latino chairs responded to the survey.

In addition, 56 chairs provided data on the number of chairs in their schools or colleges, indicating that of a total of 1,641 chairs, 236 individuals (10%) of the total chair population in their institutions are either minorities or of Hispanic ethnicity. Given the limited data available on chair demographics, these new data shed light on the predominant demographic makeup of the department chair tier. The small number of minority chairs is a matter of significant concern as institutions seek to create a representative academic bureaucracy and provide role models and mentors for increasingly diverse student populations.

Chairs also reported the demographics of their deans, and these statistics reveal an even greater representation of White males in the dean's position than in the chair's role. The sample includes 57 males and 41 females. Ninety-two of the deans are White, 5 are African American, and none of the deans are Asian or Asian American. Interestingly, 8 deans are of Hispanic/ Latino ethnicity, a much more significant representation than among the chairs themselves. In terms of sexual orientation, 88 of the survey participants (90%) indicated that they are heterosexual, 4 individuals (4%) indicated that they are lesbian or gay, 1 individual (1%) reported as bisexual, and 5 individuals (5%) did not report their sexual orientation.

Our study of the chair's role in diversity also addresses the instrumental leadership role of deans and provosts in setting the direction for diversity progress, shaping overall climate, influencing the pace of change, building accountability structures, and creating incentives for positive change. As academic leaders, deans and provosts can lead and insist on a diversity agenda in terms of hiring practices, research opportunities, curricular change, and recognition and rewards for concrete attainments. From this perspective, we believe that the approaches highlighted in this study will necessarily implicate the work of chief diversity officers, HR professionals, and university executives in their efforts to develop overarching diversity strategy and to ensure equitable outcomes in organizational processes.

Through the findings of the survey and follow-up interviews, we were able to gain a firsthand look at the challenges chairs face in their efforts to spearhead diversity change. We were impressed by the innovation, scholarship, and commitment of chairs who are engaged in the development of progressive approaches to diversity that will lead toward more inclusive campus environments.

A Conceptual Framework for Diversity Transformation

To begin the study, we first consider the conceptual foundation for diversity transformation. The concept of "inclusive excellence" introduced through the Association of American Colleges and Universities a decade ago offers a guiding principle for institutional diversity transformation that has been adopted widely by colleges and universities. Inclusive excellence counters the frequent argument that diversity and quality are antithetical by instead positing that diversity and quality form an alloy that is different from its constituent elements, yet is stronger and more durable (Clayton-Pedersen & Musil, 2005).

Of special relevance to the themes of this book is the emphasis of inclusive excellence on student learning and success through four primary elements: (a) student intellectual and social development, (b) purposeful development of institutional resources to enhance student learning, (c) attention to cultural differences that students bring to the educational experience, and (d) a welcoming community that engages diversity in student and organizational learning (Clayton-Pedersen & Musil, 2005). The four strands of inclusive excellence offer a persuasive argument for the centrality of the academic department in the student experience of diversity on college campuses.

With inclusive excellence as a unifying principle, a change model for higher education requires a data-driven framework that will enable institutions to strategically align their diversity change vision and planning with internal structures and processes (Williams, Berger, & McClendon, 2005). This framework operates bidirectionally from the institution to the department and vice versa. Furthermore, it serves as a springboard enabling the institution to be responsive to pressing external realities and to maximize its talent resources and innovative capacity. Most important, this framework provides the impetus for activating intentional change in a strategic, evidence-based, and systemic manner that emphasizes accountability (Williams, 2013).

The most widely used model in higher education is the framework developed by Daryl Smith that addresses the progressive attainment of diversity in terms of four key dimensions: student access and success, institutional climate and intergroup relations, education and scholarship, and institutional viability and vitality (D. G. Smith, 2009) (see Figure 1.2). These dimensions enhance institutional capacity to function in a diverse environment, capitalize on diversity's benefits, address persistent inequities, and create viable structures that not only serve the institution but also link the institution's core values and purposes with society's needs (D. G. Smith, 2009). The strategic diversity framework is outward looking and informed by larger global trends and social needs, while locating responsibility for diversity across all units to transform the institution as a whole (Clayton-Pedersen, Parker, Smith, Moreno, & Teraguchi, 2007).

In a similar vein, the strategic diversity goals model advanced by Damon Williams places four goals in a pyramid model with access and equity at the top of the pyramid and a multicultural and inclusive campus climate at the center of the pyramid, symbolizing the need to foster a climate in which every faculty and staff member, administrator, and student can thrive (Williams, 2013). The pyramid also includes two additional dimensions: preparing students for a diverse and global world, and domestic and international diversity research and scholarship (Williams, 2013).

The extent to which diversity programs are both localized and pervasive throughout the institution are measures of whether an institution has attained a common institutional diversity vision (Knox & Teraguchi, 2005). Building on Williams's concept of the centrality of an inclusive campus climate to diversity progress, the department is the cultural milieu that shapes how diverse individuals are supported and welcomed, the way conflicts are resolved, and how power is distributed (Evans & Chun, 2007). Given the decentralized structure of universities with varying microclimates and cultures, the experiences of diverse chairs, faculty, and staff can reflect very different realities depending on how power is operationalized in the departmental setting.

In the chapter, we will focus on the social backdrop that shapes educational access and success for diverse students and explore the ways in which exclusionary social forces can be replicated within the walls of higher education. This socioeconomic portrait provides a powerful argument for the pressing need for enhancing diversity and inclusion in the academic department.

Figure 1.2.   Framework for evaluating diversity.

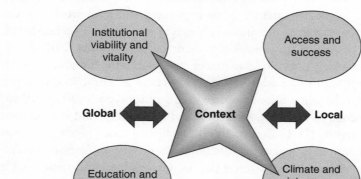

Source. A. R. Clayton-Pedersen, S. Parker, D. G. Smith, J. F. Moreno, and D. H. Teraguchi, 2007, *Making a Real Difference With Diversity: A Guide to Institutional Change,* Washington, DC: Association of American Colleges and Universities, p. 15.

To conclude the chapter, we offer a diversity self-assessment profile (Exercise 1.1) for chairs that will lay the groundwork for formulation of a specific, departmental action plan for diversity progress.

Exercise 1.1. Chair Diversity Self-Assessment Profile

Directions: This profile will assist the chair in assessing the extent and scope of your efforts to embed diversity within the department's work. Use the following scale to gauge the incorporation of diversity into your current role and responsibilities as applicable. The size of the department may determine the opportunity to implement certain dimensions such as hiring of new faculty.

Rating scale: 1 = *not applicable,* 2 = *incipient efforts,* 3 = *sporadic efforts,* 4 = *sustained efforts*

Domain	Dimension	Self-Assessment	Comment
Classroom	Promoting inclusive pedagogies		
	Providing support for marginalizing experiences of diverse faculty members		
	Assessing negative student evaluations in light of diversity issues		
Curriculum	Initiating conversations about curricular revisions to include diversity perspectives, research methods, or other aspects of diversity		
	Incorporating diversity into curricular offerings		
Research agenda	Encouraging research on diversity-related topics		
	Providing support for diversity-related and cross-cultural research in the tenure process		

(continues)

Domain	Dimension	Self-Assessment	Comment
Departmental climate	Providing day-to-day support for an inclusive work environment		
	Conducting inclusive faculty meetings		
	Ensuring inclusion of diverse faculty in departmental decision making		
	Ensuring equitable resource distribution		
	Providing support for socialization and network formation for diverse faculty members		
Recruitment and hiring of diverse faculty	Forming diverse search committees		
	Targeting outreach to diverse applicants		
	Providing concrete progress in remedying underrepresentation		
Retention of minority and female tenure-track faculty	Promoting faculty development that strengthens promotion and tenure attainment		
	Providing informal and formal mentoring		
	Providing supportive feedback on pretenure faculty evaluation		
	Assisting with research agendas of diverse faculty		

Domain	Dimension	Self-Assessment	Comment
Student development	Offering educational and psychosocial support for diverse students		
	Developing interest in departmental major through recruitment and outreach to diverse students		
Cocurricular activities	Providing inclusive cocurricular opportunities		
	Addressing diversity in symposia, forums, and learning communities		
Overall Assessment			

Synopsis

In what domains have you made the most progress? _____

The least? _____

For the areas of least progress, what are the principal barriers (e.g., resources, internal resistance, leadership support)? _____

_____

_____

What steps or factors could help you overcomes these barriers?

_____

_____

For the areas in which you have the greatest success, what factors helped you most?

_____

_____

How could you apply these factors to the areas in which you made the least progress?

_____

_____

References

Aguirre, A., Jr., & Turner, J. H. (1998). *American ethnicity: The dynamics and consequences of discrimination* (2nd ed.). Boston, MA: McGraw-Hill.

Buller, J. L. (2010). *Zen and the art of higher education administration.* Retrieved November 29, 2013, from http://www.ferris.edu/HTMLS/administration/academicaffairs/extendedinternational/ccleadership/faculty/reportacademicleadershipqualities.pdf

Buller, J. L. (2012). *The essential department chair: A comprehensive desk reference.* San Francisco, CA: Jossey-Bass.

Chu, D. (2006). *The department chair primer: What chairs need to know and do to make a difference.* San Francisco, CA: Jossey-Bass.

Chun, E., & Evans, A. (2012). *Diverse administrators in peril: The new indentured class in higher education.* Boulder, CO: Paradigm.

Cipriano, R. E. (2011). *Facilitating a collegial department in higher education: Strategies for success.* San Francisco, CA: Jossey-Bass.

Clayton-Pedersen, A., & Musil, C. M. (2005). Introduction to the series. In D. A. Williams, J. B. Berger, & S. A. McClendon (Eds.), *Toward a model of inclusive excellence and change in postsecondary institutions* (pp. iii–ix). Washington, DC: Association of American Colleges and Universities. Retrieved from http://www.aacu.org/inclusive_excellence/documents/williams_et_al.pdf

Clayton-Pedersen, A. R., Parker, S., Smith, D. G., Moreno, J. F., & Teraguchi, D. H. (2007). *Making a real difference with diversity: A guide to institutional change.* Washington, DC: Association of American Colleges and Universities.

Eckel, P. D., Cook, B. J., & King, J. E. (2009). *The CAO census: A national profile of chief academic officers.* Washington, DC: American Council on Education.

Esterberg, K. G., & Wooding, J. (2012). *Divided conversations: Identities, leadership, and change in public higher education.* Nashville, TN: Vanderbilt University Press.

Evans, A., & Chun, E. B. (2007). *Are the walls really down? Behavioral and organizational barriers to faculty and staff diversity* (ASHE-ERIC Higher Education Reports, Vol. 33, No. 1). San Francisco, CA: Jossey-Bass.

Feagin, J. R. (2010). *Racist America: Roots, current realities, and future reparations* (2nd ed.). New York, NY: Routledge.

Fry, R., & Lopez, M. H. (2012). *Hispanic student enrollments reach new highs in 2011: Now largest minority group on four-year college campuses.* Retrieved November 5, 2013, from http://www.pewhispanic.org/2012/08/20/hispanic-student-enrollments-reach-new-highs-in-2011/

Gmelch, W. H. (2004). The department chair's balancing acts. *New Directions for Higher Education, 126,* 69–84.

Gmelch, W. H., & Miskin, V. D. (2011). *Department chair leadership skills* (2nd ed.). Madison, WI: Atwood.

Gmelch, W., Reason, R., Schuh, J., & Shelley, M., II. (2002). *The call for academic leaders: The academic leadership forum evaluation report.* Ames, IA: Center for Academic Leadership and the Research Institute for Studies in Education.

Hubbard, E. E. (2004). *The manager's pocket guide to diversity.* Amherst, MA: HRD Press.

Hubbell, L., & Homer, F. (1997). The academic department chair: The logic of appeasement. *PS: Political Science and Politics, 30*(2), 209–213.

Ikenberry, S. (2013). Foreword: Academic leadership and its consequences. In R. M. Hendrickson, J. E. Lane, J. T. Harris, & R. H. Dorman (Eds.), *Academic leadership and governance of higher education: A guide for trustees, leaders, and aspiring leaders of two- and four-year institutions* (pp. xix–xxi). Sterling, VA: Stylus.

Jayakumar, U. M., & Museus, S. D. (2012). Mapping the intersection of campus cultures and equitable outcomes among racially diverse student populations. In S. D. Museus & U. M. Jayakumar (Eds.), *Creating campus cultures: Fostering success among racially diverse student populations* (pp. 1–27). New York, NY: Routledge.

Kiley, K. (2012). *Meet the new boss.* Retrieved November 2, 2013, from http://www.insidehighered.com/news/2012/07/31/business-officers-might-be-next-pipe-line-college-presidents

King, J., & Gomez, G. G. (2008). *On the pathway to the presidency: Characteristics of higher education's senior leadership.* Washington, DC: American Council on Education.

Knox, M., & Teraguchi, D. H. (2005). Institutional models that cultivate comprehensive change. *Diversity Digest, 9*(2), 10–11.

Leaming, D. R. (2006). *Academic leadership: A practical guide to chairing the department* (2nd ed.). Bolton, MA: Anker.

Lucas, A. F. (1994). *Strengthening departmental leadership: A team-building guide for chairs in colleges and universities.* San Francisco, CA: Jossey-Bass.

National Association of College and University Business Officers. (2010). *2010 profile of higher education chief business and financial officers.* Washington, DC: Author.

National Center for Education Statistics. (n.d.). *Fast facts.* Retrieved November 6, 2013, from http://nces.ed.gov/fastfacts/display.asp?id=98

Patton, S. (2013, June 9). *At the Ivies, it's still White at the top.* Retrieved August 27, 2013, from http://chronicle.com/article/At-the-Ivies-Its-Still-White/139643/

Ragins, B. R. (2007). Diversity and workplace mentoring relationships: A review and positive social capital approach. In T. D. Allen & L. T. Eby (Eds.), *The Blackwell handbook of mentoring: A multiple perspectives approach* (pp. 281–300). Malden, MA: Blackwell.

Roach, K. D. (1991). University department chairs' use of compliance-gaining strategies. *Communication Quarterly, 39*(1), 75–90.

Roberson, Q. M. (2006). Disentangling the meanings of diversity and inclusion in organizations. *Group and Organization Management, 31*(2), 212–236.

Silver, J. H., Sr. (2002). Diversity issues. In R. M. Diamond (Ed.), *Field guide to academic leadership* (pp. 357–374). San Francisco, CA: Jossey-Bass.

Smith, D. G. (2009). *Diversity's promise for higher education: Making it work.* Baltimore, MD: Johns Hopkins University Press.

Smith, E. (1996). Leader or manager: The minority department chair of the majority department. *Journal of Leadership and Organizational Studies, 3*(1), 79–94.

Stripling, J. (2013, March 5). *Falling diversity of provosts signals challenge for presidential pipeline, study finds.* Retrieved November 5, 2013, from http://chronicle .com/article/Falling-Diversity-of-Provosts/137685/

U.S. Department of Education. (2012). Washington, DC: National Center for Education Statistics, Integrated Postsecondary Education System.

Western Interstate Commission for Higher Education. (2012). *Knocking at the college door: Projections of high school graduates.* Retrieved November 6, 2013, from http://www.wiche.edu/knocking-8th

Wheeler, D. W., Seagren, A. T., Becker, L. W., Kinley, E. R., Mlinek, D. D., & Robson, K. J. (2008). *The academic chair's handbook.* San Francisco, CA: Jossey-Bass.

Williams, D. A. (2013). *Strategic diversity leadership: Activating change and transformation in higher education.* Sterling, VA: Stylus.

Williams, D. A., Berger, J. B., & McClendon, S. A. (2005). *Toward a model of inclusive excellence and change in postsecondary institutions.* Retrieved December 15, 2013, from http://www.aacu.org/inclusive_excellence/documents/williams_ et_al.pdf

Wolverton, M., & Gmelch, W. H. (2002). *College deans: Leading from within.* Westport, CT: Oryx.

2

RETOOLING THE EDUCATIONAL PLAYING FIELD

We are confronted primarily with a moral issue. It is as old as the Scriptures and is as clear as the American Constitution. The heart of the question is whether all Americans are to be afforded equal rights and equal opportunities, whether we are going to treat our fellow Americans as we want to be treated.

—President John F. Kennedy, *Civil Rights Address* (June 11, 1963)

Why is diversity transformation in American higher education an urgent matter? As Jamie Merisotis, president and CEO of the Lumina Foundation, pointed out, "College-level learning is key to individual prosperity, economic security, and the strength of our American democracy" (Lumina Foundation, 2012, p. 1). Yet at the same time, higher education must change to become responsive to the needs of a "dizzyingly diverse" twenty-first century student population—a population that is diverse ethnically, racially, socially, economically, and in terms of age and family situation (Merisotis, 2012, p. 3). Merisotis suggested we are in the midst of a perilous "Kodak moment" in which institutions of higher education must retool and redesign their offerings to meet all types of students without delay—or face the fate of the Eastman Kodak Company, which reacted too slowly to environmental change and then became irrelevant (Merisotis, 2012, p. 2). In his view, "Equity must be a non-negotiable cornerstone of a redesigned higher education system" (Merisotis, 2013).

We set the stage for the study with an overview of the structural inequality that still pervades American society and the role of higher education in recalibrating access to educational opportunity. This landscape reinforces the importance of the chair's role in diversity transformation within institutions of higher education. We explore the social context for educational access and attainment, as well as factors that may help explain lower retention rates of

21

minority students in predominantly White institutions. Then we examine how diversity is defined in the academic department and highlight particular difficulties that female and minority chairs encounter in this still predominantly White male leadership role. Our discussion concludes with examples of specific, actionable strategies that will assist chairs in formulating an agenda for diversity change within the academic department.

Why Change Is Overdue

A recent polling report of 1,006 adults conducted by CBS News found significant differences between White and Black participants on the extent to which the United States has made progress in getting rid of racial discrimination against Blacks since the 1960s (*Race and Ethnicity*, 2013). While 78% of White participants believe that the United States has made a lot of progress, 55% of Blacks perceived this to be the case (*Race and Ethnicity*, 2013). And 62% of Blacks reported a specific instance of when they felt they had been discriminated against because of race, as compared to 29% of Whites (*Race and Ethnicity*, 2013).

The two realities of what Massey and Denton termed an "American apartheid" continue to bifurcate the American experience (Massey & Denton, 1993). In this regard, the Kerner report commissioned by President Lyndon Johnson in 1967 to explain the riots arising in U.S. cities was prophetic. It concluded that the United States was "moving toward two societies, one black, one white—separate and unequal" (*Our Nation Is Moving Toward Two Societies*, n.d.). The report identified racism as a major cause of urban violence and indicated that White America bore responsibility for the rise of urban rioting. The polarization around race continues to haunt this country, even as the Supreme Court has virtually eliminated consideration of race as a measure of disadvantage in college and university admissions. More than a half century after the Kerner report, persistent inequality arises from the resegregation of housing; differential access to educational, new business, and job opportunities; and sustained patterns of subtle discrimination that penetrate the classroom, workplace, and boardroom.

Ironically, in an era in which minority populations in the United States will become the majority (by 2042), certain sectors of the economy have become enriched, whereas others have lagged far behind. A study by the Urban Institute reveals that for the past 30 years, the gaping wage inequality gap between White families and Black and Hispanic families has persisted (Lowrey, 2013; McKernan, Ratcliffe, Steuerle, & Zhang, 2013). White families earn on average $2 for every $1 earned by Black and Hispanic families.

Even more troubling is the wealth gap that has widened and deepened during the recession, with Black and Hispanic families hit disproportionately by the housing collapse. Although on average White families retained approximately $632,000 in wealth, Black families averaged $98,000, and Hispanic families averaged $110,000 (Lowrey, 2013; McKernan et al., 2013). And for undercapitalized Black businesses in which more than 90% of business owners are one-person enterprises and only 1% generates sales of a million dollars, the recession that began in 2008 has caused a heavy attrition rate (Herbert, 2012).

Is the American dream still alive and well? From a material perspective, empirical evidence indicates that Whites and Blacks represent two nations, with middle-class Blacks earning $0.70 for every dollar earned by White middle-class citizens but holding only $0.15 for every dollar of wealth possessed by middle-class Whites (Oliver & Shapiro, 2006). The rise of sophisticated philosophies of color blindness has only compounded this rather stark tale of two societies. In essence, a postracial perspective insists that the United States has attained a state in which race, ethnicity, and other differentiating characteristics no longer matter in the shaping of opportunity. Yet the "thin veneer of apparent colorblindness" is an illusion and has become a way of controlling minority groups under the facade of race-neutral policies (Picca & Feagin, 2007, p. xii). A long-dominant White racial frame undergirds the notion of color blindness, assertively accenting "a very positive view of white superiority, virtue, and moral goodness" by insisting that race is no longer relevant or considered in the United States (Feagin, 2010b, p. 11). Significant new research has suggested that individuals with color-blind racial attitudes may, in fact, have a greater tendency to engage in discriminatory behavior (see Tynes & Markoe, 2010, for review). For example, a study of 282 educational psychology students found that European Americans and individuals high in racial color blindness were more likely to be not bothered by Facebook postings that mocked Blacks and Latinos (Tynes & Markoe, 2010).

The theory of color blindness rests on the belief that the playing field is level and that status attainment is meritocratic. It places the onus for success or failure squarely on the individual and negates or overlooks the sociohistorical context that mediates the opportunity structure for education and career success. By ignoring the circumstances of the less privileged, this theory further exacerbates the fault lines so deeply etched into the American experience. And, in fact, as scholars have begun to note, color blindness can have a more toxic effect: It can reproduce White privilege and color-blind policies such as those articulated in the supreme law of the land that can impact who is able to go to college (Tynes & Markoe, 2010).

From a historical perspective, we are now in what Manning Marable termed the *fourth racial domain* since the European colonization of North America (Marable, 2006). The first domain is legal slavery that lasted nearly 250 years, the second is Jim Crow segregation that excluded Blacks from nearly all aspects of public life, the third is marked by the ghettoization and confinement of Blacks to impoverished urban areas, and the fourth era beginning in the late twentieth century represents the extreme class stratification resulting from economic and political factors that coincide with transnational globalization (Marable, 2006). The first three domains were characterized by overt discrimination that occurred through formal structural barriers. In the fourth domain, we see the evolution of forms of subtle, second-generation discrimination that are difficult to pinpoint and that take shape through microinequities or recurring patterns of devaluing messages and behavior (see Chun & Evans, 2012, for review). Nonetheless, forms of blatant discrimination still persist, as evidenced by overtly racist incidents that dominate the headlines with regularity and find expression in racist incidents on campuses.

How does persistent social inequality affect higher education? The educational experience has been viewed as the most important gateway to privilege and opportunity. Nineteenth-century educational reformer Horace Mann saw education as "our only political safety" and as "a great equalizer of the conditions of men—the balance wheel of the social machinery" that "gives each man the independence and the means by which he can resist the selfishness of other men" (Mann, 1848, para. 6). Over time, the relationship of higher education to the future of democracy has emerged as an essential context for diversity (D. G. Smith, 2009). In this sense, higher education can be seen metaphorically as the source of a river that nourishes culture and society with the potential to rectify barriers to the inclusion of talented and diverse individuals (D. G. Smith, 2009).

We also know that although the mission of universities and colleges is connected with the public good and the amelioration of social conditions, these institutions have remained socially conservative. The fact that there was no broad-based education system for Blacks until the 1920s and that African American students were admitted into most traditionally White campuses on a significant scale starting in the 1960s and 1970s speaks to this reality (Feagin, Vera, & Imani, 1996; Wise, 2005). From their inception, European American institutions have been racially hierarchical and undemocratic, and they remain so today for the most part (Feagin, 2006). Rather than leading social change, higher education could be called a late adapter. It is only the voice of the faculty, and sometimes a decidedly more radicalized faculty, that has served as a beacon of hope in galvanizing the forces of social justice that will remedy widespread inequality.

Furthermore, within the walls of higher education, institutional hierarchies replicate and intensify the effects of social hierarchies structured around race, class, gender, sexual orientation, and nationality (Feagin, 2006; Rockquemore & Laszloffy, 2008). The vulnerability of diverse tenure-track faculty and administrators arises from within a broader framework of social racial inequalities, influencing the disparate experiences of individuals from nondominant and dominant groups within the same department or institution (Chun & Evans, 2012; Rockquemore & Laszloffy, 2008). And faculty who occupy disadvantaged positions within social hierarchies structured around gender, race, class, sexual orientation, and nationality can experience a one-down status that does not end at the walls of the institution (Rockquemore & Laszloffy, 2008).

Researchers have identified the *systemic* nature of institutional discrimination that still pervades organizational hierarchies, processes, and cultures and that can be mediated, buffered, or solidified by individual actors within academe (see, e.g., Bonilla-Silva, 2006; Chun & Evans, 2012; Feagin, 2006, 2010b; Razack, 1998). From this perspective, socially based discrimination is replicated within the norms, culture, and practices of institutions through dominance, hierarchical interaction, and legacies of White privilege (Feagin, 2006, 2010a). *White privilege* refers to implicit opportunities and power that have persisted within different domains of American life, including higher education (Brown, Hinton, & Howard-Hamilton, 2007). And this privilege is sustained and reproduced through economic, social, and cultural capital that reinforces the group-based nature of advantage (DiTomaso, 2013).

Those in power determine what is seen as normal and correct through a hegemonic process of cultural domination that is accomplished through the consent of those who are disempowered (Chun & Evans, 2009; Hardiman & Jackson, 1997). As a consequence, the dynamics of unequal and asymmetrical power alter and affect the day-to-day experiences of nondominant individuals within the academy. For example, a White female chair of education in a private master's-level western university explicitly connects diversity in higher education with power inequality:

> To me, diversity represents a range of power that is represented in the room. For most of us in higher ed, that power doesn't generally exist for women or for younger faculty, or for folks who have come out of lesser respected institutions. I think it's a slippery slope when we start talking about evaluating diversity and understanding what it is.

Significant scholarly attention, particularly by female academics, has been devoted to the differential experiences of women and minorities in the tenure process (see Chun & Evans, 2012, for review). As Rockquemore and Laszloffy (2008) explained with reference to Black faculty,

> Who receives the benefit of the doubt, whose opinion is valued, who gets mentored, and who is invited into collaborative opportunities are subtly shaped by often unconscious racialized assumptions about who is an insider and who is an outsider, who does and does not belong in the academic club, and whose presence is welcomed and whose is tolerated. (pp. 2–3)

Black academics and members of other nondominant groups struggle with domination, marginalization, and even subjugation both within the walls of their own institution and outside their respective campuses in the communities in which they live (Evans & Chun, 2007; Rockquemore & Laszloffy, 2008). Take the observations of a White female history chair on a predominantly White, religiously affiliated western campus who describes the double isolation of minority and female faculty both in the classroom and in the surrounding community:

> I think there are only half a dozen faculty of color on our faculty. . . . Feeling isolated and invisible comes with the territory. . . . Feeling isolated and invisible in our city is unavoidable. Unless we do things like change the way we evaluate faculty, at least think about what role gender and race play in student evaluations, that's going to be a problem. . . . On a largely White Protestant campus, many of our students come in without significant diversity experience themselves. They relate well to young White men teaching their classes, despite the fact that we have a majority female population. People [faculty] have trouble in classrooms here if they don't fit that profile.

Because diversity is shaped by social forces linked to the structural position of nondominant groups in society, institutions of higher education need to develop diversity strategies that communicate their commitment to long-term change that will benefit society (Aguirre & Martinez, 2007). In other words, higher education must counteract rather than replicate regressive external social forces and instigate social change from the inside out.

Nonetheless, campuses tend to maintain homogeneity and adapt only when necessary, such as when limits are set on access for Asian Americans because of the fear of overrepresentation in the student body or on access for African Americans and Latino students and faculty in the name of quality (D. G. Smith, 1990). If creating a multicultural campus is seen as a diversion from, but not central to, the purpose of education, then the campus climate will not change (D. G. Smith, 1990). By contrast, transforming the *system* for diversity means reinventing everything: new mind-sets, new infrastructures, new frames, and new business models (Scharmer, 2009). Transformational leadership for diversity needs to be focused on changing the organizational culture and enhancing the campus's ability to adapt (Aguirre & Martinez, 2007).

As a result, we emphasize the importance of actualizing inclusive practices within the culture of the university as embodied in the academic environment, interactional relations, and learning outcomes. A values-based framework that embraces the trilogy of demography, diversity, and democracy offers us the opportunity to address regressive social forces, build support for the new American majority, and create an inclusive learning experience that prepares students for participation in a global, knowledge-based society (Chun & Evans, 2009).

Social Justice Revisited: Conservative Backlash and the Legal Shift

To offset the forces of social inequality, higher education policy has, for the past three decades, espoused an agenda of access with the objective of making the benefits of a college education available to all Americans regardless of economic background (Gumport & Zemsky, 2003). For this reason, affirmative action has become a major battleground for colleges and universities seeking to ensure such access (Gumport & Zemsky, 2003). Yet the tide has turned and virtually closed the door on affirmative action in admissions through the determination of a very conservative Supreme Court in *Fisher v. University of Texas at Austin et al.* (2012). In this case, Abigail Fisher, a White undergraduate denied admission to the University of Texas, claimed that her race prevented her admission to the University of Texas while less-qualified minority students were admitted.

The *Fisher* decision essentially represents the crystallization of a White backlash against affirmative action expressed through the medium of a far-right court, with five of the six justices expressing highly conservative views. In contrast to the moderate and liberal perspectives of the American public that resulted in the 2012 election of Barack Obama, the Supreme Court's shift to the right suggests a failure to represent the views of the newly emerging, increasingly diverse American majority. The determination in *Fisher* validates a view of reverse discrimination that insists on the prevalence of social meritocracy and negates centuries-old legacies of privilege.

Why is this decision so critical for higher education? In *Fisher*, the Court took an unprecedented step into the administrative domain of higher education admissions by requiring a reviewing court to determine if a university's use of race is necessary to achieve the educational benefits of diversity. Furthermore, the ruling indicates that "the reviewing court must ultimately be satisfied that no workable race-neutral alternatives would produce" these benefits (*Fisher v. University of Texas at Austin et al.*, 2012, p. 2). As a result, colleges and universities now bear the burden of proof that such alternatives have been exhausted when seeking to consider race and/or ethnicity as one factor among others in a holistic review of admissions applications. As Eric Lewis, a prominent litigator, put it, this decision represents "a complete rout for pragmatic remedies to the continuing legacy of racial discrimination" (Lewis, 2013). Another commentator noted that the Court's views represent "an extremely active and aggressive colorblindness" (Troutt, 2013).

Compounding this decision, just a day after the *Fisher* ruling, in the *Shelby County v. Holder* decision, the Court invalidated a key part of the landmark Voting Rights Act of 1965. Chief Justice John Roberts summarized the Supreme Court's view of the United States' progress in overcoming discrimination with his insistence that "today, our nation has changed" (*Shelby County, Alabama v. Holder, Attorney General, et al.*, 2012, p. 29).

Inequities in Educational Access, Persistence, and Success

The Supreme Court's optimistic depiction of how the United States has changed contrasts with a significant body of research indicating that the playing field for racial and ethnic minority students is far from level in terms of access, persistence, and degree attainment. For example, a Georgetown University study demonstrates that American higher education has two separate and unequal tracks: the 468 selective colleges and the 3,250 open-access institutions (Carnevale & Strohl, 2013). The divergence between these tracks is increasing and not diminishing. Carnevale and Strohl identified two prominent themes that characterize these tracks: (a) racial stratification in the 4,400 two- and four-year colleges analyzed for the study and (b) polarization between the most selective schools and the open-access schools.

Between 1995 and 2009, despite increases in the enrollment of African American and Hispanic students attending postsecondary institutions, more than 8 in 10 of new White students enrolled in the 468 most selective institutions, accounting for 78% of the growth in these institutions, whereas more than 7 in 10 new Hispanic and African American students have gone to open-access two- and four-year colleges, composing 92% of the growth in these schools (Carnevale & Strohl, 2013). Stratification by income is marked in more selective colleges, with high-income students overrepresented relative to population share by 45 percentage points and African American and

Hispanic students underrepresented relative to population share by 9 percentage points (Carnevale & Strohl, 2013). This disadvantage is magnified by preexisting geographic (spatial) isolation in the location of high schools, as well as economic and educational deprivation in the precollege years. And from a student perspective, the study concluded, "Disadvantage is worst of all when race and class collide" (Carnevale & Strohl, 2013, p. 37).

The 468 most selective schools spend two to nearly five times more per student and have higher ratios of full- to part-time faculty, higher completion rates, and greater access to graduate schools, even when considering equally qualified students (Carnevale & Strohl, 2013). The college completion rate for the most selective schools is 82%, compared with 49% for open-access two- and four-year institutions (Carnevale & Strohl, 2013).

Another study reveals that the six-year postsecondary persistence rates of Latinos (68%) and Blacks (66%) fall behind their White (79%) and Asian American counterparts (86%). Six-year graduation rates for African Americans are over 20 percentage points lower than those rates for Whites, and African American men in particular have low enrollment and high dropout rates (see Arcidiacono & Koedel, 2013, for review). First-generation college students are less likely to persist than other students, and Latino students are more likely to be first-generation students than other groups (see Nunez, Hoover, Pickett, Stuart-Carruthers, & Vazquez, 2013, for review).

What accounts for the differential retention rates for minority students? In addition to factors of academic preparedness and financial aid, the campus climate and the student's social and academic integration are critical factors related to retention (Swail, Redd, & Perna, 2003). Research on minority student adjustment finds that race and ethnicity often elicit less friendly treatment, and minority students frequently function in a more constricted and separated social world (see Fleming, 2012, for review). On predominantly White campuses, first-generation minority students may feel socially isolated and experience loneliness, stress, and anxiety. For example, a longitudinal research study of 10 Latino students found that students who came from areas where Latinos constitute a critical mass do not view themselves as minorities until they arrive on a predominantly White campus (Torres, 2003).

Perceived discrimination has been identified as a unique source of major and chronic stress apart from everyday life stresses, affecting the mental and physical well-being of its targets (see Evans & Chun, 2012, for review). In this regard, a study of 161 freshman minority students on a predominantly White campus (56% White) identified *minority status stress* as a separate risk factor for maladjustment, noting that sociocultural and contextual stresses are important factors in minority student adaptation to a White university (Smedley, Myers, & Harrell, 1993). Among social climate stresses identified by students in this study were not having enough professors of their own race, negative treatment of minority students by faculty, and expectations of poor academic performance by White students and faculty (Smedley et al., 1993).

Similar to the barriers encountered by minority students, sexual minority students on campus face challenges that can inhibit their academic progress and inclusion. A 2003 study of 14 campuses and a respondent sample of 1,669 self-identified lesbian, gay, bisexual, and transgender (LGBT) individuals found that more than one third of LGBT students reported harassment within the past year, with derogatory remarks as the most frequent form of harassment (see Rankin, 2005, for review). Most faculty, students, administrators, and staff surveyed in the study reported that their campus climate for LGBT individuals was homophobic (see Rankin, 2005, for review).

Diverse students can experience culture shock as they encounter stereotypes and misconceptions that challenge the formation of a positive identity. Racialized issues may increase minority students' reluctance to approach instructors of a different race. And stereotypic perceptions of minority students' academic ability or competence can impact performance through the phenomenon of self-fulfilling prophecy (Fleming, 2012; Steele, 1997).

The retention of diverse students is affected by a number of factors at both the institutional level and the departmental level. A biracial male music department chair in a midwestern liberal arts college noted specific differences in the type and competitiveness of institutions in terms of the challenges of minority student retention and shared the perspective of his institution in its effort to bring all students to a certain point so that they can compete equally:

> We try institutionally to bring all students to a certain point, so then when they are in the classroom they're competing equally. We are also not a highly competitive institution, which might be an aspect of all this kind of thing. If you took Ivy League schools, you would be getting a whole different population. . . . Those norms depend on whether it is competitive or not so competitive even in terms of admission. It impacts everything that happens after they come to the institution too.
>
> So we are more of a kind of nurturing institution than highly competitive. That is also an aspect of liberal arts colleges: There you get personal attention; there you get help; it's not like competing with everyone. . . . We're also focused as a liberal arts college . . . on the whole person rather than just them taking courses. We're focused on them developing as a whole person. Part of that has to do with how they deal with diversity. . . . So part of our mission inherently is toward opening people up to understand these kinds of issues, and it's at the institutional level. It's more at the institutional level than at the departmental level.

Factors in the academic department that impact minority student retention include the presence of diverse faculty as role models; interactional diversity with faculty, staff, and other students; the diversity of curricular offerings; the cultural competency of faculty and their ability to make course materials relevant to the students represented in the classroom; and departmental climate. For these reasons, we now further explore the meaning of *diversity* within the academic departmental context.

Defining *Diversity* in the Academic Department

Moving from a broad view of the educational landscape, we now consider how *diversity* is defined and operationalized within the academic department through the lens of department chairs in this study. The definition of what constitutes optimal diversity in the academic department will provide the foundation for the development of an actionable agenda.

Our interviews reveal a clear awareness by chairs of a holistic view of diversity that not only includes ethnicity, race, gender, and sexual orientation but also addresses socially acquired characteristics. Interview participants frequently articulated this multidimensional view of diversity. A number of interviewees reflected a high degree of sophistication, moving beyond the broad palette of diversity characteristics to implicate notions of power and privilege. Consider how a White female sociology chair in a southwestern research university described her department's active engagement with the meaning of diversity:

> That's a complex question. I think diversity can mean diversity in terms of race, ethnicity, composition; it can be diversity in terms of background and class; it can be diversity in terms of outlook and perspective. This is something that our department talks about and struggles with and . . . we frequently talk about this.

And in the view of a White male psychology chair from a private midwestern college, defining *diversity* as "everything" in the context of the role of the department chair avoids the salient question of racial underrepresentation among faculty and students in higher education. As he explained,

> For purposes of the department chair and for work with faculty and students, I define diversity around social identity; for me, primarily race. I think that is historically the central issue in U.S. history, also gender, sexual orientation, religion, nationality, in terms of social identities, frankly with an emphasis on race.

To define diversity too generally is to make the concept kind of useless. Certainly we want it to include attitudes and experience; I don't think that's our problem in higher ed. I think the problem is the historical underrepresentation of certain groups, race being the predominant one, gender likewise, but in my discipline of psychology, gender is increasingly more equally represented. In many graduate schools, women are now the majority. I don't know, it seems to me that defining diversity as everything is sort of a cop out.

Similarly, a White female chair of higher education in a western public research university differentiates two clear strands in the definition of *diversity*: The first involves difference, and the second necessarily brings into play issues of power and privilege. As she explained,

When I think about diversity, I think about it in two ways. One is equated with difference, in terms of race, in terms of class, in terms of sexual orientation, and also even diversity of ideas and disciplinary differences. . . . Another component of diversity goes way beyond difference, in that when I think about diversity, I also really think about power and privilege difference and sort of underlying constructs that go with diversity that privilege certain groups over others.

So when I think about diversity, I think about two things: On the one hand it's difference and . . . notions of plurality, but on the other hand, recognizing that where there is difference there are almost always issues of power and privilege difference that we need to be cognizant of.

The biracial male chair of music in a private midwestern liberal arts college cited earlier articulated his view of the social construction of diversity and clearly differentiated between institutional and personal definitions of *diversity*:

I don't like the word [*diversity*], particularly, truthfully, because there is one human race. . . . So everyone who is a human is essentially equal. Now in society diversity gets defined by how people perceive other people, in various groupings, often which are artificial, often which are based on the color of one's skin . . . so I think it depends on the context of whatever society you are in. In the institution, diversity would tend to be defined by national origin, ethnic origin, color, and possibly along with national origin, linguistic origin. . . . This other question came up in our recent faculty meeting. The admissions person had separated out persons of color and then people of more than one race . . . because he said you could check off more than one box in a category.

If I am working in an institution, then I am looking at diversity from the institution's perspective in terms of what it is after in terms of its diversity goals. In my own personal life, everyone is diverse. I think everyone in essence is the same because they are human, and everyone is totally different because they are individuals. So a person who might be of black-colored skin who has been raised in upper-class economic society is going to be very different from the person with very dark skin who has been in a very poor situation. So economic diversity is almost as important at this point in this country as racial diversity.

Survey responses indicate that chairs are aware of the complexity and layers of meaning involved in the definition of *diversity*, as well as the continuing salience of race, ethnicity, gender, sexual orientation, and disability as the principal barriers to inclusion.

The Challenges of Chairs From Nondominant Groups

The chair's leadership in diversity remains a key and even contested role in academic institutions. And our interviews reveal particular challenges that remain for minority, female, and LGBT chairs in a largely White male heterosexist hierarchy. Such challenges can range from lack of support to personal attacks on their credibility, attacks that are sometimes even launched by members of nondominant groups. Minority and female chairs can be caught in the battle of proving their competence, because allegations of incompetence are a frequent stereotype used to undermine their performance. And, ironically, when individuals from nondominant groups are high performers, their competence may be viewed as a threat. A White female chair of education in a private western master's-level university described the vicious nature of attacks that involve mobbing or collective efforts to exclude or humiliate a targeted individual (see Westhues, 2004, for review): "It's that response of individuals who feel intimidated by competence." She noted that she "was shocked by the ferocious response that the mob can have against someone."

Chairs from nondominant groups may be viewed with a lack of respect that results in their not being taken seriously, making frequent end runs to higher administrators, seeing their initiatives blocked, and even having faculty members attribute routine business decisions that do not go their way to race/ethnic issues (E. Smith, 1996). And in some religiously affiliated institutions, openly LGBT individuals cannot be considered for faculty or administrative appointments. As a female chair in a Catholic university commented, "There is almost no diversity at all here. Sexual orientation diversity is a taboo since we are a Catholic institution, so we can't address the issue openly."

A study of 800 chairs in 100 institutions found that minority chairs experienced particular stress in their efforts to resolve collegial conflicts and make decisions affecting others. The uncertainty of the level of support they receive in their administrative capacity likely contributes to this stress (see E. Smith, 1996, for review). Attempts to redress structural imbalances in the face of faculty resistance coupled with the demands of research, scholarship, and teaching can tax a minority, female, or LGBT chair's reservoir of energy, time, and resources. Consider the experiences of a White female chair of educational leadership in a western public research university who explained how her leadership has come under attack, especially by other women, and is focused on a personal level:

> What I've observed for myself, I think there is a tendency especially [for] other women who challenge . . . I feel like they want to be the leader, and therefore they criticize my leadership at a pretty personal level. And I'm not saying this to sound pompous, but I feel like that's the only way they can kind of get me . . . because they can't discount my productivity. They can't discount [the fact that] I take initiatives; I hire people; I've done a lot of good things. And I'm not saying I'm above reproach and people shouldn't have comments about my leadership at all, but I feel like there is a tendency for people to get personal pretty quickly as a way to discount my leadership and question what I'm doing.

The chair recounted the way in which a departmental staff person openly challenged her authority on the simple matter of rearranging furniture:

> Just recently we were talking about, of all things, rearranging furniture, and a departmental staff person said, "Who says I have to do it that way?" . . . That's not something she would have said to a man, in no way. I feel like a lot of times as a result of being a woman . . . people do feel like they can challenge me in ways that I am certain if I were a man they would not be bringing those things up.

Similarly, an African American male sociology chair in a private southern research university describes the tenuous circumstances under which minority chairs can be selected and how other colleagues may be suspicious of their abilities:

> I chaired a couple of departments, predominantly White. And one of the first things you know if you are a person of color or you're not in the major-

ity is that people are always suspicious of your abilities. And they may not say it, but you know. . . . And so you're given a job for whatever reason: Usually it's like the football coach, the non-White football coach, who is given a chance to coach the team. It's usually the worst team in the league and at the bottom of the barrel. So they give it to you for a number of reasons: You know, hopefully you'll fail or you bring a different type of leadership style. You want to be honest; you want to be straight; you don't want to play games. So the administration knows I've got this person who, excuse my French, will kick some butt, and he is coming in and won't take the crap.

He underscored the vulnerability of minority chairs to end runs by colleagues to upper administration that undermine the chair's authority. As a result, the chair emphasized the importance of support from the dean:

The biggest challenge is getting your supervisor, be it vice president or whoever you report to, to respect your position to the extent that they're not going to let the end run exist so that you're not spending half of your work week having to deal with the dean or provost or vice president or somebody defending some anonymous claim from your department that you're not fair, that you don't spread the money around correctly. So for me the biggest challenge is to say, "You hired me for this position, I'm going to run this department like every other chair, and I can't have people coming to you before they come to me." And I have made that clear in every position I've had. I've been involved in enough chairs conversations and chairs meetings and conferences to know that other chairs of color, female chairs, this also is a big, big challenge, not being undermined.

And a White female chair of urban education in a midwestern regional university reported that her experiences of being marginalized in her earlier career enhanced her sensitivity to the importance of diversity:

But I had the experience of feeling discrimination and feeling I'd been marginalized in my early career. . . . I wasn't expecting it quite to the degree in an academic institution that I saw when I came in. Some of the struggles that were put upon me just seem to be sexist. Other women had felt that and seen that too. And the president developed a commission on the status of women years ago and started really looking at that kind of thing. Hopefully that helped turn the tide. And so I think that my sensitivity was greater.

When isolated in a predominantly White male academic infrastructure, chairs from nondominant groups can represent the singular voice advocating diversity change. As a Black male chair of Hispanic ethnicity in an elite private research university observed, "When one is a minority advocating for diversity, White colleagues believe one is advancing a political agenda." Individuals who represent the single diverse member of the faculty in a given academic department can be perceived as the diversity advocate, the individual predictably focused on issues of diversity. In this regard, a White male psychology department chair in an urban midwestern university explained how the minority leader of the diversity committee stepped down as a result of negative perceptions of her "agenda":

> At one point we were down to one minority individual. . . . We have in our department a standing committee populated by faculty members and students to promote diversity and to bring awareness about diversity to the department. That group has a faculty leader so to speak, and this individual was a leader of that for a while. And she actually stepped down; she felt that after a certain point, she was doing more harm than good by being the head of that committee because people came to see her as "Oh yes, you are always going to bring up the minority issues because you are a minority."
>
> She actually stepped down as the head of that position, because she wanted a nonminority person to be speaking up for minority issues, because she . . . (and I agreed with her) . . . sometimes perceived people thinking, "OK, this person (if she wants to speak up at faculty meetings) . . . is going to bring up the minority issues again" in a negative way. I definitely have seen people perceived as "OK, that's their only agenda." . . . In fact that was her responsibility in this position, but it became entangled with her as a natural minority.

In this case, White faculty leadership of the diversity committee was seen as more effective in gaining the support of other White faculty for the contested diversity change effort. Throughout this chapter, we have shared the persistent structural inequities in the social landscape that demand that institutions of higher learning serve as catalysts of change. The perspectives of chairs in our study clearly reveal an awareness of the need to shift the representational balance in the department to create a more intellectually rich and diverse learning environment.

Concluding Perspectives: Strategies for Attaining Consensus on a Diversity Agenda

In the effort to build a common diversity agenda, strategies suggested by department chairs provide specific approaches that will help build consensus for diversity change within the academic department. Although some of these strategies may seem surprising, they reflect the actual, lived experience of chairs in their efforts to foster more inclusive departmental environments.

Develop a common understanding of the meaning of diversity and inclusion in both an institutional and departmental context through open dialogue and in-depth discussion. A reflective definition of *diversity* honed within the departmental context needs to take into account the institution's strategic diversity agenda, its affirmative action program and goals, its research-based and disciplinary perspectives, and its personal interpretations and experiences. In this regard, the National Institute for Intergroup Dialogue approach at the University of Michigan provides an exemplary, critical-dialogic methodology for discussing commonalities and differences among social identity groups, with an emphasis on sustained communication and involvement (Zúñiga, Nagda, Chesler, & Cytron-Walker, 2007).

Link departmental discussions to the campus dialogue on diversity. The campus framework for diversity plays a critical role in shaping and reinforcing departmental dialogue. For example, in a far-reaching, self-critical report by a trustee committee on diversity, Princeton University cited a number of critical, reinforcing elements necessary for an inclusive campus, including (a) articulating diversity as a core value by campus leaders, (b) creating forums for diversity, (c) building a common language that promotes open dialogue, and (d) strengthening cultural competencies (*Report of the Trustee Ad Hoc Committee on Diversity*, 2013). As a second example, in its 2011–2016 Diversity Strategic Action Plan titled "To Form a More Inclusive Learning Community," the California State University at Chico identified the need to develop a shared understanding of "inclusive community" as one of its eight priorities (The Diversity Scorecard Committee, 2010).

Participate in national disciplinary forums to develop greater awareness of disciplinary barriers. National disciplinary discussions about the relevance of diversity to a specific discipline will also strengthen awareness of the obstacles to diversity within a particular field of specialization. For example, a two-and-a-half-day workshop attended by 43 chemistry chairs in 50 top-ranked institutions in 2007 was found to impact the sensitivity of the department chairs to the obstacles that underrepresented minority faculty members face in academic chemistry (Greene, Lewis, Richmond, & Stockard, 2011). The seminar affected the views of department chairs on hiring underrepresented minorities, with four times as many respondents after the workshop viewing the need to change current faculty members' attitudes as a factor in increasing the likelihood of hiring underrepresented faculty (Greene et al., 2011). Such national discussions are particularly important in the science, technology, engineering, and mathematics (STEM) fields, because these disciplines do not have a readily apparent curricular tie to diversity.

Build a critical mass of faculty from dominant and nondominant groups to lead and support diversity progress. A White male chair of economics in a public southwestern university explained the importance of obtaining a critical mass of faculty to take concrete action in support of diversity:

> The chair has to take the leadership role, has to be proactive, has to get a critical mass of people on his or her side to try to take the proactive measures that are necessary. Obviously a chair or a dean . . . who simply gives lip service to diversity but doesn't do anything concrete to make it happen is not going to make any progress.

Our interviews also reveal that minority chairs in predominantly White departments may be viewed as pushing a particularistic agenda, making their leadership of diversity initiatives more problematic. For example, a female Asian American chair indicated that other faculty could view her promotion of diversity as driven by personal, selfish interests. And a female African American chair reported a challenge she has faced in promoting diversity due to "misunderstandings as well as perceptions about 'why' I'd promote diversity." These observations underscore the heightened vulnerability of minority chairs in predominantly White institutions when they promote a diversity agenda.

Recognize that White faculty may also face challenges to their legitimacy or authenticity in leading diversity efforts. A White male chair of modern languages and literatures in an eastern urban private religiously affiliated university explained how his legitimacy as a diversity advocate can be questioned:

> I am a White male and therefore privileged, in some sense, just by being who I am. I think I get an airing for my views with certain constituencies. So I acknowledge that I have used my position of privilege to try to work toward this goal and that my privileged position has been an advantage for doing so. At times, though, I think also the fact that because I am a White male, there are those who might question my legitimacy as an advocate for diversity simply because I simply don't "have an understanding of" or I "don't necessarily" come from a diverse background.

Similarly, a White female chair of occupational therapy in a private southern university shared her perspective on the importance of sharing the "diversity burden":

> I think that sometimes it is hard for me to further that agenda because of who I am and what I am. I am a typical American White female OT [occupational therapist], so it's hard for me, even when I am talking in class about the importance of diversity in the discipline. I feel like it sounds awkward coming from me, but at the same time, that burden, being the diversity burden, should not fall completely on the shoulders of people from diverse groups.

And a White male chair of psychology in a midwestern liberal arts college pointed out that White leaders that are committed to a diversity agenda can be viewed as predictably focused on this issue, causing pushback among other faculty:

> The first chair of psychology that I worked with was utterly committed to the cause of diversity. She was White, but she was kind of criticized as being one-note, of being too excessive, so the pushback was in that regard.

A White female chair of educational leadership in a western research university noted how her ideas on diversity are sometimes dismissed when she is viewed as part of the hierarchical system she represents:

> I think sometimes as a woman I get passed over with some of my ideas, a discounted sense that I attribute to gender. I also feel like age is part of it, where younger students committed to diversity think I don't "get it." I also feel like [because I am] a White woman, students and faculty of color think I don't "get it" and that as chair I'm part of the "system." I feel like I "get it," but I'm not always able to just "fix" it in ways that are immediately apparent. Challenging!

Insist on welcoming departmental climates free of harassment. Chairs, deans, and chief diversity and human resource officers need to be aware of the subtle dynamics that can create differential standards for chairs from nondominant groups. Organizational development interventions such as workshops and seminars that discuss unconscious bias and subtle discrimination can provide the opportunity to strengthen awareness of subtle behavioral barriers. As a White male economics chair in a public southwestern university emphasized,

> The other thing I had in my department and the dean's office had was zero tolerance for any kind of racial or ethnic or sexual harassment. And even beyond that we expected departments to create climates that were welcoming and in which everybody could feel that they were included in the department.

Work with the dean's office to ensure equitable treatment of all departments within a college or school. The dean's office plays a critical role in how resources are distributed, including faculty lines, research opportunities, and incentives. The dean can provide the necessary support for the chair's efforts to formulate a progressive diversity agenda. Yet when disparities exist in how certain departments are treated, perceptions of inequity can hinder the full participation of women and minority chairs in college-wide decision making.

For example, a White female chair in a private southern research university observed that the dean's office in her institution reflects a male-dominated perspective that can cause women in the college to be taken less seriously:

> My discipline, and therefore my department, is female dominated. However, the dean's office is very male dominated. While not overt, it feels as though the women in the college are taken less seriously.

We shall explore further dimensions of the chair's relationship with the dean in chapter 4. Given the crucial socioeconomic framework shared in this chapter and its implications for higher education, in the next chapter we will examine the external, internal, and disciplinary factors that impact the chair's role as diversity change agent within the campus environment.

References

Aguirre, A., Jr., & Martinez, R. O. (2007). *Diversity leadership in higher education* (ASHE-ERIC Higher Education Reports, Vol. 32, No. 3). San Francisco, CA: Jossey-Bass.

Arcidiacono, P., & Koedel, C. (2013). *Race and college success: Evidence from Missouri.* Retrieved August 26, 2013, from http://www.nber.org/papers/w19188

Bonilla-Silva, E. (2006). *Racism without racists: Color-blind racism and the persistence of racial inequality in America.* Lanham, MD: Rowman & Littlefield.

Brown, O. G., Hinton, K., & Howard-Hamilton, M. (2007). Unleashing suppressed voices at colleges and universities: The role of case studies in understanding diversity in higher education. In O. G. Brown, K. G. Hinton, & M. Howard-Hamilton (Eds.), *Unleashing suppressed voices on college campuses: Diversity issues in higher education* (pp. 3–14). New York, NY: Peter Lang.

Carnevale, A. P., & Strohl, J. (2013). *Separate and unequal: How higher education reinforces the intergenerational reproduction of White racial privilege.* Retrieved August 26, 2013, from cew.georgetown.edu/separateandunequal/

Chun, E., & Evans, A. (2009). *Bridging the diversity divide: Globalization and reciprocal empowerment in higher education* (ASHE-ERIC Higher Education Reports, Vol. 35, No. 1). San Francisco, CA: Jossey-Bass.

Chun, E., & Evans, A. (2012). *Diverse administrators in peril: The new indentured class in higher education.* Boulder, CO: Paradigm.

DiTomaso, N. (2013). *The American non-dilemma: Racial inequality without racism.* New York, NY: Russell Sage Foundation.

The Diversity Scorecard Committee. (2010). *To form a more inclusive learning community: The CSU, Chico 2011–2016 diversity action plan.* Retrieved November 29, 2013, from California State University website: http://www.csuchico.edu/prs/dap/12-13-2010.pdf

Evans, A., & Chun, E. B. (2007). *Are the walls really down? Behavioral and organizational barriers to faculty and staff diversity* (ASHE-ERIC Higher Education Reports, Vol. 33, No. 1). San Francisco, CA: Jossey-Bass.

Evans, A., & Chun, E. (2012). *Creating a tipping point: Strategic human resources in higher education.* San Francisco: Jossey-Bass.

Feagin, J. R. (2006). *Systemic racism: A theory of oppression.* New York, NY: Routledge.

Feagin, J. R. (2010a). *Racist America: Roots, current realities, and future reparations* (2nd ed.). New York, NY: Routledge.

Feagin, J. R. (2010b). *The White racial frame: Centuries of racial framing and counterframing.* New York, NY: Routledge.

Feagin, J. R., Vera, H., & Imani, N. (1996). *The agony of education: Black students at White colleges and universities.* New York, NY: Routledge.

Fisher v. University of Texas at Austin et al. (2012). Retrieved from www.supremecourt.gov/opinions/12pdf/11-345_l5gm.pdf

Fleming, J. (2012). *Enhancing minority student retention and academic performance: What we can learn from program evaluations.* San Francisco, CA: Jossey-Bass.

Greene, J., Lewis, P. A., Richmond, G. L., & Stockard, J. (2011). Changing the chairs: Impact of workshop activities in assisting chemistry department chairs in achieving racial and ethnic diversity. *Journal of Chemical Education, 88*(6), 721–725.

Gumport, P. J., & Zemsky, R. (2003). Drawing new maps for a changing enterprise. *Change, 35*(4), 30–35.

Hardiman, R., & Jackson, B. W. (1997). Conceptual foundation for social justice courses. In M. Adams, L. A. Bell, & P. Griffin (Eds.), *Teaching for diversity and social justice: A sourcebook* (pp. 16–29). New York, NY: Routledge.

Herbert, B. (2012). *The destruction of Black wealth: Businesses owned by African Americans are suffering at higher rates than most during the downturn.* Retrieved November 11, 2013, from http://prospect.org/article/destruction-black-wealth

Kennedy, J. F. (1963). *Civil rights address.* Retrieved November 25, 2013, from http://www.americanrhetoric.com/speeches/jfkcivilrights.htm

Lewis, E. (2013, June 26). Five justices in a bubble: The court's step back on race. *The New Yorker.* Retrieved August 22, 2013, from http://www.newyorker.com/online/blogs/newsdesk/2013/06/fisher-and-shelby-county-the-courts-cynicism-on-race.html

Lowrey, A. (2013, April 28). Wealth gap among races has widened since recession. *The New York Times.* Retrieved August 22, 2013, from http://www.nytimes.com/2013/04/29/business/racial-wealth-gap-widened-during-recession.html?ref=todayspaper&_r=1&

Lumina Foundation. (2012). *A stronger nation through higher education: How and why Americans must achieve a big goal for college attainment.* Retrieved November 29, 2013, from www.luminafoundation.org/publications/A_stronger_nation.pdf

Mann, H. (1848). *Horace Mann on education and national welfare.* Retrieved August 22, 2013, from http://www.tncrimlaw.com/civil_bible/horace_mann.htm

Marable, M. (2006). *Living Black history: How reimagining the African-American past can remake America's racial future.* New York, NY: Basic Books.

Massey, D., & Denton, N. (1993). *American apartheid: Segregation and the making of the underclass.* Boston, MA: Harvard University Press.

McKernan, S.-M., Ratcliffe, C., Steuerle, E., & Zhang, S. (2013). *Less than equal: Racial disparities in wealth accumulation.* Retrieved August 22, 2013, from http://www.urban.org/UploadedPDF/412802-Less-Than-Equal-Racial-Disparities-in-Wealth-Accumulation.pdf

Merisotis, J. P. (2012). More than mere data, "stronger nation" report is a call for change. In Lumina Foundation (Ed.), *A stronger nation through higher education: How and why Americans must achieve a big goal for college attainment* (pp. 1–3). Retrieved November 29, 2013, from www.luminafoundation.org/publications/A_stronger_nation.pdf

Merisotis, J. P. (2013). *A stronger nation through higher education.* Retrieved November 29, 2013, from http://www.luminafoundation.org/about_us/president/speeches/2013-09-09.html

Nunez, A.-M., Hoover, R. E., Pickett, K., Stuart-Carruthers, A. C., & Vazquez, M. (Eds.). (2013). *Latinos in higher education and Hispanic-serving institutions: Creating conditions for success.* San Francisco, CA: Jossey-Bass.

Oliver, M. L., & Shapiro, T. M. (2006). *Black wealth, White wealth: A new perspective on racial inequality.* New York, NY: Routledge.

Our nation is moving toward two societies, one Black, one White—separate and unequal: Excerpts from the Kerner report. (n.d.). Retrieved August 22, 2013, from http://historymatters.gmu.edu/d/6545/

Picca, L. H., & Feagin, J. R. (2007). *Two-faced racism: Whites in the backstage and frontstage.* New York, NY: Routledge.

Race and ethnicity. (2013). Retrieved November 24, 2013, from http://www.pollingreport.com/race.htm

Rankin, S. R. (2005). Campus climates for sexual minorities. In R. L. Sanlo (Ed.), *Gender identity and sexual orientation: Research, policy, and personal perspectives* (pp. 17–24). San Francisco, CA: Jossey-Bass.

Razack, S. (1998). *Looking White people in the eye: Gender, race, and culture in courtrooms and classrooms.* Toronto, ON: University of Toronto Press.

Report of the trustee ad hoc committee on diversity. (2013). Retrieved from www.princeton.edu/reports/2013/diversity/report/

Rockquemore, K. A., & Laszloffy, T. (2008). *The Black academic's guide to winning tenure—Without losing your soul.* Boulder, CO: Lynne Rienner.

Scharmer, C. O. (2009). *Field based leadership development.* Paper prepared for the Round Table Meeting on Leadership for Development Impact, The World Bank, The World Bank Institute, Washington, DC. Retrieved September 18, 2013, from http://www.ottoscharmer.com/publications/articles.php

Shelby County, Alabama v. Holder, attorney general, et al. (2012). Retrieved www.supremecourt.gov/opinions/12pdf/12-96_6k47.pdf

Smedley, B. D., Myers, H. F., & Harrell, S. P. (1993). Minority-status stresses and the college adjustment of ethnic minority freshmen. *Journal of Higher Education, 64*(4), 434–452.

Smith, D. G. (1990). Embracing diversity as a central campus goal. *Academe, 76*(6), 29–33.

Smith, D. G. (2009). *Diversity's promise for higher education: Making it work.* Baltimore, MD: Johns Hopkins University Press.

Smith, E. (1996). Leader or manager: The minority department chair of the majority department. *Journal of Leadership and Organizational Studies, 3*(1), 79–94.

Steele, C. M. (1997). A threat in the air: How stereotypes shape intellectual identity and performance. *American Psychologist, 1*(6), 613–629.

Swail, W. S., Redd, K. E., & Perna, L. W. (2003). *Retaining minority students in higher education: A framework for success.* San Francisco, CA: Jossey-Bass.

Torres, V. (2003). Influences on ethnic identity development of Latino college students in the first two years of college. *Journal of College Student Development, 44*(4), 532–547.

Troutt, D. D. (2013). *The Supreme Court's race impatience.* Retrieved August 22, 2013, from http://blogs.reuters.com/great-debate/2013/06/28/the-supreme-courts-race-impatience/

Tynes, B. M., & Markoe, S. L. (2010). The role of color-blind racial attitudes in reactions to racial discrimination on social network sites. *Journal of Diversity in Higher Education, 3*(1), 1–13.

Westhues, K. (Ed.). (2004). *Workplace mobbing in academe: Reports from twenty universities.* Lewiston, NY: Edwin Mellen.

Wise, T. J. (2005). *Affirmative action: Racial preference in black and white.* New York, NY: Routledge.

Zúñiga, X., Nagda, B. A., Chesler, M., & Cytron-Walker, A. (2007). *Intergroup dialogue in higher education: Meaningful learning about social justice.* San Francisco, CA: Jossey-Bass.

3

THE CHAIR'S VANTAGE POINT ON DIVERSITY

Much as the identity of a living organism is reflected in its every cell, the identity of a university can be found in the structure of departments and the relationship among faculty and administrators.

—Clayton M. Christensen and Henry J. Eyring (2011, p. 20)

From an institutional perspective, great variation exists among colleges and universities in terms of their readiness, commitment, and demonstrable progress in the attainment of more inclusive learning and working environments. This chapter examines the differential context for the department chair role in diversity progress based on a range of factors such as institutional type, mission, affiliation, geographic location, size, unionization, and disciplinary focus. Although these variables can significantly impact the chair's ability to contribute to diversity progress, department chairs in differing institutional types are strategically positioned to reshape educational curricula, increase diverse faculty representation, and promote the success of a diverse student body. As the first level in the administrative hierarchy, they play a crucial role in making the university work in a broad sense (Esterberg & Wooding, 2012). If presidential initiatives or strategic plans are going to work, chair participation is critical (Esterberg & Wooding, 2012). And conversely, chair dissatisfaction coupled with faculty discontent can derail initiatives launched by upper administration.

Within the relatively decentralized organizational structure of colleges and universities, department chairs represent the nucleus of academic governance in terms of their structural location between the faculty and the administration. As such, they play a boundary-spanning role that enables them to be an agent of normative change.

Boundary-spanning leadership. Chairs operate at the heart of the value creation process in the university, and as crucial local line leaders, they are professors who serve "on loan" as managers (Senge, 2000). In this capacity, chairs have the opportunity to actualize *boundary-spanning leadership* in what has been termed a "nexus effect" through the possibilities that result from bridging the academic and administrative spheres (Ernst & Chrobot-Mason, 2011, p. 12). As boundary-spanning leaders, chairs have six leadership practices: (a) they *buffer* the boundary between faculty and administration, (b) they can *reflect* on boundaries to strengthen respect and promote understanding, (c) they *connect* and build trust between the two groups, (d) they can *mobilize* stakeholders in a common purpose and reframe the boundaries, (e) they *weave* together diverse experiences and discover new frontiers, and finally (f) they can *transform* boundaries through intergroup reinvention (Ernst & Chrobot-Mason, 2011).

In their boundary-spanning role, chairs are key players in the political dynamics of the department that involves the sometimes conflicting interests of long-term tenured faculty, tenure-track junior faculty, and adjunct or part-time faculty. Trapped between dealing with the pressure of performing as an administrator and being a productive faculty member, chairs function in a Janus-like position with divided loyalties, heightened role conflict, and conflicting commitments between the freedom and the independence of the academic core and the tightly coupled, often mechanistic managerial core (Gmelch, 1995).

Some faculty may be angered if their chair appears to be an agent of the administration, while the administration can become irritated with a chair who persistently argues for departmental needs in the midst of an institutional crisis such as a budgetary reduction (Hecht, Higgerson, Gmelch, & Tucker, 1999). As an African American male sociology department chair in a predominantly White private southern university put it,

> The dean's relationship is very important, and I think that it is probably the most important. And at the same time you have to convince your faculty that you are not in the pocket of the dean. The guy who took over after me when I was done, every faculty meeting we had, he would start off with "the dean said, the dean said." And it got to be nauseating.

Faculty can view the chair's effort to represent institutional interests as having sold out to the administration (Hecht et al., 1999). At the same time, the same male sociology chair stressed the importance of a collegial relationship with the dean: "I always felt that every place I have worked, you have to be good colleagues with the dean, and better yet, if you can, establish some kind of friendship."

Innovative influence. Because of their structural location within the institution as boundary-spanning leaders, chairs are positioned to be the focus of innovation within higher education institutions. Peter Senge predicted that the innovation needed within universities will center on faculty clusters and potentially on chairs (Senge, 2000). Department chairs who are committed to innovation have the ability to deal with problematic conflicts arising between academic expectations and relevance, such as the exploration of new intellectual territory and the expansion of the tenure process beyond the "methodological mainstream" (Senge, 2000, p. 294). And the chair's structural location enables these academic leaders to impact multiple dimensions of diversity through classroom experiences, student engagement, faculty representation, departmental climate, and curricular offerings.

Selected from the faculty ranks for this unique management role, chairs can be compared to an orchestra conductor who needs to marshal the talents and participation of individual musicians to contribute to the whole. Like musicians, each faculty member possesses his or her own expertise and autonomous perspective. Similar to an orchestra conductor's role, the chair's authority derives from the faculty's respect for his or her accomplishments and ability. In this regard, a White female chair of educational leadership in a western public research university explained how her research background makes a difference in the level of respect she receives as chair:

> You know, I have been studying these things for 20 years, and now I get to practice it. That's been really helpful. And then, you know, I sort of have nothing to lose, right? I'm a full professor; I work with the people who have gotten away, in my opinion, with a lot of b.s., at the risk of being a little crass, for a lot of years, and no one really called them on stuff. And I kind of just feel like I have nothing to lose by saying, "You see it that way, but other people don't." You know, just prompting the conversation. So I think having a research background makes a difference. . . . Our previous chairs have not had strong research agendas, and I do, so people can't question my credibility, in terms of, you know, I'm active with research, I have grants, I have doctoral students, so they can't really say I don't get it, because I do.

The chair also emphasized how her scholarly accomplishments and her own level of personal confidence have enabled her to work on improving the university as a whole and to help faculty think critically about diversity:

I've always been pretty confident as a person and as a colleague, and now as a chair I'm trying to use that confidence to call it like I see it. A big part of my commitment as a faculty member is improving the college and university as a whole, and I think part of it is thinking critically about diversity. And when I have an opportunity, just bringing that up.

Yet in contrast with an orchestra conductor, chairs often do not have the leverage or authority to insist on a common pathway and must lead by influence, negotiation, and persuasion. They cannot act with impunity, and they suffer from a lack of power because they must seek the consent of the faculty, be cautious about making immediate changes, and often take on what could be viewed as routine or even demeaning tasks (Hubbell & Homer, 1997, p. 210). In this regard, a White male psychology chair in a midwestern urban research university explained how he wished he had more power to address faculty diversity:

I think chairs would be more successful if they were given more authority by their deans. So, for example, one of the ways I was able to hire a minority faculty member was by asking someone to come give a colloquium and discovering after that that the faculty response to that individual's presentation was really, really good, and in casual conversation I learned this person was interested in moving from the current location. First thing I did was jump on that, and I went to the dean and said, "Guess what I just learned." If chairs and heads were told that part of their job is to find ways to bring in talent, underrepresented faculty and . . . if the dean were supportive of less conventional approaches, chairs and heads would be more successful.

As can be seen in this commentary, chairs may not have the organizational latitude to develop new approaches without the direct support of the dean and the administration.

Commonalities in the Chair Role

Across the higher education spectrum, certain commonalities pertain to the chair role, regardless of institutional and departmental typology. Since the evolution of the chair role in the nineteenth century, chairs have overseen the department's disciplinary offerings in a field of specialty focused on the education of students and that consists of curriculum, budget, faculty, students, and support staff (Seagren, Creswell, & Wheeler, 1993; Smith, 2004).

Some institutions differentiate between department chairs and department heads. In these institutions, department heads carry a higher level of authority and a broader scope. On campuses with faculty unions, this differentiation can also reflect management layers in which department heads are considered management and not represented by collective bargaining units. In other institutions, however, the terminology is used interchangeably.

Often drawing on faculty input, chairs recommend faculty for appointment, promotion, and tenure; address faculty workload and teaching schedules; represent their faculty to the institution, as well as external professional organizations; promote research in the discipline; and set the tone for departmental culture (see Carroll & Wolverton, 2004, for review). As appointees for a specific term typically of three to five years, they can be appointed by the dean or elected by a faculty vote, and sometimes their selection can occur in a situation of conflict between the faculty and the administration.

Chairs tend to see themselves as scholars who, from a sense of duty and for the good of the department, take on the administrative assignment (Gmelch, 1991). In fact, chairs can view their roles as career disruption rather than career advancement, accepting the job reluctantly at personal sacrifice in terms of their research and teaching (Hancock, 2007). For example, a study of 40 department chairs in a public university with 22,000 students and 66 department chairs found that the most frequently cited reason for becoming chair was a sense of duty and the desire to effect change (Hancock, 2007). Pay, status, and career benefits were ranked as less important (Hancock, 2007).

Given the duality of their role, chairs may take on heavy workloads and can suffer from significant stress. A national study of 576 department chairs conducted in 1990, for example, found that 6 of every 10 chairs suffered from heavy workloads, compared with 4 out of 10 of their faculty counterparts as measured in a parallel study of faculty stress (Gmelch, 1991). These stressors included the pressures of performing as an administrator, resolving collegial differences and confrontation among colleagues, and meeting institutional requirements (Gmelch, 1991).

As a result of this national study, Gmelch and Miskin developed the Chair Stress Inventory, which consists of five stressors: administrative tasks, faculty role (staying current in field and publishing), role ambiguity (responsibilities without training/information), perceived expectations (additional professional and social responsibilities), and hierarchical authority stress (resolving difficulties with dean; lack of authority or recognition) (see Gmelch & Miskin, 2011, for review). Add to these stressors the temporary dimension of a chair's responsibilities, a constrained budgetary environment, and a limited ability to recruit and hire new faculty, and the chair can find it particularly difficult to effect change.

Further evidence of the delicate tightrope chairs walk between the faculty and the administration can be found in the 1999 North American Academic

Survey Study of 1,645 faculty, 807 administrators, and 1,607 students in 140 colleges and universities. The study found divergent views between faculty and administration that could cause the two groups to work at cross-purposes (Rothman, Kelly-Woessner, & Woessner, 2011). Administrators, for example, were more positive in assessing their own institutions than were faculty and students and were more confident in their ability to influence the institution (Rothman et al., 2011). When faculty raise concerns or are critical of the institution, administrators may be seen as defensive or unresponsive, whereas, conversely, faculty can be viewed as making the administrator's ability to present the institution in a positive light more difficult (Rothman et al., 2011). These internal tensions resulting from divided authority between faculty and administration can make it difficult to provide a unified vision, and the lack of a coherent message can lead to public confusion (Rothman et al., 2011).

As we have noted, the chair's approach to diversity leadership is affected by external, internal, and disciplinary factors. From an external perspective, the institution's mission; vision; affiliation; leadership focus; geographic location; demographic makeup of faculty, staff, and students; organizational culture; and historical legacy shape the institutional climate for diversity. Factors internal to the department and disciplinary factors also affect the direction the chair sets for diversity within the academic department. We now turn to a more detailed examination of these intersecting factors on the chair's diversity leadership role within higher education through a discussion of (a) external environmental forces, (b) campus-specific factors, and (c) internal departmental differences that include the chair's own positionality with respect to diversity.

External Environmental Forces

Dramatic changes in the external environment are reshaping the higher education landscape, with significant impact on the chair's leadership role in diversity. These pressures have been described as a "perfect storm" in which sea, wind, and rain combine with cataclysmic force (Tierney, 2004), and this storm, in turn, powers diversity's emergence as a strategic priority in higher education (Williams, 2013).

How has this occurred? Globalization has transformed ways of sharing and developing knowledge by eroding barriers of distance and compressing both time and space. The porousness of these boundaries means that universities and colleges must find new ways to engage creative intellectual capital and recruit and deploy a diverse workforce to meet educational needs. In an era of explosive change in which the currency of knowledge is critical, students need to be prepared for a workplace that demands not only cultural competency but also new forms of global and diversity intelligence that enrich intercultural sensitivity and engagement (Chun & Evans, 2014).

As the mission statements of many universities and colleges attest, higher education plays a pivotal and multifaceted role in a global environment. Institutions of higher learning must prepare students for citizenship in a globally connected society; they must collaborate to advance knowledge across local, national, and international boundaries; and they have to compete for diverse talent in a highly competitive global marketplace (see Evans & Chun, 2007, for review). The engaged campus moves beyond a one-way relationship where knowledge flows outward to a relationship in which the synergy between knowledge in and knowledge out involves the community voice (see Ward, 2003, for review). Consider the expansion of campuses to overseas locations such as Duke University's plan to build a full campus in Kunshan, China, and New York University's identification as a "global network university" that includes the 2010 opening in Abu Dhabi of the first comprehensive liberal arts and science campus to be operated abroad by a major American research university (*The Global Network University*, n.d.).

Consider how a White female chair of urban education in a geographically isolated midwestern regional university explained the intersection of globalization with the goals of her institution and her department:

> The university really has looked at a global perspective. . . . One of our strategic priorities is global solutions. So I think that in our department the fact that 25% of our students are international speaks well to a midwestern regional university. And we are able to provide an experience for those students that they're able to take when they are in this country back to their home countries and build upon that. I and my Ghanian colleague go to Ghana every other year, and we recruit students and we take American students there for field studies and engage in that kind of an exchange, and various faculty members have done that in different regions of the world.

Yet campus responses to global imperatives can be addressed with surface-level initiatives that do not change the fundamental institutional demography or culture. In this regard, an African American male sociology department chair in a predominantly White southern university described the frequent tendency to sprinkle a few diverse faces across the campus to satisfy the espoused need for diversity:

> When I look at academe and what makes the heart of the institution, we're talking about, at least for me, the curriculum, the students, the faculty. Then you have the people that run the institution, the administrators, the top level. And so when all this discussion of diversity comes about, the

thing that annoys me is if you're talking about sprinkling a few non-White faces wherever they come from—Central America, Africa, or Harlem.

When you sprinkle a few of these faces in the classroom, you say, "Oh we have diversity; we now have a diversity officer." Once you move outside of that little bubble and start walking across the campus, and it could be any campus . . . you begin to realize that 99.9% of these institutions are still predominantly White, and they count diversity in the most superficial ways. So when I think of diversity, I'm thinking about the kids who have to come to class in a wheelchair because they don't have legs. I'm thinking about diversity when the faculty member standing up in front of the class in physics and mathematics, etc., is female.

Accountability and budgetary constraints. The demand for accountability in higher education has intensified amid budgetary pressures and created new challenges for academic department chairs. All institutions face accountability pressures in terms of how they fulfill a variety of public purposes and are accountable to various publics (Siegel, 2010). Beginning in the 1980s, the assessment movement resulting from changes in U.S. education policy has forced universities and colleges to reconsider and even defend their missions (Rothman et al., 2011). Accountability takes shape in external forms such as through accreditation; compliance with federal, state, and local regulatory bodies, governing boards of trustees, or regents; and unionization, as well as internally through internal reviews and assessments that ensure the maintenance and improvement of quality (Trow, 1998).

Following the recession in the United States and the global economic decline that began in late 2007, shortfalls in state budgets have led to increased demands by legislatures to create terms and conditions of employment for faculty and staff that are more favorable to management and offer fewer employment protections. For example, because of constricting state budgets, following the election in 2010, newly elected Republican governors and GOP-controlled legislatures responded to budget deficits by making efforts to eliminate bargaining rights, increase contribution rates for health insurance and pensions, and restrict wage increases (see Evans & Chun, 2012, for review). In 2011, an unpopular bill signed into law by Republican governor John Kasich in Ohio would have reclassified faculty as management employees and stripped them of their collective bargaining rights (Evans & Chun, 2012). Through the collection of 915,000 signatures in a voter referendum, the bill was overturned (Evans & Chun, 2012).

In a similar move to curtail union rights in Wisconsin, in 2011 legislation was signed by Republican governor Scott Walker that limited state government workers to bargaining on anything except wages, required public unions to hold an annual election to see whether members wish the union to continue representation, and barred unions from withdrawing dues from members' paychecks (Richmond & Bauer, 2013). A federal appeals court upheld the contentious law (Richmond & Bauer, 2013). In 2012, Walker became the first governor to survive a recall election in 2012, representing a severe setback to the state's public college faculty unions who had backed the recall effort (Schmidt, 2012).

States have also adopted an increased emphasis on performance-based funding formulas for public higher education as a way of strengthening institutional accountability. A dozen states have implemented performance-based funding, another 20 are considering it, and four are moving in that direction (Milligan, 2013). The emphasis on graduation rates, although positive, can also create pressures on chairs and faculty in the educational process. In Ohio, Governor John Kasich in concert with committees of higher education leaders has revamped the funding formula for higher education, with 50% of operating funds for the state's 14 universities and 23 community colleges derived from graduation rates (Kiley, 2013). This funding ratio is the highest in the nation (Kiley, 2013).

With the rise of economic pressures, some theorists see the trajectory of higher education as a social institution shifting in more corporate directions with the advent of what has been termed "academic capitalism" (see, e.g., Gumport, 2001; Morphew & Eckel, 2009; Rhoades & Slaughter, 2004; Slaughter & Rhoades, 2004; Tuchman, 2009). This trend can have an adverse effect on the attainment of diversity. As universities seek to generate revenue through entrepreneurial, market-like behaviors, efforts to increase access to low-income and minority students have been replaced by an emphasis on accessibility and pursuits of "privileged, niche student markets" (Rhoades & Slaughter, 2004, p. 52).

Faculty workload and productivity are under constant scrutiny as budgets tighten. The vise of dwindling budgets and increased accountability creates dilemmas for chairs in their efforts to sustain the viability and quality of academic programs under their direction while generating sufficient student credit hours to sustain these programs. With funding linked to student credit hour production, department heads across a variety of settings have begun to focus on "educational entrepreneurialism" rather than research-oriented entrepreneurialism as they seek ways to increase undergraduate credit hours such as by packaging programs to attract more students (Rhoades & Slaughter, 2004, p. 41). Department heads have noted with concern, frustration, and even anger the increased pressure from academic administration to generate new revenue, find new sources of federal grants or contracts, and enhance productivity (Rhoades & Slaughter, 2004).

Funding shortfalls also mean dwindling teaching resources, including a lack of funds for sections taught by part-time faculty. For chairs, balancing curricular and program needs with available teaching resources has become increasingly difficult. And academic program review and pressures to ensure sufficient enrollment in certain majors have created conflicts between the aims of a liberal education and the financial viability of programs with limited enrollment.

Take the devastating impact of budget cuts on language programs. At the State University of New York at Albany, new majors in French, Italian, Russian, and the classics were suspended. Similar moves occurred at a number of other institutions such as at Louisiana State University, where majors in German and Latin were phased out, and basic instruction in a number of other languages was eliminated (Foderaro, 2010). As critics have noted, such pressures are at cross-purposes with the aims of the academy to prepare students for their role in a global society. In other examples, in 2010 the University of Nevada, Reno, closed 23 degree programs, releasing 20 tenured professors, and at the University of Nevada, Las Vegas, 18 degree programs were eliminated (American Association of University Professors, 2013). In March 2012, the University of Northern Iowa announced the elimination of more than 50 programs (American Association of University Professors, 2013).

The increasing role of administrators in determining program closures that affect the curriculum has caused a firestorm of protest among faculty. In the view of the American Association of University Professors, such moves have further eroded the discretionary power of the tenured professoriate and, by extension, the department chair (American Association of University Professors, 2013). Noting the damaging effect of budget reductions on educational quality, Elizabeth Capaldi, provost at Arizona State University, noted that boards often focus on the academic program as the primary unit of analysis rather than recognize that academic administrative units—departments and schools—are how universities are managed (Capaldi, 2011). External pressures have exacerbated internal tensions between administration and the governance process, tensions that cause decision making to be "mired by gridlock and inaction" (Rothman et al., 2011, p. 15).

Faculty unionization. Faculty unionization is a significant factor that can intensify the difficulty of building bridges between the faculty and the administration. In public institutions, just over half of the full-time faculty are unionized in four-year and comprehensive institutions, and about one third are in doctoral institutions (Benjamin, 2006). Overall, public sector representation in two- and four-year public institutions is just under 50%, with nearly half of the institutions with faculty unions located in California and New York (Benjamin, 2006; Cain, 2013; Hedrick, Henson, Krieg, &

Wassell, 2011). By contrast, representation of full-time faculty is much lower in private institutions because of the 1980 *NLRB v. Yeshiva* decision that found faculty in private institutions to be managerial employees, excluding them from protection under the National Labor Relations Act (Benjamin, 2006; DeCew, 2003). Few private college union cases have succeeded since this decision, with a handful of exceptions, although it remains possible for a private institution to voluntarily agree to collective bargaining with the faculty (DeCew, 2003).

The inclusion or exclusion of department chairs from the faculty bargaining unit varies among institutions with faculty unions. In our survey sample, 21% of the chairs are represented by a union and serve in public institutions, whereas 10% of the chairs who are not represented by a union work in institutions in which the faculty are represented. Even when faculty are excluded from the bargaining unit as administrators, the faculty contract may contain provisions pertaining to the selection of chairs.

The ambiguities of the chair role as "neither fish nor fowl" coupled with the uneasy feeling of administration and faculty about trusting someone from the "other side" can amplify the difficulties of the chair in the context of collective bargaining (Brown, 2003, p. 157). In some institutions such as St. John's University, the University of Bridgeport, and the Minnesota system, faculty can even initiate recall proceedings of their own chairs (Brown, 2003).

We now explore the impact of campus-specific factors on diversity progress and how these factors interrelate with the academic department chair's efforts to implement diversity-related change.

The Interrelationship of the Campus and Departmental Diversity Progress

A constellation of factors such as the college's or university's mission, affiliation, or geographic location and other variables provide the campus-wide backdrop for the chair's role in facilitating diversity progress. University or college leadership plays a critical role in setting institutional direction and providing support for diversity efforts.

Mission. Symbolic forms of diversity leadership take place in mission statements that then require enactment in the crucible of university culture. When an institution links diversity with its core educational mission and vision, this fundamental message provides the groundwork for connecting diversity programs with resources, accountability, and expected outcomes. In this regard, a study of the websites of 80 institutions of public higher education in 2009 found that 75% mentioned diversity in their mission statements and 65% had a separate diversity statement, with 25% to 35% of these institutions not including diversity as a core focus in their public statements (Wilson, Meyer, & McNeal, 2012). Interestingly, even with the institution that did express a commitment to diversity, the tendency was to emphasize diversity as integration of "others" rather than in terms of the transformation of all in the campus community (Wilson et al., 2012).

Yet having a mission statement that connects with diversity is not sufficient, because campus stakeholders do not automatically accept the institutional mission without leadership investment. Individuals must be socialized to the mission, and the mission has to be reinforced through conversations and meetings or a process called "sensemaking" (Kezar, 2005). Researchers have noted that colleges and universities frequently engage in impression management to portray themselves as diverse organizations through brochures, websites, and other materials (Aguirre & Martinez, 2007). In such cases, institutions of higher education can resort to co-optative approaches to diversity that provide lip service to diversity and serve as window dressing rather than change the existing culture (Aguirre & Martinez, 2007). Diversity strategic plans can suffer from this phenomenon as well. For example, when we contacted chief diversity officers for a review of diversity strategic plans cited in our earlier research (Evans & Chun, 2007), a number of these top diversity leaders indicated that the practices identified in the plans had not been actualized.

Affiliation. Our study includes institutions that have a religious affiliation and, for example, require that faculty and staff be professing members of a specific faith. The religious affiliation of an institution can present certain difficulties in attracting diverse faculty and students. A White female department chair at a religiously affiliated institution described how the geographic location of the college coupled with the makeup of students coming from a particular religious affiliation have made it more difficult to attain diversity:

> It's kind of a vicious cycle where the city is a very homogeneous city. The school relies on a certain population, basically kids that want to go to an evangelical Christian school. . . . A lot of the major evangelical denominations are predominantly White. It's a gross generalization. . . .
>
> So I think honestly that it was a largely White school in a White region with pretty mostly White students. . . . I think if the students kind of banded together and said, "Look the curriculum has to change; the situation has to change," that would have been very powerful, but . . . what is happening now is really a push from the faculty, not from our clientele.

According to the chair, the recent hiring of a chief diversity officer has galvanized efforts to increase the college's faculty diversity.

Leadership focus. One of the most significant factors in diversity trans-formation is the direction set by institutional leadership. Although the role of president or chancellor is pivotal, the leadership of academic institutions is multifaceted, complex, and interactional. It includes the board of trustees, cabinet-level leadership, the dean, and academic governance such as through the faculty senate (see Evans & Chun, 2007, for review).

Contrary to the tendency for diversity leadership studies to empha-size the structural framework of presidential leadership, academic leaders depend on diffused power by negotiating coalitions both within and out-side the organization (Kezar, Eckel, Contreras-McGavin, & Quaye, 2008). Such power can be informal and based on influence rather than hierarchical relationships.

A White female department chair of urban education in a regional midwestern university described the strategic alignment of the university's diversity direction with the values in her department. She explained this alignment as resulting in the creation of both a top-down synergy and a department-level-up synergy:

> Leadership does count. We can be just really movers in the trenches, but I think we have to have leadership that embraces the concept of diversity and understands what it takes to bring diversity about. . . . So because that's embraced by the president and his cabinet, that seems to move both direc-tions from the department level up and from the top level down. And you know really what I am saying is our values are aligned. And I think that's what it takes, is to have values aligned.

In chapter 7, we will discuss further the alignment of institutional diver-sity policy with departmental practices.

Faculty demographics. The extent to which a campus has explicitly focused on faculty diversity has significant influence on programs and ini-tiatives at the departmental level. As shown in Table 3.1, despite increases in the percentages of full-time women and minority faculty between 2001 and 2011, the faculty in the six institutional types represented in this study remain predominantly White, with White males garnering the most signifi-cant percentage of full-time faculty appointments. The low rates of represen-tation of African American men and women, Asian American women, and Hispanic or Latino men and women have persisted over more than three decades, indicating a pervasive structural inequality within the academic hierarchy (Evans & Chun, 2007). By contrast, White women have gained a larger share of full-time faculty employment during the decade in ques-tion, with significant gains in private master's and private research doctorate institutions. Table 3.1 does not include nonresident aliens, those faculty of

TABLE 3.1

Percentage Change in Demographics of Full-Time Faculty From 2001 to 2011

Institution Type

Demographic	Private			Public			
	Bacc.	*Master's*	*Research/Doctorate*	*Bacc.*	*Master's*	*Research/Doctorate*	*Total*
Asian men							
% change	13.0	49.3	25.9	43.6	27.7	27.3	28.7
% of total	1.1	1.6	4.2	1.8	2.8	4.3	3.1
Asian women							
% change	14.2	57.6	35.0	35.6	19.3	19.6	24.8
% of total	1.5	2.2	5.0	1.8	3.1	4.2	3.3
Black or African American men							
% change	50.1	105.4	90.0	59.0	33.8	26.4	47.4
% of total	7.1	6.0	4.2	6.4	5.3	4.4	5.2
Black or African American women							
% change	59.6	113.2	142.3	48.8	27.5	19.0	49.4
% of total	11.8	11.7	9.8	10.2	8.7	6.6	8.9

Hispanic or Latino men							
% change	63.3	92.7	76.8	43.2	88.9	76.0	78.0
% of total	4.8	5.8	5.9	6.4	5.6	5.4	5.6
Hispanic or Latina women							
% change	80.1	85.1	79.1	22.4	78.2	68.5	71.7
% of total	7.0	8.7	8.6	8.9	8.2	6.7	7.7
White men							
% change	7.3	35.7	18.8	12.5	15.3	8.0	14.0
% of total	27.1	26.9	27.1	30.1	29.2	33.8	30.1
White women							
% change	13.4	34.7	40.0	7.4	6.7	2.3	11.9
% of total	40.0	37.0	35.0	34.0	37.0	35.0	36.0

Source. U.S. Department of Education, 2012, Washington, DC: National Center for Education Statistics, Integrated Postsecondary Education System. Analysis by authors.

Note. Bacc. = Baccalaureate.

two or more races, Native Hawaiians, and those whose race or ethnicity is unknown.

Because of increasing diversity in student enrollment, chairs play an active role in recruitment and hiring strategies that will build a more diverse faculty representative of the demographics of the student body. Although Table 3.1 reveals appreciable increases in minority hiring over the decade, minorities still occupy only a small percentage of full-time faculty positions, indicating that much work still remains to be done to create a more representative faculty.

Student demographics. As we have shared earlier, one of the primary arguments for campus diversity focuses on the student experience and the preparation of students for citizenship and careers in a globally interconnected workplace. Recent social science research indicates that campuses that are racially diverse tend to provide more varied and enriched educational experiences that facilitate engagement and participation in a democratic society (see Chang, Denson, Saenz, & Misa, 2006, for review). The educational potential of diversity, however, depends on whether the presence of diversity leads to greater levels of engagement such as through interpersonal interactions with peers (Chang et al., 2006).

Researchers have indicated that students' perceptions of an institution's overall commitment to diversity influence their determinations of whether they are able to benefit from diversity. On campuses that implement more comprehensive diversity programs, students are more likely to perceive greater institutional commitment to diversity (Milem, Chang, & Antonio, 2005). Conversely, when students from nondominant groups are underrepresented, they can be subjected to negative social stigma, stereotype, and "minority status stressors" (see Milem et al., 2005, for review). In support of this thesis, a survey of 9,750 Latino and African American students at eight University of California campuses found that they perceived the campus racial climate as more inhospitable following the state ban on affirmative action and low diversity, which has led students to believe that they are less respected by their peers (Kidder, 2013).

Geographic location. Geographic location was cited by a significant number of respondents as a barrier to attaining greater faculty diversity in the academic department. When a predominantly White university is located in an isolated geographic area with relatively little population diversity, attracting members of nondominant groups presents a substantial hurdle to attaining diversity. For universities and colleges located in urban areas, attracting faculty from nondominant groups is a less difficult proposition.

In discussing what would constitute optimal diversity for their departments, several chairs interviewed for the study described the need to serve an increasingly diverse student body and to have faculty representative of both student diversity and the diversity of the surrounding geographic area and state. A White male psychology chair in a midwestern urban university explained what would constitute optimal diversity for his department:

> For my particular department, optimal diversity would closer resemble the diversity of the student body. . . . We're one of the most diverse universities in the nation in the sense that we don't even have a majority population that exceeds 50%. I think, optimally, our faculty and staff would be more in line with that particular diversity, which actually is in line with the diversity of the United States itself.

And a White female chair of journalism in a master's-level university described the challenge of her university's rural location, coupled with limited hiring opportunities:

> One of our challenges is that our city does not have a diverse population. We are living in one of the most diverse states in the country, and we are in the least diverse part of the state. The challenge for us is for faculty members, people of color in particular, to come here and be happy, find a place that they can like as home and that they can feel comfortable here. The challenge is just where we are, and how small our faculty is. One shift, hiring one Black faculty member, is a huge percentage when you only have about six or seven or eight faculty members. And recruitment is difficult. The economy meant that we were not able to hire for a while.

Historical legacy. The historical legacy of a campus can shape campus climate in terms of the readiness to implement diversity and the prevailing mindset, beliefs, and assumptions about diversity that pervade the campus culture. The vestiges remaining from institutionalized discriminatory practices in all areas of the United States can continue to affect the climate for racial and ethnic diversity on college campuses (Feagin, Vera, & Imani, 1996; Milem et al., 2005). The starting line for diversity efforts cannot be viewed as uniform, because receptivity to the need for diversity change is affected by historical forces exhibited through community influences, institutional practices and structures, and behavioral climate. In this regard, a White female sociology chair in a southwestern public research university described the efforts of her department to overcome the historical legacy of inequality in her state:

> So we're sociologists, and sociologists are concerned particularly with the study of inequality, the reproduction of inequality, and hopefully the dismantlement of inequality. One of the things that we hope we are very

mindful about is diversity in terms of racial and ethnic composition as reflected in the United States population. . . .

Our university has a tradition that emphasizes tradition. It has a conservative image, I think. Of course . . . we have right down the road a HBCU, and this serves as a reminder of the racial history. We have this image issue. People have worked very hard to overcome the image. One thing I want to make clear is that it is not just "image": There is an obvious racial discrimination history as evidenced by the history of segregated schools.

The chair sees the work of the department as a force that helps counteract historical legacies of inequality in the state and the university's environment.

Factors Internal to the Academic Department

Within the department, the context for diversity is affected by the disciplinary focus, the historical approach to diversity, and the predominant representation of faculty in terms of race, ethnicity, gender, and sexual orientation. For example, the White female sociology chair cited earlier described how the "forefathers" and "mothers" of the department created the norm for considering diversity:

I think it partly was the commitment early on in the department which we kind of structured, and people, I guess we call them the ancestors, the forefathers and mothers of the department, emphasized it and created a norm for considering that type of issue. . . . And we have supportive administrators . . . a supportive dean and department heads who kind of emphasize diversity and the importance of it. And so the development of these norms and the access to resources are the crucial components.

She further explained how, as a social psychologist, her focus is on the structure of the department and its norms rather than on individual characteristics:

As a sociologist, I would say that we have to think not about individual characteristics but more about the structure of the department setup to encourage diversity and help people from diverse backgrounds navigate through more traditional kinds of settings. In that way, it is important to set up policies and norms, and I emphasize norms, because you might have policies that when written look great, but if they are not enforced in the terms of kind of everyday life, it's not going to work. In that way, chairs are important for sustaining the norms and also modeling the behavior. But in my department . . . because of the great history of the department and the support . . . it's kind of set up: The norms are already there, and so it's important just to nourish them.

A chair's own positionality and framing of values necessarily impacts his or her approach to diversity. This approach is shaped by identity, background, experience, and other contextual factors (Kezar, 2000). Positionality theory is based on the acknowledgment that individuals in an organization have multiple, overlapping identities and the assumption that the power relations in an organization can change (Kezar, 2002). Prevailing legacies of structural inequality, for example, situate individuals differently in the power structure and influence how individual leaders approach their roles and their ability to implement change (see Chun & Evans, 2009, for review). The White female sociology chair explained how her own implicit biases affect her view of diversity:

> You never really know your own biases as well as other people might be able to [laughs]. . . . I'm a social psychologist as well, so I am thinking about this response. I think there are a lot of hidden biases that I have that I am not very aware of, but I try to keep myself honest by encouraging people to tell me what they really think. I feel that I'm very committed as a department to the idea of diversity recruitment and retention. I hope that I am.

In support of this perspective, a study of 36 faculty and administrators in a community college reinforces the notion of positionality in diversity leadership. It found that women and people of color were more likely to incorporate experience with oppression into their personal philosophy of leadership and to emphasize the servant leadership model of nonhierarchical, collective, empowerment-based leadership (Kezar, 2002). This model derived from their personal, vivid experiences of how they had been devalued for their leadership style in past positions (Kezar, 2002).

A White female lesbian psychology chair in a midwestern liberal arts college explained with candor how her positionality and skills in assisting minority students in their identity development were affected by her growing up in a "lily-white community":

> I think I personally was pretty hapless in that regard, especially with African American students. I received no formal training about how to do that. . . . I grew up in a pretty lily-white community and certainly felt those social values . . . but I personally didn't have any skills, and I am sure that I had negative skills, of not really knowing how to do it. . . . I am probably a racist

in some strange ways that I did not appreciate at the tender age of 30. It's
not unlikely. . . . I'm sure my efforts to do it were ham-handed.

Nonetheless, this chair, like other chairs interviewed in this study,
brought a concern and level of understanding of her diversity role that
derives from her reflecting critically on her own experiences, assumptions,
and presuppositions.

In small departments in which all the faculty are tenured, the absence of
new faculty lines is the main obstacle to compositional diversity. Furthermore,
when a department does take the extra step to hire an underrepresented minority, and that individual is not successful, this experience can present additional
challenges, particularly in small departments that have few untenured lines.
A White lesbian female psychology department chair in a midwestern liberal
arts college described how her active efforts to diversify the department with a
minority hire failed and what she learned from the experience:

> In a department of eight people without an African American, the great
> challenge was to fill that void. . . . I did actually succeed in hiring someone,
> but she was a one-woman disaster area. She had excellent recommenda-
> tions, but she had no clue how to teach; in fact we had to pull her from
> teaching after one semester and give her an administrative job for the sec-
> ond semester, after which she had to leave. . . . Her students had come in
> and complained to me and to the dean very early on.
>
> And I went to sit in on her class and try to help. Her teaching
> method was to outline the textbook and to read her outline in class to
> be transcribed by the students. . . . I tried to give her lessons on lectur-
> ing, having myself been given formal lessons by a great teacher. . . . She
> just had some huge anxiety issues and really couldn't do public speaking.
> Helping her was completely beyond what I could offer as a chair. . . .
> So those were some of my challenges. I thought I did great. I was very
> proud to bring her in. Actually my first or second year as chair, first hire,
> someone who, at least on paper, looked fabulous but became a disap-
> pointment.

The chair described her department as "overtenured," with only a single
line available for diversity hiring at the time. Because of her failed attempt to
hire a minority, her perspective shifted:

> It made me a little gun-shy. I think I went into that first hire with the
> criterion: Let's find an African American. And after that, I thought let's
> find somebody good and to leave race as a deciding point between two
> candidates.

The decline in the number of full-time faculty lines due to budgetary factors has intensified the pressure on chairs in their efforts to increase faculty diversity.

Concluding Perspectives: Strategies for Overcoming Environmental Hurdles

The most prominent environmental obstacle to diversity identified by survey participants is the lack of funding for new faculty lines. The absence of funding has hampered the efforts of departments to remedy underrepresentation and to offer areas of specialization that enhance curricular diversity. Complex approval processes and levels of faculty compensation are also cited frequently as barriers to enhancing faculty diversity. And geographic location plays a significant role in departments' ability to attract diverse faculty. The following strategies have been employed at the institutional and departmental levels to address these obstacles.

Consider creating opportunities for bringing new faculty into the department by offering a voluntary university-wide early retirement/severance program that offers service credit and/or a substantial incentive payment. Voluntary severance plans are usually distinct from state retirement plans, but they can be combined to increase the incentive for separation. The revenue gained from such plans allows the hiring of less senior faculty, providing both salary savings and the ability to meet projected curricular needs (see Evans & Chun, 2012, for review). Examples of such plans include those offered at Kent State University and other Ohio universities, including Wright State University, Ohio University, and Bowling Green State University (Evans & Chun, 2012). A decentralized version of this plan was offered by Ohio State University in which each college could offer a payment of 12 months of salary but no more than $75,000 for separating employees (see Evans & Chun, 2012, for review).

Once new lines become available through the voluntary severance plan, direct funding toward areas that will enhance representational and curricular diversity by establishing new faculty lines. With the increased availability of funding, chairs have the opportunity to broaden the areas of curricular specialization and work to attract a diverse pool of candidates. For example, an English department chair cited the broadening of offerings in African American literature in her department, without the ability to obtain funding for an additional line in Hispanic literature. The addition of this area of specialization would enhance the university's responsiveness to the growing Hispanic population.

Make the "business case" for the need for greater departmental diversity to the dean and provost to enhance hiring flexibility and overcome bureaucratic approval processes. Making a business case for the need for representational diversity to the dean and provost and obtaining greater flexibility in the hiring process can assist in building a more diverse department. A number of chairs cited bureaucratic formal approval processes as a barrier to increasing faculty diversity. In this regard, a White male chair of psychology in an urban midwestern university emphasized the importance of representing the interests of diverse students in terms of both representational diversity and areas of academic specialization. Within his first two years as chair, he lost all but one of the four minority faculty members in the department of 30 faculty to other universities that offered higher salaries. His concerns were twofold:

> One of the obvious reasons is that we don't represent the students in terms of how we look on diversity, but . . . it takes away from the academic status of our department because the individuals of color often are the people who are studying issues related to diversity. So it wasn't just a loss of the diverse individuals, but it was the loss of an important field of study. They weren't studying just racial diversity: We have people studying sexual and gender identity, racial identity, personality development, access to health resources, and things of that nature.

As a result, the chair approached the dean and requested a faculty line that he could use immediately to help rebuild the department's representational diversity:

> So I went to the dean and said I would like to have a hire that I can just have in my pocket . . . such that if we encounter a highly qualified person I can make an offer. One of the first things I tried to do was to increase the physical presence of diversity.

Take advantage of diversity hiring incentives offered by the office of the provost or the chief diversity officer. A number of institutions have developed special funding incentives to enhance faculty diversity. At Kent State University, for example, the Division of Diversity, Equity, and Inclusion has developed a program of incremental funding for tenure-track hires from underrepresented groups, with up to $15,000 a year provided for six years to the hiring dean (Chun & Evans, 2014). The dean is required to provide a plan for the success of the new faculty hire that helps acclimate the faculty member to the university through mentoring and research support (Chun & Evans, 2014). At Stanford University, the vice provost for faculty development and diversity offers a faculty incentive fund designed to help departments and schools make appointments that will bring diversity to the faculty ("Recruitment Programs," n.d.). Because of low faculty turnover, the uneven distribution of minority and women scholars in the academic disciplines, and the fact that hiring opportunities may not occur in departments with diversity needs, the fund facilitates opportunities for hiring diverse scholars ("Recruitment Programs," n.d.).

Enhance budgetary resources through grant opportunities designed to strengthen diversity. A primary example of federal funding directed toward strengthening faculty diversity is the National Science Foundation's (NSF) ADVANCE program (*ADVANCE*, n.d.). This program is designed to enhance systemic approaches to increase the representation and career advancement of women in academic science and engineering fields. It is specifically focused on institutional transformation and overcoming external factors that hinder women's advancement unrelated to individual ability such as implicit and explicit bias, organizational constraints, differential family and work demands, and the lack of women in leadership positions (*ADVANCE*, n.d.). Since 2001, the NSF has invested over $130 million at more than 100 institutions of higher education. ADVANCE programs at Case Western Reserve University and the University of North Carolina at Charlotte, for example, have focused specifically on faculty recruitment, with an emphasis on training to reduce and eliminate bias in evaluative processes and conducting ongoing, proactive recruitment with representationally diverse search committees (Bilimoria & Buch, 2010).

Additional opportunities for funding can also be garnered through corporate partnerships. For example, a White female chair in journalism in a western master's-level university identified the major obstacle to diversity as "money, money, money" and indicated that partnership with a media news group has provided nearly $80,000 in donations for scholarships and internships in her department, mainly for first-generation students.

For campuses in isolated geographic locations, consider approaches that create an inclusive faculty environment through retreats and social interactions that create a sense of community and belonging. A White female chair of special education in a geographically isolated western public research university described her efforts to create an inclusive departmental environment for faculty, staff, and students through programs that enhance human interaction such as orientation programs, retreats, dinners, potlucks, and other events. She emphasized going "one step further" by "valuing each other as human beings," as expressed through activities that facilitate personal involvement. Coupled with campus workshops and support systems, this inclusive approach helps overcome the lack of diversity in the surrounding community and enables students, faculty, and staff to form close bonds across all identity groups. The chair also works to facilitate inclusion in her discipline across all of the university's four campus locations, each of which has its own distinct climate. In other words, the chair's work does not stop at the boundaries of the department but facilitates the inclusion of diverse faculty as part of the overall campus community.

Moving forward with our exploration of the chair's role in diversity, in chapter 4 we examine the structural design of the academic organization in terms of how this design can facilitate or hinder the process of diversity transformation. In particular, we focus on the roles of the dean and provost as influential drivers of diversity efforts who can set the tone and vision for diversity attainment and provide the instrumental resources needed to make concrete progress.

References

ADVANCE: Increasing the participation and advancement of women in academic science and engineering careers. (n.d.). Retrieved November 29, 2013, from http://www.nsf.gov/funding/pgm_summ.jsp?pims_id=5383

Aguirre, A., Jr., & Martinez, R. O. (2007). *Diversity leadership in higher education* (ASHE-ERIC Higher Education Reports, Vol. 32, No. 3). San Francisco, CA: Jossey-Bass.

American Association of University Professors. (2013). *The role of the faculty in conditions of financial exigency.* Retrieved August 31, 2013, from http://www.aaup.org/file/FinancialExigency.pdf

Benjamin, E. (2006). Faculty bargaining. In E. Benjamin & M. Mauer (Eds.), *Academic collective bargaining* (pp. 23–51). New York, NY: American Association of University Professors.

Bilimoria, D., & Buch, K. K. (2010). The search is on: Engendering faculty diversity through more effective search and recruitment. *Change, 42*(4), 27–32.

Brown, W. R. (2003). Academic politics: Faculty unions and the academic perception. In J. W. DeCew (Ed.), *Unionization in the academy: Visions and realities* (pp. 139–166). Lanham, MD: Rowman & Littlefield.

Cain, T. (2013). *The research on faculty unions.* Retrieved September 15, 2013, from http://iprh.wordpress.com/2013/02/09/the-research-on-faculty-unions/

Capaldi, E. D. (2011). *Budget cuts and educational quality: Policy makers—and the public—need to understand the potentially devastating effects of cuts to higher education.* Retrieved August 31, 2013, from http://www.aaup.org/article/budget-cuts-and-educational-quality

Carroll, J. B., & Wolverton, M. (2004). Who becomes a chair? *New Directions for Higher Education, 126,* 3–10.

Chang, M. J., Denson, N., Saenz, V., & Misa, K. (2006). The educational benefits of sustaining cross-racial interaction among undergraduates. *Journal of Higher Education, 77*(3), 430–455.

Christensen, C. M., & Eyring, H. J. (2011). *The innovative university: Changing the DNA of higher education from the inside out.* San Francisco, CA: Jossey-Bass.

Chun, E., & Evans, A. (2009). *Bridging the diversity divide: Globalization and reciprocal empowerment in higher education* (ASHE-ERIC Higher Education Reports, Vol. 35, No. 1). San Francisco, CA: Jossey-Bass.

Chun, E., & Evans, A. (2014). *The new talent acquisition frontier: Integrating HR and diversity strategy in the private and public sectors and higher education.* Sterling, VA: Stylus.

DeCew, J. W. (2003). *Unionization in the academy: Visions and realities.* Lanham, MD: Rowman & Littlefield.

The Diversity Scorecard Committee. (2010). *To form a more inclusive learning community: The CSU, Chico 2011–2016 diversity action plan.* Retrieved November 29, 2013, from http://www.csuchico.edu/prs/dap/12-13-2010.pdf

Ernst, C., & Chrobot-Mason, D. (2011). *Boundary spanning leadership: Six practices for solving problems, driving innovation, and transforming organizations.* New York, NY: McGraw-Hill.

Esterberg, K. G., & Wooding, J. (2012). *Divided conversations: Identities, leadership, and change in public higher education.* Nashville, TN: Vanderbilt University Press.

Evans, A., & Chun, E. B. (2007). *Are the walls really down? Behavioral and organizational barriers to faculty and staff diversity* (ASHE-ERIC Higher Education Reports, Vol. 33, No. 1). San Francisco, CA: Jossey-Bass.

Evans, A., & Chun, E. (2012). *Creating a tipping point: Strategic human resources in higher education.* San Francisco, CA: Jossey-Bass.

Feagin, J. R., Vera, H., & Imani, N. (1996). *The agony of education: Black students at White colleges and universities.* New York, NY: Routledge.

Foderaro, L. W. (2010, December 3). Budget-cutting colleges bid some languages adieu. *The New York Times.* Retrieved August 31, 2013, from http://www.nytimes.com/2010/12/05/education/ 05languages.html?pagewanted=all&_r=0

The global network university. (n.d.). Retrieved from http://www.nyu.edu/students/undergraduates/the-global-networkuniversity.html

Gmelch, W. H. (1991). Paying the price for academic leadership: Department chair tradeoffs. *Educational Record, 72*(3), 45–48.

Gmelch, W. H. (1995). Department chairs under siege: Resolving the web of conflict. *New Directions for Higher Education, 92,* 35–42.

Gmelch, W. H., & Miskin, V. D. (2011). *Department chair leadership skills* (2nd ed.). Madison, WI: Atwood.

Gumport, P. J. (2001). Restructuring: Imperatives and opportunities for academic leaders. *Innovative Higher Education, 25*(4), 239–251.

Hancock, T. M. (2007). The business of universities and the role of department chair. *International Journal of Educational Management, 21*(4), 306–314.

Hecht, I. W. D., Higgerson, M. L., Gmelch, W. H., & Tucker, A. (1999). *The department chair as academic leader.* Phoenix, AZ: Oryx.

Hedrick, D. W., Henson, S. E., Krieg, J. M., & Wassell, C. S., Jr. (2011). Is there really a faculty union salary premium? *Industrial and Labor Relations Review, 64*(3), 558–575.

Hubbell, L., & Homer, F. (1997). The academic department chair: The logic of appeasement. *PS: Political Science and Politics, 30*(2), 209–213.

Kezar, A. (2000). Pluralistic leadership: Incorporating diverse voices. *Journal of Higher Education, 71*(6), 722–743.

Kezar, A. (2002). Reconstructing static images of leadership: An application of positionality theory. *Journal of Leadership and Organizational Studies, 8*(3), 94–109.

Kezar, A. (2005). Moving from I to we: Reorganizing for collaboration in higher education. *Change, 37*(6), 50–57.

Kezar, A., Eckel, P., Contreras-McGavin, M., & Quaye, S. J. (2008). Creating a web of support: An important leadership strategy for advancing campus diversity. *Higher Education, 55*(1), 69–92.

Kidder, W. C. (2013). Misshaping the river: Proposition 209 and lessons for the Fisher case. *Journal of College and University Law, 39*(1), 53–125.

Kiley, K. (2013, July 23). Personalities and policies. *Inside Higher Ed.* Retrieved September 2, 2013, from http://www.insidehighered.com/news/2013/07/23/ohio-state-president-steered-state-policy-two-years-thanks-relationship-governor

Lumina Foundation. (2012). *A stronger nation through higher education: How and why Americans must achieve a big goal for college attainment.* Retrieved November 29, 2013, from www.luminafoundation.org/publications/A_stronger_nation.pdf

Merisotis, J. P. (2012). More than mere data, "stronger nation" report is a call for change. In Lumina Foundation (Ed.), *A stronger nation through higher education: How and why Americans must achieve a big goal for college attainment* (pp. 1–3). Retrieved November 29, 2013, from www.luminafoundation.org/publications/A_stronger_nation.pdf

Merisotis, J. P. (2013). *A stronger nation through higher education.* Retrieved November 29, 2013, from http://www.luminafoundation.org/about_us/president/speeches/2013-09-09.html

Milem, J. F., Chang, M. J., & Antonio, A. L. (2005). *Making diversity work on campus: A research-based perspective.* Retrieved August 22, 2013, from http://siher.stanford.edu/AntonioMilemChang_makingdiversitywork.pdf

Milligan, S. (2013). *Graduation rates, test scores drive higher education funding.* Retrieved September 14, 2013, from http://www.pewstates.org/projects/stateline/headlines/graduation-rates-test-scores-drive-higher-education-funding-85899488906

Morphew, C. C., & Eckel, P. D. (Eds.). (2009). *Privatizing the public university: Perspectives from across the academy.* Baltimore, MD: Johns Hopkins University Press.

Recruitment programs. (n.d.). Retrieved from https://facultydevelopment.stanford.edu/recruitment/recruitment-programs

Rhoades, G., & Slaughter, S. (2004). *Academic capitalism in the new economy: Challenges and choices.* Baltimore, MD: Johns Hopkins University Press.

Richmond, T., & Bauer, S. (2013). Scott Walker's collective bargaining law upheld by federal appeals court. *The Huffington Post.* Retrieved September 15, 2013, from http://www.huffingtonpost.com/2013/01/18/scott-walker_n_2507376.html

Rothman, S., Kelly-Woessner, A., & Woessner, M. (2011). *The still divided academy: How competing visions of power, politics, and diversity complicate the mission of higher education.* Lanham, MD: Rowman & Littlefield.

Schmidt, P. (2012, June 5). *Wisconsin governor survives recall attempt in setback for faculty unions.* Retrieved September 15, 2013, from http://chronicle.com/article/Wisconsin-Governor-Survives/132151/

Seagren, A. T., Creswell, J. W., & Wheeler, D. W. (1993). *The department chair: New roles, responsibilities, and challenges.* San Francisco, CA: Jossey-Bass.

Senge, P. M. (2000). The academy as learning community: Contradiction in terms or realizable future? In A. F. Lucas (Ed.), *Leading academic change: Essential roles for department chairs* (pp. 275–300). San Francisco, CA: Jossey-Bass.

Siegel, D. (2010). *Organizing for social partnership: Higher education in cross-sector collaboration.* New York, NY: Routledge.

Slaughter, S., & Rhoades, G. (2004). *Academic capitalism and the new economy: Markets, state, and higher education.* Baltimore, MD: Johns Hopkins University Press.

Smith, E. (2004). The end of the reign: Department chair no more. *New Directions for Higher Education, 126,* 85–92.

Tierney, W. G. (2004). Introduction: A perfect storm: Turbulence in higher education. In W. G. Tierney (Ed.), *Competing conceptions of academic governance: Negotiating the perfect storm* (pp. 1–32). Baltimore, MD: Johns Hopkins University Press.

Trow, M. (1998). On the accountability of higher education in the United States. In W. G. Bowen & H. T. Shapiro (Eds.), *Universities and their leadership* (pp. 15–64). Princeton, NJ: Princeton University Press.

Tuchman, G. (2009). *Wannabe U: Inside the corporate university.* Chicago, IL: University of Chicago Press.

U.S. Department of Education. (2012). Washington, DC: National Center for Education Statistics, Integrated Postsecondary Education System.

Ward, K. (2003). *Faculty service roles and the scholarship of engagement.* San Francisco, CA: Jossey-Bass.

Williams, D. A. (2013). *Strategic diversity leadership: Activating change and transformation in higher education.* Sterling, VA: Stylus.

Wilson, J. L., Meyer, K. A., & McNeal, L. (2012). Mission and diversity statements: What they do and do not say. *Innovative Higher Education, 37*(2), 125–139.

4

BUILDING A NEW TAXONOMY FOR DIVERSITY IN THE ACADEMIC DEPARTMENT

The academic leader's challenge is to create a dynamic collective culture that bridges the differences of gender, race, ethnicity, and age to promote the development of a team.

—Walter H. Gmelch and Val D. Miskin (2011, p. 25)

We now turn to key elements in academic organizational design that create the opportunity structure for the chair's role in diversity progress. As Burton Clark pointed out, higher education has developed "its own massive structure and bounded procedures that provide some insulation and strengthened hegemony over certain tasks and functions" (Clark, 1983, p. 3). This infrastructure is characterized by the metainstitutional nature of the disciplines across the higher education system, with the extensive professionalization of academic work based on the fields of study in which individuals have obtained advanced training and from which they receive symbolic and material rewards (Clark, 1983). The merger of professionalization with organizational bureaucracy produces powerful social actors (Clark, 1983).

Although a number of studies have examined the theoretical underpinnings of college and university organization (see, e.g., Bess & Dee, 2008), limited recent research actually deconstructs the prevailing model of academic organization and examines the multidimensionality of this formal structure (Gumport & Snydman, 2002). The scarcity of recent research on the interrelationship among the structural components of academic organizational design suggests a certain immutability of these practices without critical examination of their impact on institutional capacity and effectiveness in the face of increasingly complex social and environmental demands.

These accelerating external demands, for example, can coalesce in the forces of *disruptive innovation* that have intruded into the higher education sphere in terms of online learning, the formation of MOOCs (massive open online courses), and other nontraditional forms of instruction that increase access (Christensen & Horn, 2013, p. B31). Most institutions of higher learning often seek "to be all things to all people" in their effort to build prestige and have become vulnerable to such disruption (Christensen & Horn, 2013, p. B31). For universities to thrive in this situation, tighter organizational structure could enable them to home in on the clear job to be done, while discarding everything that doesn't assist the institution in doing that job (Christensen & Horn, 2013). Consider the mission of comprehensive state universities that are geared toward specific regional economies but have drifted from this purpose (Christensen & Horn, 2013). These institutions could focus on creating autonomous divisions that help local employers fill needed skill gaps (Christensen & Horn, 2013).

Or, as a second example, interdisciplinary instruction foregrounds the importance of learning across traditional disciplinary boundaries and suggests the potential for different models of academic organization. The formation of larger clusters that are interdisciplinary in nature could constitute the core of divisional majors or create methods of delivery of liberal or general education (Clark, 1983). Apropos to formation of interdisciplinary clusters, the argument for "consilience" made by E. O. Wilson emphasized the interlocking nature of knowledge across all disciplines that promotes interconnectedness and convergence (Wilson, 1998). Consilience refers to the "jumping together" of knowledge by linking facts and fact-based theory across disciplines to develop a common groundwork of explanation (Wilson, 1998). This framework could bridge the natural and social sciences and offer a new vista in understanding the human condition, because real-world problems exist in a realm where the disciplines intersect without maps and with few concepts and words (Wilson, 1998). In this context, an emphasis on cross-disciplinary approaches that draw on the life and social sciences, as well as social justice education, could provide a viable framework for implementing diversity change (Evans & Chun, 2007).

The components of academic organizational design not only are simply structural but also include the roles, processes, lateral interrelationships, and human resource capabilities that help the organization attain optimal effectiveness (see Williams & Wade-Golden, 2013, for review). We shall examine these different components in this chapter, with a view to determining their impact on the realization of optimal diversity within the academic department. And as Gmelch and Miskin (2011) pointed out, the challenge of the chair as leader is to build a team within the context of the departmental structure.

Perhaps most important, organizational design serves as the medium for the transmission of power and authority. Such power is manifested in decision making, particularly in employment processes such as hiring, tenure, promotion, compensation, and termination, as well as in the informal atmosphere and climate of a department. In the next chapter, we will examine the dimensions of formal processes in the context of the prevailing power structure and the prism of departmental culture.

Principal Components of Organizational Design

Two primary structural aspects characterize the organization of colleges and universities: *bureaucratic* (schools, divisions, departments) and *programmatic* (degree programs offered) (Gumport & Snydman, 2002). Together, the bureaucratic and programmatic elements of academic organizational structure serve as a "powerful symbolic mechanism" that transmits the intention, if not the ability, of higher education to respond to competing expectations in the external environment (Gumport & Snydman, 2002, p. 377). These expectations include the role of colleges and universities in preserving existing knowledge, while advancing new knowledge and responding to the priorities and budgetary constraints represented in external mandates (Gumport & Snydman, 2002).

Both the bureaucratic components and the programmatic components of academic organizational design have vertical and horizontal dimensions. From a horizontal perspective, the bureaucratic structure consists of academic departments that are organized around a field of study and have a physical location, budgetary resources, and personnel, whereas the vertical aspect is reflected in "nested levels of bureaucracy" (Gumport & Snydman, 2002, p. 385). The programmatic dimension reflects an array of programs differentiated horizontally by subject and differentiated vertically by certification or degree level (Gumport & Snydman, 2002). In essence, academic department chairs mediate the complex vertical and horizontal components of the bureaucratic and programmatic structures.

The most common structural design for academic administration consists of three hierarchical layers: provost, dean, and department head or department chair. As noted earlier, in some institutions, the department head designation can designate a broader level of responsibility with greater decision-making and budgetary authority over larger departments.

Interestingly, the chair role has its origins in the guild model of medieval universities, with master professors who oversaw student apprentices with the assistance of a few journeymen (Clark, 1983). Chair leadership was the model in most European and Latin American universities and took on its modern form in the evolution of the German research university (Clark, 1983). As such, chair organization has assumed even greater importance than departmental organization, which represents a relatively new phenomenon developed most extensively in the United States (Clark, 1983). What the guild model suggests is oversight of the chair as a guide to the attainment of junior faculty. Yet the limited authority of the chair perched between faculty and administration, as well as the rapid rotation and lack of substantive additional compensation associated with chair leadership, can undermine the influence of this role.

Unlike other administrative appointments, academic leadership positions usually require a terminal degree with the credentials including publications and research that qualify for tenure in a discipline related to the specific position. In general, the positions of provost and dean carry tenure in an academic department with retreat rights from the administrative position to the faculty. Chairs are typically also tenured and most frequently are full professors. One of the dangers of tenured associate professors serving as chairs is that the demands of their roles may cause them to alienate senior faculty who have influence in the promotion process. An African American male chair of sociology in a private southern research university described this dynamic and the perils of chairs who do not have tenure and might try to advocate for diversity:

> You have to get along with colleagues or you're dead in the water. And if your colleagues have groups in the department and cliques, and you say you want to bring in women or minorities, and they're saying, "No way, are they qualified?" then you might decide, that's a battle I can't fight right now. And there's a lot of institutions letting associate professors chair departments. I think it's the kiss of death, because as an associate professor, you still have to go through the review process to get promoted. And that's where you get killed—where people are saying, "You know, I have a vote." And if you want to get through that last level of professorship, you can't antagonize certain people. So it's tough.

Similarly, Thomas Miller, chair of the history department at the University of Wisconsin, observed that it becomes difficult for tenured faculty to separate their evaluation of the chair's performance as teacher and scholar from their feelings about him or her as chair (Jacobson, 2002). Nonetheless, in a tightening economy, some departments have called on untenured faculty to assume the chair role when they have lost senior scholars to retirement, have been unable to replace faculty lines, and already have rotated the chair role among existing tenured faculty (Jacobson, 2002).

Two Pathways: Academic and Nonacademic Administration

Like the metaphorical pathways that diverge in a wood in Robert Frost's famous poem "The Road Not Taken," the administrative and academic pathways within higher education are, in many respects, separate trajectories guided by differing principles and employment conditions. Although academic administration involves some degree of hierarchy in terms of the existence of three layers of management, the protections of tenure accorded to senior faculty members significantly counterbalance the impact of hierarchical authority and buttresses the peer-based, consensus-oriented nature of decision making within the department.

By contrast, nonacademic administrators such as those who serve in facilities, human resources, finance, student affairs, and information technology operate within a more corporate and hierarchically defined environment. In the nonacademic administrative universe, positions at the level of director or department head and above usually serve "at will," without employment protections and are subject to the oversight and determinations of a single supervisor (see Chun & Evans, 2012, for review). Unlike faculty whose careers promote individual accomplishments solidified through tenure and protected by academic freedom, nonacademic administrators work without employment protections for the success of the whole institution (Chun & Evans, 2012). As Gaye Tuchman pointed out in her critique of the fictional "Wannabe University," these administrative employment conditions can foster an accountability regime for administrators that emphasizes a politics of control, surveillance, centralized power, and market management (Tuchman, 2009). As a result, the dichotomy between the nonacademic world and the academic world can, in fact, accelerate the tendency toward competing centers of power, multiple goals, and vulnerability to external forces (Chesler, Lewis, & Crowfoot, 2005).

In essence, the nonacademic administrative model is at variance with the faculty model of autonomy and functional independence (see Chun & Evans, 2012, for review). Faculty see themselves more as individual scholars rather than employees, whereas administrators' efforts to respond to the demands of the entire campus and external constituencies often contradict faculty values (Esterberg & Wooding, 2012). Faculty employment in the tenured ranks emphasizes autonomy and the principles of academic freedom. As the legitimizing concept of the academic enterprise, academic freedom creates a zone of protection and self-regulation in areas of academic inquiry (Menand, 1996). The iconic 1940 statement by the American Association of University Professors (AAUP) indicates that academic freedom is premised on the importance of tenure in protecting the rights of faculty in their research, in their publication of results, and in the classroom (AAUP, 2006). As a result, court decisions in tenure denial cases have deferred to academic judgment in the evaluative review of tenure qualifications (see Evans & Chun, 2007, for review).

As a measure of their ability to exercise academic judgment, tenured senior faculty serve on tenure and promotion review committees that make critical recommendations on promotion and tenure at the department level. These recommendations are typically passed on to higher levels of review at the college and then to the university-wide level. By contrast, junior untenured faculty do not share similar authority or influence, because they are subject to nonrenewal, and have a more tenuous employment status. Chairs are especially important to junior faculty in the tenure process because they create a climate of equity and transparency and provide mentoring support and opportunities for collaboration (see Trower, 2012, for review).

Yet at the same time, the power of tenured faculty can limit the chair's ability to change departmental direction and to build an academic team. Despite the existence of nested levels of academic hierarchy, the chair operates as a leader among peers within the relatively democratic and nonhierarchical faculty ranks (Hubbell & Homer, 1997). And chairs too often are seen as responsible for a department yet do not have the ability to sway the direction of the faculty. As a White male chair of modern languages and literatures in a religiously affiliated eastern university explained,

> Leadership is important, but in academics leadership is different from other kinds of organizations. One cannot simply dictate to tenure-track faculty. . . . Quite frankly the chair doesn't have a whole lot of tools, doesn't have a whole lot of leverage for pressing colleagues to do things a little bit differently. So in some sense, the chair is almost always in a difficult position. Even if the chair is a clear advocate and even if the chair does have allies in the department, it doesn't mean the department as a whole is easily going to do the right thing. So for me it's a challenge, it's an extreme challenge, and it's unfair to judge a chair for having been unsuccessful.

The intradepartmental tug-of-war. The intradepartmental dynamic between senior faculty and junior faculty with the strongholds of power held by tenured faculty can influence the level of commitment and energy devoted to diversity work. Consider the observation of a White male chair of social psychology in a predominantly White, private midwestern college who differentiated between active support for diversity and lip service that preserves the status quo:

> Tenured faculty are supporting [diversity] verbally and in establishing policy. However, they want "others" to do the actual diversity work. As a result, their support is not oppositional, but it is inactive and therefore supports the status quo. When there is resistance, it takes the form of, "Are you saying I did something wrong?" From the chair's perspective, I'm not saying you did something wrong, but not blocking [diversity initiatives] is not the same as being proactive.

A Black chair of Hispanic background in a predominantly White department of an elite private university reported, "Most White colleagues assume 'diversity' is for people of color and do not do much in recruitment." In such a departmental climate, opportunities for diversifying the faculty may be curtailed by the internal power dynamic and not given priority or addressed as an important need.

Similarly, the White male chair of modern languages and literatures cited earlier observed the tension among tenure-track faculty regarding their view of disciplinary specialization and diversity competence:

> Even though we are a department where one might expect great diversity of outlook, support for multiculturalism, and a focus on intercultural understanding, many tenure-track faculty in my department are ensconced in a narrow view of disciplinary specialization. They are generally unwilling to engage in genuine "border-crossing" dialogue or thought (either cross-cultural or cross-disciplinary).

And a White male chair of economics in a predominantly White southwestern public research university shared his observation of a disparity in the level of interest in diversity between junior faculty and senior faculty that has improved over time: "Junior faculty tended to be more interested in diversity than tenured faculty, almost all of whom were White males." Furthermore, an African American female chair of foreign languages in a western master's-level university also observed that when there is no post-tenure review of consequence, senior faculty may not be willing to engage in activities outside their core teaching responsibility:

> The sad part about it is given the view and perceived rights of full tenured faculty, especially when there is no tenure review with consequences, you will have senior faculty who will say they accept [the need for diversity] but will not participate in helping. And that's in everything: They don't

participate on committees; they just do their teaching. It's particularly destructive in supporting the climate for newly hired diverse persons, especially when it's someone who is the first or the only.

These perspectives provide insight into the difficulties chairs face in leading diversity change among tenured faculty, a role that Brown and Moshavi (2002) compared to "herding academic cats" and that requires greater charismatic influence than needed in other situations. The tendency for faculty to be autonomous agents and the existence of departmental factions that involve senior tenured faculty can curtail and exacerbate the chair's efforts to reach consensus on the need for diversity progress and to take meaningful action.

Convergence Through Shared Governance

The framework of shared governance is a primary component of organizational design in higher education since it represents the site of convergence for administration and faculty decision making. The AAUP's "1966 Statement on Government of Colleges and Universities" articulates principles of joint effort within institutions of higher education in terms of the respective and interdependent responsibilities of the administration and the faculty (AAUP, n.d.). Shared governance refers not only to systems and structures ("hard" or rational governance) but also to social interactions and connections that define group and individual norms ("soft" governance) (Birnbaum, 2004, p. 8).

In essence, shared governance differentiates the legal and managerial authority of the administration from the professional authority of the faculty in matters of research and instruction (Birnbaum, 2004). For example, when an educational goal has been established, it is primarily the faculty's responsibility to determine the appropriate curriculum for student instruction (AAUP, n.d.). Similarly, with reference to the selection of academic deans and other chief academic officers, the AAUP statement indicates that this selection is the responsibility of the president in consultation with the faculty (AAUP, n.d.).

In changing times, questions of shared governance such as who has responsibility for a particular decision, which processes are used, and what level of involvement is required (review or approval) create a high-stakes environment for university decision making (Eckel & Kezar, 2006). Shared governance has become an area of contention between the faculty and the administration in difficult budgetary decisions, such as in the declaration of financial exigency when it involves the elimination of departments and tenured faculty. For example, in 2013 the AAUP cited "chilling" violations of shared governance principles at Southern University in Baton Rouge, Louisiana, and National Louis University in Chicago, Illinois (Flaherty, 2013). At Southern, the university declared financial exigency in 2011 and eliminated 19 tenured professors, while National Louis eliminated four departments and terminated 63 faculty, including 16 tenured professors, because of revenue shortfalls (Flaherty, 2013). The AAUP questioned faculty exclusion from the decision-making process and the doubling of the athletic program subsidy at Southern, while at National Louis, the AAUP found that the university had not formally declared financial exigency and had not consulted faculty in the downsizing process (Flaherty, 2013).

A particularly relevant perspective on shared governance is the cultural framework proposed by Minor and Tierney (2005) that links governance to quality through the institution's symbolic and communicative processes. The view that culture and governance are integrated spheres supports an institution's progress toward diversity through the integration of systems, social interactions, and values that support inclusion (see Evans & Chun, 2007, for review). From this perspective, shared governance needs to be seen as a means to an end, a collaborative process that results from collegiality and is concerned with change and innovation in the academy (Crellin, 2010). As such, shared governance can offer the potential for transmitting the values of diversity, inclusion, and empowerment through the hard governance of systems and structures and the soft governance of interactions and cultural norms. Nonetheless, conversations about diversity and inclusion in the context of shared governance often seem to be the exception rather than the rule—a missed opportunity for meaningful dialogue between the faculty and the administration.

The Provost's Leadership Role in Diversity Transformation

The provost or chief academic officer (CAO) represents the locus of academic power in educational institutions, because the academic organization occupies the largest percentage of an institution's budget and includes the college's or university's faculty. A survey of 1,715 CAOs found that 67% serve as second in command to the president or chancellor, whereas 23% reported that they were one of several fairly equal positions, and 11% reported that another position is the clear number two (Eckel, Cook, & King, 2009). In large research universities, the provost can hold the title of executive vice chancellor, such as at the 10 individual campuses of the University of California.

The provost's office typically consists of vice provosts for functions such as budget, diversity, and academic personnel and has responsibility for academic personnel matters including oversight of tenure and promotion processes. In some institutions, a vice provost for diversity position has emerged as the chief diversity officer (CDO), because the focus of diversity initiatives and efforts is most strongly reflected in curricular and academic practices. The presence of a joint title like "vice provost for diversity and academic affairs" signals a connection between diversity and academic excellence, integrating two areas of responsibility with units and responsibilities in both areas (Williams & Wade-Golden, 2013). Provosts also frequently have diversity councils that provide them with strategic advice on matters of diversity.

The average length of service for CAOs is only 4.7 years, less than half the length of the average presidential tenure (Mann, 2010). These individuals typically rise through the academic ranks, with 27% having served as deans, and spend an average of 12 years during their career in faculty positions, 5 years in positions with split academic and administrative responsibilities such as department chair or head, and 12 years as full-time administrators (Eckel et al., 2009). Surprisingly, only 42%, or less than half, have tenured status in their current positions (Eckel et al., 2009).

The trend toward short tenure and rapid turnover among CAOs has been a source of skepticism of new provost-led initiatives among faculty critics. As a faculty leader from a private New England university wrote in response to a 2013 *Chronicle of Higher Education* survey of provosts and faculty leaders,

> "We have constant injections of new presidents and provosts who think everything in the past was bad and all of their shiny new initiatives must be implemented immediately with little or no—or only symbolic—faculty buy-in." (quoted in Schmidt, 2013, para. 38)

Similarly, in her study of the fictional Wannabe University, Gaye Tuchman shared the faculty perspective on rapid CAO turnover: "Provosts come and go. Each one brings his own policies. This may just be a temporary policy. *How long do you think we can put off doing what this [provost] wants us to do?*" (Tuchman, 2009, p. 109, italics in original). And an interview study of 50 deans found that deans who had been at their institution from 4 to 7 years had usually experienced at least two or more changes in the provost position and one in the presidency (Gmelch, Hopkins, & Damico, 2011).

Yet when CAOs leave their positions and, for example, assume a highly compensated, tenured 9-month teaching position, they may receive considerable support from faculty who view administration and its responsibilities as burdensome and somewhat unrewarding, with relatively little value added to the core academic enterprise. John Wooding described his return to the faculty from the provost position at the University of Massachusetts at Lowell as follows (Esterberg & Wooding, 2012):

When I returned to the faculty, I felt relief that I was no longer responsible for the institution. I had time to read and think again and be with students. No more board of trustees meetings, no more "welcome" events, no more budget meetings and no more daily crises. (p. xvi)

He also indicated that he watched the faculty adaptation to a new set of administrators with sympathy and occasionally with horror, underscoring the fact that most faculty have little idea of what administrators do (Esterberg & Wooding, 2012). As he put it, "the university's administration remains impenetrable to most faculty" (Esterberg & Wooding, 2012, p. xvii). This lack of understanding can create disconnection between the administration and the faculty.

The provost or CAO role is integral in terms of conveying authentic commitment to diversity and ensuring accountability in process outcomes, including recruitment and appointment, evaluation, and promotion and tenure. The provost provides leadership in curricular matters, program creation, research support, and faculty development and can allocate budgetary resources that support the hiring of diverse faculty. Because CDOs often report directly to the provost, provosts have the opportunity to initiate a strategic diversity agenda and operationalize this agenda in academic priorities and policies, organizational infrastructure, and curricular initiatives.

A study of 38 provosts in liberal arts colleges found that all the respondents measured their success in terms of the level of diversity among the student population, whereas 97% saw diversity in the faculty and academic professionals as an important factor (Winston & Li, 2003). Only 65% identified institutional climate as an important factor, and only 5% felt that there were available resources to support diversity efforts (Winston & Li, 2003).

Examples of innovative programs for department chairs launched by CAOs include the University of Minnesota's Provost's Department Chairs and Heads Leadership Program, a yearlong program for new department chairs and heads that represents a collaboration between the office of the provost and human resources (*Provost's Department Chairs*, 2013). This program reinforces the key role of the department chair as an academic leader who is "pivotal in the University's strategic goal to be one of the top three public research universities in the world" (*Provost's Department Chairs*, 2013). Similarly, the provost's office at the University of South Carolina offers a series of department chair and academic program director workshops that include workshops on retention of women faculty, bullying and other forms of harassment, and legal issues (*2012–2013 Department Chair*, n.d.).

The Heart of the Matter: The Chair's Relationship to the Dean

The dean, like the department chair and associate dean, plays an essential academic leadership role that balances the interests of faculty with those of the administration. As such, deans represent the crucial yet delicate backbone of university decision making, linking the professional bureaucracy of colleges with the professional bureaucracy of the university (Wolverton & Gmelch, 2002). Our 98 survey respondents, on average, rated support from their dean in the area of diversity on a scale of 1 to 5 as 4.5. By contrast, they rated support from university leadership for diversity at a slightly lower level as 4 on a scale of 5.

As our interview study reveals, the dean's leadership is a critical component in diversity progress, and ambivalence or lack of direction from the dean can leave department chairs unsure of overall direction and support. Yet, ironically, from the university's perspective, the more direct and decisive a dean is, the more effective he or she is, whereas from the college's perspective, reliance on the direct use of power can lead to the dean's demise (Wolverton & Gmelch, 2002). Attainment of the necessary balance among the perspectives of administration, department chairs, and faculty can be a challenging proposition for deans.

In the typical academic organizational structure, chairs report to the dean, although, on occasion, this model may vary, with chairs reporting to the provost, especially in smaller institutions. Deans also typically have an associate dean or associate deans who interface with department chairs on issues such as research funding and assessment of learning outcomes (Stone & Coussons-Read, 2011). In fact, the associate dean role can serve as an entry point for faculty into administration. Associate deans face communication challenges in their relations with chairs, because the power differential between chairs and associate deans is smaller than that between chairs and deans (Stone & Coussons-Read, 2011). Some department chairs and faculty can perceive the associate dean as "having gone to the dark side" of administration and hold the associate dean responsible for policies that they do not agree with (see for review, Stone & Coussons-Read, 2011, p. 65). Associate deans typically have bifurcated academic and administrative appointments. Because associate deans deal with all the disciplines in their college, at times they may be forced to go against the wishes of their home department, while still serving as faculty in their academic department (Stone & Coussons-Read, 2011).

An interview study of 50 deans found that they report spending a major portion of their time in both informal and formal meetings with associate deans, department chairs, faculty, and staff, often working through changing curricular or programmatic issues (Gmelch et al., 2011). In terms of managing upward, their relationship with the provost is critical for the colleges they represent (Gmelch et al., 2011). At the same time, deans in this interview study reported the importance of creating a college climate of respect where people feel valued (Gmelch et al., 2011).

In the pyramid of academic administration, deans yield extensive influence in their academic discipline, and their academic stature can be pivotal in building the resources of a school, attaining national recognition, drawing outstanding graduate students, and attracting star faculty. Take the example of Dean Wilfred Bain of the Indiana University School of Music, who from 1947 to 1973 led the transformation of the music school from a regional institution to international stature, expanding the faculty from 25 to 150, founding the Opera Theater, and bringing world-class faculty to teach there ("Wilfred C. Bain," 1997).

In certain environments, the compensation of deans can even exceed that of the chancellor or CAO. Law and medical school deans clearly top the compensation list. Take, for example, the salary of the longtime dean of the New England School of Law, John F. O'Brien, who could be the highest paid law school dean in the United States, garnering more than $867,000 a year in salary and benefits, with a salary as high as that of the president of Harvard (Rezendes & Pazzanese, 2013). In another example, the University of Michigan's Medical School dean, James O. Wooliscroft, was reappointed to a five-year term following a salary increase of 13.2% or $69,500 for an annual salary of $593,980, just under the salary of President Mary Sue Coleman, who earned $603,357 (Woodhouse, 2012).

With the demands for accountability and increasing economic constraints, deans have been called on to lead fund-raising efforts for their schools and ensure the viability of academic programs under their direction. Yet a sampling of 50 postings of deanship requirements in 2004 and 2009 found a significant drop in the requirement for demonstrated fund-raising experience and a corresponding rise in references to vision and indices of professional accomplishment (Gmelch et al., 2011). This shift suggests that deans must keep the vision alive and advance the discipline while at the same time raise funds to support these efforts (Gmelch et al., 2011).

A study that involved 865 responses for individuals reporting through 22 academic deans in a western research-based doctoral extensive university identified differential responses between department chairs and faculty in their views of the dean (Rosser, Johnsrud, & Heck, 2003). Department chairs rated the deans more strongly as effective leaders than did the faculty, perhaps because of their more privileged role in the communication process, their closer interpersonal relationship, and their ability to receive greater rewards from the deans such as input into decision making, reduced teaching loads, and so on (Rosser et al., 2003). Within the academic hierarchy, the relationship of the chair to the dean influences the chair's effectiveness and ability to access scarce budgetary resources. This relationship is particularly important for chairs who are members of nondominant classes and when the departmental faculty are largely White males.

As an African American male sociology chair in a private southern research university observed, "The chair-dean relationship cannot be adversarial . . . you have to have a good relationship." He described one of the primary challenges for minority and female chairs as not being undermined by his or her supervisor:

> People are always suspicious of your abilities, they may not say it. . . . The biggest challenge is getting your supervisor, dean or VP, to respect your position so that they won't let the end run exist, so you are not spending half of the workweek defending anonymous claims that you are not fair, that you don't spread money around fairly. . . . I've been involved in enough chairs' conversations and chairs' meetings and conferences to know that for other chairs of color, female chairs, this also is a big, big challenge, not being undermined by your supervisor.

Describing his relationship with his dean, he indicated, "We had trust. He wasn't going to see faculty without them seeing me first. I can't tell you how important that is, that faculty have to talk to the department chair first."

The dean's leadership in the area of diversity sets the tone for the academic departments in his or her purview and can provide both the vision and the direction for diversity within the college as a whole. The level of support naturally varies considerably based on the individual's own commitment to diversity and willingness to take risks. In this capacity, the dean can buffer faculty reactions to the department chair's efforts to implement diversity initiatives. Consider how a White female chair of educational leadership in a western public research university described the impact of a new dean who is willing to step out on a limb for diversity issues. The new dean has relieved her of the pressure she experienced previously when faculty raised objections to diversity initiatives:

> I felt like previously as the chair I was the one having to give some of that rationale and take the heat. Whereas now the dean says, "They have a problem with it? Tell them to come see me." I felt like with my old dean he used me as a scapegoat and a couple of times threw me under the bus. It was pretty horrific actually, especially when I was a new chair. And the dean that we have now, when we're having these conversations and they're difficult dialogues and people are [saying], "Why are we hiring so and so at that salary when I've been here for 10 years and I don't have that salary?"

He'll basically just say, "All right, well bring me your résumé, and we'll have a conversation."

The chair further explained the dean's commitment to stand up with courage and confidence for his diversity vision:

With our new dean, I feel like he has a real strong vision, and diversity is part of his vision, and he realizes that to achieve that diversity both demographically and people-wise, and also diversity in terms of ideas, that it requires stepping out on a limb, and he is willing to do it. And he is willing to stand up for it.

By contrast, a White male sociology chair in a midwestern private liberal arts college described the dean's reluctance to support a faculty-led diversity initiative that had led to an AAUP report calling for greater faculty and student diversity:

The dean at the time didn't feel a particular passion for the issue; he didn't get it. His major problem was he didn't want any failures. He was a guy who had a pretty large ego. . . . His response to the AAUP report was "This is a pointless battle; I don't want to expend resources and effort on something we know that is going to fail." But there was significant support on campus. He certainly didn't try to block anything and in fact decided that he needed to take some leadership in this, and he visited a number of historically Black colleges and graduate programs to do some recruiting of faculty. And he was the best person to do that.

A number of the interview respondents mentioned the rapid turnover among academic administration at their institutions. For example, one White male chair in a midwestern public research university, indicated that over the past 8 years, he has had five deans with one semi-interim dean. Of the four permanent deans, three of the four were clearly supportive in the area of diversity. Another White female chair in a western religiously affiliated university described academic administration as a "revolving door" with high turnover at the provost level. Such high turnover can make it difficult to sustain departmental diversity efforts in terms of the resources and instrumental support needed for concrete progress. A White male chair of economics in a southwestern public research university similarly described the shift he has observed under new leadership:

In the past couple of years, we've had a new dean, new upper administration, so the whole university is in kind of a state of flux. And I honestly don't know if we are on same path as we were a couple of years ago. There are some disheartening data and incidents that suggest that we have fallen back a little bit.

A White female chair of urban education in a midwestern regional university described the high turnover in the deanship and the resulting reliance on the academic vice president and president's office for sustained diversity leadership:

We have a new dean, and she was on for just 2 years, and now she is on an assignment in an acting position in the administration. So we have had a lot of transitions with deans. We had a dean leave, we had an interim dean, then we have an appointed dean, and the appointed dean was in place for 2 years, and we are going to have an acting dean. We have had a lot of transition, so I can't say the dean has contributed a lot. We have had a supportive academic vice president who has left, and we hope that the new academic vice president will be as good in that respect. That's where a lot of the impetus came from, the academic vice president and the president's office.

And, at times, chairs resist the dean's initiatives either on principle or because of their perceived need to protect their faculty (Esterberg & Wooding, 2012). One chair, for example, indicated that he always waited three times for a dean to make a request, to ensure that it was important and that the dean would follow through (Esterberg & Wooding, 2012). As a result, the chair's relationship with the dean would vary considerably. And as a former dean of nursing, Florence Richman, pointed out, faculty "can get rid of a dean or even a president if they want to" (Kelly, 2010, p. 12). This power requires deans to be engaged and listen to their constituents (Kelly, 2010).

Because of the tenure status of most chairs, some of our interview respondents seemed to see it as their individual responsibility to pursue their diversity objectives even when faced with changes in upper administration. At times the provost or CAO provides the leadership needed as transitions in the deanship take place, or cultural norms that were established under previous administrations have left a legacy in place that supports diversity. Nonetheless, as we have indicated, these efforts can be more difficult for chairs to negotiate without leadership support and budgetary resources.

Structural Considerations in Chair Appointments

A number of factors impact chair appointments, including the method of selection, the term of service, compensation, and whether chairs are represented by a union. These structural considerations can have an impact on the level of support chairs receive from departmental faculty, their job satisfaction, and their willingness to take on this role.

Chairs are selected in several different ways. They can be elected from the tenured and tenure-track full-time faculty in a department and then appointed by the dean, provost, or president; they can be elected by tenured, tenure-track, and part-time faculty and then appointed by the dean, provost, or president; they can be selected and appointed following a search with a faculty search committee; or they can be directly appointed by the dean. In some departments, they serve in a rotational process among tenured faculty. A survey of over 400 department chairs in the California State University system found that 60% were selected by election of tenured and tenure-track faculty (Chu & Veregge, n.d.). The method of selection can impact the chair's acceptance by faculty colleagues, with election from the tenured and tenure-track faculty viewed as the most democratic approach and the one most likely to obtain greater faculty acceptance.

The average chair serves for 6 years, although some serve only one three-year term and others continue for an indefinite time period (Cipriano, 2011). For example, 59% of the chairs in the California State University study indicated that the typical term of service is 3 years (Chu & Veregge, n.d.). Chairs can serve on 12-month appointments, although some serve on 9- or 10-month contracts.

Chairs vary in their own reasons for serving in this capacity. Some assume the chair position for extrinsic reasons such as responding to the request of a dean or faculty in the department or feeling forced to take it when no one else will take the role (Gmelch & Miskin, 2011). Others assume the role for intrinsic reasons such as to help their departments or advance their own personal development (Gmelch & Miskin, 2011). In fact, a survey of department chairs conducted in 1990 found that 321 chairs or 60% served for personal development (intrinsic reasons), whereas 251 or 46.8% also responded that they had been drafted by the dean or other colleagues (see Gmelch & Miskin, 2011, for review). Nonetheless, chairs may see their role as being about more than money, career aspirations, or a necessary burden (Cipriano, 2011). They may view their role as meaningful in shaping the legacy of their department in terms of the profound influence they have on faculty and students (Cipriano, 2011). Sometimes chairs put aside their own research and long-overdue sabbaticals to continue in this role because of their commitment to seeing new hires through the tenure and promotion process and to ensure that their new faculty survive (Esterberg & Wooding, 2012).

The methodology for compensating chairs varies significantly. For half of our sample, chairs receive a salary that is determined by expertise and experience within a salary range, whereas 21% receive a monthly stipend ranging from $1,000 to $2,200 per month for an 11- or 12-month appointment or a fixed salary amount. Other chairs are compensated by course releases for the academic year, as well as summer stipends, or by formulas that take into account chair rank and number of FTEs (full-time equivalent students) in the department.

A final structural consideration is whether chairs are represented by a faculty bargaining unit. In the California State University system, department chairs are not officially considered as administrators but are considered faculty, and as such they are represented by the faculty union (Chu & Veregge, n.d.). In other institutions with unionized faculty, such as the University of Illinois at Chicago, chairs can be excluded from the bargaining unit and considered as part of university administration. This distinction can make a significant difference in how university or college administration views the participation and inclusion of chairs in decision-making processes.

Concluding Perspectives: Proactive Strategies to Navigate the Academic Infrastructure

This chapter has examined structural components of university or college organizational design that impact the chair's leadership role in diversity. These interrelationships include strengthening vertical communication through interactions with the dean and provost while fostering collaborative horizontal relationships among departmental faculty and across departments within the governance structure. We have also noted the distinctive features of chair leadership, which includes the dual responsibilities of representing the interests of the department and also leading the department in the change process. The following strategies have emerged from the chair narratives and from best practices nationwide.

Recognize that the chair must take a proactive role in diversity as both leader and manager, with a clear goal of improving the quality of the academic environment. In this regard, an African American female chair of foreign languages in a public western master's-level university differentiated between leading and managing in her view of chair leadership:

> A good leader represents the people they lead. It's not one or the other. If you are just a manager, that's a whole other thing. The question is are you administering or just managing if you don't really care about the overall individuals you represent? A good leader absolutely represents them but is trusted to make judgments and decisions that are good for the overall whole.

Leverage the shared governance process as a powerful vehicle for institution-wide diversity transformation. Although shared governance represents the powerful voice of faculty, this avenue of diversity transformation has been significantly underutilized. Because nondominant faculty are often not in a position to alter the organizational distribution of power and privilege because of their location outside the mainstream, they must often lead from the margins (Aguirre & Martinez, 2002). The governance process, by contrast, offers the opportunity for formation of a coalition of tenured faculty at the core of an institution that includes members of nondominant groups. Such a coalition can undertake a consolidated approach to changing mindsets, transforming organizational culture, developing policies, and impacting long-standing arrangements of power and privilege. The participation of faculty from nondominant groups in the governance process can influence the development of institutional policies and ensure the inclusion of diverse viewpoints in institutional policies (Aguirre & Martinez, 2002).

As a best practice example, a number of institutions have formed standing committees of the academic or faculty senate on diversity and inclusion. Such committees can function in single institutions or in statewide multicampus systems. The Committee on Diversity and Equal Opportunity at the University of California at Los Angeles provides advice to the administration on programs and policies to advance faculty diversity including women and underrepresented minorities (*Committee on Diversity and Equal Opportunity*, n.d.). The university-wide faculty senate of the State University of New York's 64 college campuses has a Committee on Diversity and Cultural Competence that focuses on issues relating to inclusiveness and access in the curriculum, student body, and personnel (*Diversity Committee*, 2013). Topics discussed at the committee's plenaries include how to make diversity count in employee development and review, general education requirements for diversity, conversations in the disciplines, and equitable decision making in program closures (Ortiz, 2012).

Work collaboratively with the dean to clarify and communicate funding resources for diversity-related programs. Because of the shortage of fiscal resources, departments within a given college may question how resources are allocated when programs are associated with diversity. An African American male sociology chair hired to head up a new ethnic studies department in a private southern research university described the open backlash he experienced from other department chairs at a meeting to discuss courses that might fit with the new unit:

> When I was hired, I asked the dean the summer coming in to set up a meeting with all the department chairs in the college. . . . So we get to the restaurant, and there are about 15 department chairs, one of them was a female; none of these people were persons of color. And so I'm at one end of the table and the dean is at the other. . . .
>
> Everybody was nice and respectful, but the guy from English was a little edgy, and at one point he burst out, "Where did the money come from to start this unit? We haven't had money in our department for years. Now here's a new unit . . ." and he was talking to me. And my response

was, "I'm sorry, you need to ask the dean those questions." And the whole table went silent.

And so later I find out that the way the new department was funded was through a donor, a gift, which also funded my own position, what they called a named chair, and it came with the appointment. And then over time, the way the contract read, the university would put in a greater percentage of the funding . . . so over the years, the unit would be funded every other year by the college. But I just thought it was interesting that this chair was so annoyed that this new ethnic studies unit was being funded that he had the audacity to ask me in a public meeting about the funding. And I'm thinking, "This is ridiculous." I didn't fund the unit, that's for sure, nor did I steal money from other units to fund it, which was sort of the implication, that they lost money because my unit was being funded. So the dean had to say, "This money came from elsewhere."

This scenario vividly illustrates the contested nature of funding for diversity in tight budgetary environments, the criticism that can arise related to diversity initiatives that are viewed as secondary to departmental purposes, and the importance of support at the dean's level.

Partner with the dean's office in the development of diversity accountability structures. A White male economics chair in a southwestern public research university explains how the dean implemented a series of accountability measures in the area of diversity. The dean pressed department chairs to increase the diversity of the faculty, the graduate students, and the curriculum. In addition, the dean built a reward structure for departments that modestly rewarded departments for making diversity progress. According to the chair,

He went to a system of differential allocations to departments in their merit pools and the same thing with allocations of faculty positions. And it wasn't just based on diversity, it was based on a number of factors, but diversity was one of them. And departments were essentially ranked and put into categories like excellent, good, satisfactory. If your department was in an excellent category, it got a slightly higher merit allocation. In terms of faculty positions . . . he wanted a statement in the proposal itself of what they were going to do to attract a diverse candidate pool and how the person who filled the position would contribute to diversity in one way or another.

The chair noted that these actions did provoke some backlash. Yet the dean developed strong linkages with the university administration and the dean of the faculty in overcoming this internal resistance. As the chair explained,

Looking back there was some backlash, some resistance under the surface that we were doing too much in the way of diversity. I heard that occasionally, "The dean is too preoccupied with diversity." But I think we actually made demonstrable accomplishments during those years.

To overcome intradepartmental conflict, create an evidence-based ethos of respect for individual perspectives, recognizing that even statements by the chair can contribute to diversity tensions. A White male chair of modern languages and literatures in an urban religiously affiliated university strives to bring an evidence-based, collegial ethos to his department, while recognizing that his own personal irritation can exacerbate existing tensions:

> I think there are a number of things that contribute to this. Some of it is, shall we say, "disciplinarily ideological"; that is, it arises from our divergent conception of our disciplines and what we should be doing with them professionally. So there are times when there is definitely tension in the department. I have tried to make clear that no one has a lock on the truth, and that we all need to be respectful of points of view of other folks, and that we need to truly look at evidence, and I do think that that ethos has penetrated more or less in the department.
>
> That said, there are still folks who want what they want, and they are willing to be unfair to others to get it. And sometimes that makes folks who are a little bit different feel like they are excluded or pushed out or that their point of view is not particularly welcome or that they must struggle to make their voice heard. So there are always challenges.
>
> My department is definitely not a "nest of vipers," so to speak, but on the other hand all of us could be a lot better at being respectful of each and every member, even though some points of view might be very different from our own. And that's human nature. Part of our problem, quite frankly, is leadership; I am not sure I have done a consistent job of trying to lead us in the direction of tolerance. And sometimes I let my own personal irritation push me to say things and do things in a way that I know are not welcoming and inclusive. So I'm part of the problem as well.

Given our discussion of components of academic organizational structure in this chapter, we next consider the chair's diversity leadership in formal and informal processes that support the creation of a positive and inclusive work climate.

References

2012–2013 department chair and academic program director workshops. (n.d.). Retrieved November 18, 2013, from University of South Carolina website: http://www.sc.edu/provost/acadadmin/workshops/

Aguirre, A., Jr., & Martinez, R. O. (2002). Leadership practices and diversity in higher education: Transitional and transformational frameworks. *Journal of Leadership Studies, 8*(3), 53–62.

American Association of University Professors. (n.d.). *1966 statement on government of colleges and universities.* Retrieved November 16, 2013, from http://www.aaup.org/report/1966-statement-government-colleges-and-universities

American Association of University Professors. (2006). *1940 statement of principles on academic freedom and tenure with 1970 interpretive comments.* Retrieved November 2, 2013, from http://www.aaup.org/file/principles-academic-freedom-tenure.pdf

Bess, J. L., & Dee, J. R. (2008). *Understanding college and university organization: Theories for effective policy and practice.* Sterling, VA: Stylus.

Birnbaum, R. (2004). The end of shared governance: Looking ahead or looking back. *New Directions for Higher Education, 127,* 5–22.

Brown, F. W., & Moshavi, D. (2002). Herding academic cats: Faculty reactions to transformational and contingent reward leadership by department chairs. *Journal of Leadership and Organizational Studies, 8*(3), 79–93.

Chesler, M. A., Lewis, A., & Crowfoot, J. (2005). *Challenging racism in higher education: Promoting justice.* Lanham, MD: Rowman & Littlefield.

Christensen, C. M., & Horn, M. B. (2013, September 30). *How disruption can help colleges thrive.* Retrieved October 30, 2013, from http://chronicle.com/article/How-Disruption-Can-Help-/141873/

Chu, D., & Veregge, S. (n.d.). *The California State University department chair survey report.* Retrieved November 18, 2013, from http://www.calstate.edu/AcadSen/Records/Reports/CSU_Chairs_survey_report.pdf

Chun, E., & Evans, A. (2012). *Diverse administrators in peril: The new indentured class in higher education.* Boulder, CO: Paradigm.

Cipriano, R. E. (2011). *Facilitating a collegial department in higher education: Strategies for success.* San Francisco, CA: Jossey-Bass.

Clark, B. R. (1983). *The higher education system: Academic organization in cross-national perspective.* Los Angeles, CA: University of California Press.

Committee on diversity and equal opportunity (CODEO): Committee members. (n.d.). Retrieved December 9, 2013, from UCLA website: http://www.senate.ucla.edu/committees/codeo/

Crellin, M. A. (2010). The future of shared governance. *New Directions for Higher Education, 151,* 71–81.

Diversity committee: University faculty senate committee on diversity and cultural competence. (2013). Retrieved December 9, 2013, from State University of New York website: http://www.suny.edu/facultysenate/diversitycommittee.cfm

Eckel, P. D., Cook, B. J., & King, J. E. (2009). *The CAO census: A national profile of chief academic officers.* Washington, DC: American Council on Education.

Eckel, P. D., & Kezar, A. (2006). The challenges facing academic decision making: Contemporary issues and steadfast structures. In P. D. Eckel (Ed.), *The shifting frontiers of academic decision making: Responding to new priorities, following new pathways* (pp. 1–14). Westport, CT: Praeger.

Esterberg, K. G., & Wooding, J. (2012). *Divided conversations: Identities, leadership, and change in public higher education.* Nashville, TN: Vanderbilt University Press.

Evans, A., & Chun, E. B. (2007). *Are the walls really down? Behavioral and organizational barriers to faculty and staff diversity* (ASHE-ERIC Higher Education Reports, Vol. 33, No. 1). San Francisco, CA: Jossey-Bass.

Flaherty, C. (2013). *Budget woes are no excuse.* Retrieved November 16, 2013, from http://www.insidehighered.com/news/2013/06/17/aaup-censures-two-institutions-following-violations-shared-governance-amid-financial

Gmelch, W. H., Hopkins, D., & Damico, S. (2011). *Seasons of a dean's life: Understanding the role and building leadership capacity.* Sterling, VA: Stylus.

Gmelch, W. H., & Miskin, V. D. (2011). *Department chair leadership skills* (2nd ed.). Madison, WI: Atwood.

Gumport, P. J., & Snydman, S. K. (2002). The formal organization of knowledge: An analysis of academic structure. *Journal of Higher Education, 73*(3), 375–408.

Hubbell, L., & Homer, F. (1997). The academic department chair: The logic of appeasement. *PS: Political Science and Politics, 30*(2), 209–213.

Jacobson, J. (2002, November 6). *In charge without tenure.* Retrieved November 2, 2013, from http://chronicle.com/article/In-Charge-Without-Tenure/46107/

Kelly, R. (2010). *Becoming a more mindful leader.* Retrieved November 18, 2013, from http://www.ferris.edu/HTMLS/administration/academicaffairs/extendedinternational/ccleadership/faculty/reportacademicleadershipqualities.pdf

Mann, T. (2010, June 27). *Turnover of chief academic officers threatens strategic plans.* Retrieved November 2, 2013, from http://chronicle.com/article/Turnover-of-Chief-Academic/66064/

Menand, L. (1996). The limits of academic freedom. In L. Menand (Ed.), *The future of academic freedom* (pp. 3–20). Chicago, IL: University of Chicago Press.

Minor, J. T., & Tierney, W. G. (2005). The danger of deference: A case of polite governance. *Teachers College Record, 107*(1), 137–156.

Ortiz, P. (2012). *Report from the committee on diversity and cultural competence (CDCC).* Retrieved December 9, 2013, from State University of New York website: http://www.suny.edu/facultysenate/diversitycommittee.cfm

Provost's department chairs and heads leadership program. (2013). Retrieved November 18, 2013, from University of Minnesota website: http://www.academic.umn.edu/provost/faculty/dept_chairs.html

Rezendes, M., & Pazzanese, C. (2013, January 13). New England law head draws scrutiny for his pay: A princely paycheck for dean of unheralded school. *The Boston Globe.* Retrieved September 14, 2013, from http://www.bostonglobe.com/metro/2013/01/13/law-school-dean-salary-may-nation-highest/r59QMPRZANUkeJOkxhne1K/story.html

Rosser, V. J., Johnsrud, L. K., & Heck, R. H. (2003). Academic deans and directors: Assessing their effectiveness from individual and institutional perspectives. *Journal of Higher Education, 74*(1), 1–25.

Schmidt, P. (2013, October 7). *Campus relations aren't as frayed as you might think.* Retrieved November 2, 2013, from http://chronicle.com/article/Campus-Relations-Arent-as/142143/

Stone, T., & Coussons-Read, M. (2011). *Leading from the middle: A case-study approach to academic leadership for associate and assistant deans*. Lanham, MD: Rowman & Littlefield.

Trower, C. A. (2012). *Success on the tenure track: Five keys to faculty job satisfaction*. Baltimore, MD: Johns Hopkins University Press.

Tuchman, G. (2009). *Wannabe U: Inside the corporate university*. Chicago, IL: University of Chicago Press.

Wilfred C. Bain, music educator, 89. (1997, March 16). *The New York Times*. Retrieved November 18, 2013, from http://www.nytimes.com/1997/03/16/nyregion/wilfred-c-bain-music-educator-89.html

Williams, D. A., & Wade-Golden, K. C. (2013). *The chief diversity officer: Strategy structure, and change management*. Sterling, VA: Stylus.

Wilson, E. O. (1998). *Consilience: The unity of knowledge*. New York, NY: Vintage Books.

Winston, M., & Li, H. (2003). *Diversity and organizational success: A survey of chief academic officers in liberal arts colleges*. Retrieved November 16, 2013, from http://www.ala.org/acrl/sites/ala.org.acrl/files/content/conferences/pdf/winston.pdf

Wolverton, M., & Gmelch, W. H. (2002). *College deans: Leading from within*. Westport, CT: Oryx.

Woodhouse, K. (2012, December 17). 2012 salary report: 20 University of Michigan deans collect $7.28M in base pay. *The Ann Arbor News*. Retrieved September 14, 2013, from http://www.annarbor.com/news/post-203/

5

THE CHAIR'S LEADERSHIP ROLE IN FORMAL AND INFORMAL ORGANIZATIONAL PROCESSES

If equality of opportunity is the bedrock on which the United States was built, diversity is the litmus test of whether this equality is being truly achieved.

—Princeton University, *Report of the Trustee Ad Hoc Committee on Diversity* (2013, p. 7)

What actions can department chairs take to foster team-based, collaborative environments in which the contributions of all members of the department are nurtured and valued? And how do chairs help ensure equitable outcomes for diverse faculty in formal processes of hiring, tenure, evaluation, and promotion? In search of these answers, we first explore the chair's leadership role in surmounting informal behavioral barriers that preclude the creation of an inclusive departmental climate. Next we examine key formal processes that impact faculty diversity and share forward-looking strategies chairs have adopted to diversify the academic department and provide instrumental support for diverse faculty in the complex pathway to tenure.

We do not wish to overstate the impact of a single position in changing departmental dynamics, although it may be considerable. As the chapter unfolds, the narratives reveal the difficulties faced by chairs who may be a singular voice attempting to persuade resistant colleagues. We also share the perspectives of individuals who represent the first female and the first African American chair in their departments. The insights of courageous and insightful chairs illuminate the subtle skill set and nuanced understanding of the mechanisms of workplace inequality needed to ensure equity in formal processes and promote the inclusion of diverse faculty and staff in the working environment. In addition, these efforts are strengthened by partnerships with the dean, provost, and chief diversity officer, as well as alignment with overall institutional diversity objectives.

Our focus on both informal and formal processes in this chapter is based on how inequality in the workplace transpires in the workplace today. Subtle, cumulative forms of discrimination that find expression in the behaviors, interactions, and dynamics of employment processes have replaced the egregious forms of blatant discrimination addressed through civil rights legislation more than half a century ago. The covert, cumulative nature of contemporary discrimination makes it hard to pinpoint and even more complex to litigate (see Chun & Evans, 2012, for review). Instances of second-generation discrimination are often hidden, difficult to document, and easily overlooked or explained away by third parties or bystanders. Yet in the narratives of chairs in the study we also see forms of overt discrimination that can go unchecked if not addressed. And both covert and overt discrimination have serious and long-lasting effects that can create chronic stress and increase the risk for stress-related diseases (see Chun & Evans, 2012, for review).

In cultures of power within the university, patterns of exclusion in everyday work reinforce existing hierarchies, resulting in outcomes that are often beyond the control of members of subordinate groups who may be the subjects or targets (Chun & Evans, 2012; Kivel, 2004; Roscigno, 2007; Roscigno, Garcia, & Bobbitt-Zeher, 2007). We shall see an example of this later in the chapter in terms of what one chair described as the "turnstile" effect that occurs through subtle mechanisms such as student evaluations that can be used to drive individuals from the workplace. A process-based perspective will alert us to patterns that strengthen privilege through acts of social closure by dominant group members and to the counter efforts of nondominant groups to resist such stratification (Roscigno, 2007).

Chairs as leaders with positional authority can identify and take active steps to eradicate exclusionary practices so that those individuals who are at the margins are not the only ones challenging the status quo (Hale, 2004). In the course of this chapter, we shall see examples of chairs who are willing to leverage their credibility and status to insist on equity within the academic department.

Psychological and Behavioral Barriers to Diversity in the Academic Department

In the view of Santa Ono, the first Asian American president of the University of Cincinnati, because of the assumption of meritocracy in academic institutions, "unconscious bias might, perversely, be harder to address where intellectual rigor and fairness are already presumed to be in place" (Ono, 2013, p. B27). Nonetheless, as Ono reminds us, social and psychological barriers "are the more imposing for being invisible" (Ono, 2013, p. B27).

In essence, discrimination can occur through the intersection and interdependence of institutional ("macro") forms of exclusion and individual ("micro") acts of marginalization and discrimination (Feagin & Feagin, 2012). From an individually mediated perspective, the emergence of microinequities has been called the new scaffolding for discrimination in the twenty-first century (Rowe, 2008). Microinequities are small micro-incursions that undermine individuals and send devaluating messages that can hinder performance and erode the targets' self-esteem (Young, 2003). A comprehensive taxonomy of microinequities identifies microassaults, micro-insults, and microinvalidations as the ways in which microinequities are delivered and reproduced in the workplace (Sue, 2010).

In this regard, DiTomaso's (2013) interview study of 225 participants is particularly relevant in uncovering how subtle acts of discrimination transpire through behavioral interactions. DiTomaso argued that the mechanism for reproducing racial inequality essentially transpires through acts of opportunity hoarding and favoritism. Such acts or exchanges of social and cultural capital among White actors represent the principal mechanism by which racial inequality is transmitted through the exchange of social capital and contributes to continued inequality (DiTomaso, 2013). The exchange of social capital involves social solidarity in terms of who is likely to help whom and the use of social resources that include social, cultural, and economic capital to confer advantage (DiTomaso, 2013).

In substantiation of this theory, a White female professor of international programs in a private religiously affiliated western university shared how the "old boys' network" in her college has been perpetuated by the selection of White male faculty for leadership positions. This opportunity hoarding among the White male network has been noticed by the female faculty, who find it relatively easy to predict who will be offered the next award or will be groomed to be the chair or director:

> Even though it is very sort of understated, there is still sort of an old boys' network that works at the university, so if there are any challenges, there are still enough people who don't think diversity is a problem or issue that we need to think or talk about. . . . Definitely, I see some evidence that there is a guys' club, and they watch out for each other, and they put each other up for awards or for particular offices, or they groom them to be the next chair or the next director of a program. I think that [network] in some ways makes it more difficult for women and faculty of color. There is kind of a

core group of White men who take care of each other in the next genera-
tion, and there's definitely evidence of that in who is the next person to be
director of the honors program. . . . They are grooming the next genera-
tion, and it's pretty obvious to women in particular in the college in terms
of moving into leadership positions or things like that sometimes.

Because the chair role is the typical pipeline to a deanship, the notable absence of diverse department chairs indicates the continuing existence of legacies of inequality in the academic hierarchy. Furthermore, when
diverse department chairs assume leadership roles, their leadership and that
of their majority counterparts may be evaluated differently. For example,
four research studies involving undergraduates, MBA students, and graduate
students in situations revealed that Whites are viewed as more prototypical
leaders and evaluated more favorably than racial minority leaders (Rosette,
Leonardelli, & Phillips, 2008). When vague conditions surround the evaluation of leaders, negative bias against racial minorities is more likely to occur,
particularly when evaluations stemming from negative stereotypes can be
rationalized or justified (see Rosette et al., 2008, for review).

Although some may question whether subtle acts of discrimination still
occur in academe, consider the findings of an independent investigative
study at the University of California, Los Angeles. This study was conducted
by an external review team based on interviews with 18 faculty members in
individual interviews and 10 written statements submitted after a town hall
meeting found instances of discrimination and bias in two academic departments (Moreno, Jackson-Triche, Nash, Rice, & Suzuki, 2013).

Allegations of systematic exclusion of minority and female faculty in
"Department A" ranged from comments made to junior faculty of color
about how they would not attain tenure, to discriminatory remarks such as
"I thought Asian women were supposed to be submissive" (Moreno et al.,
2013). A White faculty member who was tenured and subsequently left
the department indicated that he had spoken out against such conduct and
been retaliated against by the department chair through a recommendation
against a merit increase in pay; he then retired rather than continue in that
atmosphere (Moreno et al., 2013).

In "Department B" two faculty members alleged that the department
was divided along racial lines, indicating that they had experienced incidents
of bias or discrimination by other faculty members, including senior faculty.
One faculty member indicated what he perceived to be a clique of Caucasian
male professors who ran the department, and he said he had personally wit-
nessed senior faculty use racially or ethnically insensitive language (Moreno
et al., 2013).

And faculty from nondominant groups may feel that they must portray themselves as positive and nonthreatening and engage in what has been called "smile work" in their relations with White faculty in order to be successful (Tierney & Bensimon, 1996, p. 85). Marginalized individuals may only be able to function on terms that are unfavorable and determined at others' discretion, hiding who they are to participate in the predominant culture (Kivel, 2004). Women and minorities may experience pressure to falsify or disguise their identities and be more accommodating, agreeable, and even submissive in order to fit in (Tierney & Bensimon, 1996). Such pressure can lead to feelings of powerlessness and loss of self-confidence (Tierney & Bensimon, 1996). In this regard, a White male psychology professor from a midwestern liberal arts college described the price paid by a minority faculty member by being "doggedly reassuring" in order to gain the cooperation of other White faculty in his administrative role:

> In our department one of the African American faculty members was highly, highly regarded, and he was not chair yet, but he had a number of administrative roles. And I think he had the cooperation of the people. But I think the price of that was that he was everybody's friend. He had positions, strong positions . . . but he was just doggedly nonthreatening, and whereas the other admin leaders had sharp edges, John had none, so I guess he had earned the role. . . . The price . . . was to sort of constantly be the Black man who is reassuring the White faculty.

He emphasized the cost of such efforts: "Chairs of color have been able to join the club, but I would imagine at a very high personal price, the price of anxiety and pressure."

An African American male history chair in a midwestern religiously affiliated university described his journey as the first African American chair in his institution and only one of a few African American faculty members in the university. He endured 10 years of mistreatment by a White faculty member in religious studies who resented his hiring from an adjunct to a full-time professor. The White faculty member refused to speak to him for a decade, even though their offices were adjacent to each other. Only when the African American faculty member later became chair did the White faculty member have to respond to him, when asked a question in a departmental meeting. As he explained,

> There was a man who retired now, a religious studies professor, which is kind of odd. His office is right next door to mine. He didn't talk to me for 10 years, not a word. . . . He didn't believe I was qualified, he didn't believe that I was a real intellectual, I was only hired so that the university could say

that we had Black professors. This is somebody who would engage in those kinds of conversations . . . with the door open right next to my office. . . . That's when I started closing my door. . . . Near the end, I became chair just before he retired, so then he had to say something, because then I could sit in a meeting and actually ask him a question. He had to engage me. I always made the subject diversity, and he always made the answer, "I think we're already diverse." Needless to say, I wasn't invited to his retirement dinner.

The chair noted that as the first African American chair in his institution, his presence in diversifying the all-White hierarchy and his research and stance on social justice have had a discernible, informal impact on the climate in his department. As he explained,

I think it helps just by my mere presence. I am the first African American department chair at this university. So in an institutional context, I think that matters. I think my research on Dr. King, my own commitment to social justice, racial justice, and racial equality, and so on impact at least tangentially and informally the discussions which we have in the department. I think the people that were here when I got here, the people who were hired on before I became chair, and the ones I was able to hire as chair through those searches, all the faculty truly believe in what the true ideal of diversity and inclusiveness means. There is an implicit understanding in our own dialogue within the department of the importance of this issue.

Take the case of a White female history department chair who was the first female to hold that position in her department in a western religiously affiliated liberal arts college. She persistently sought to overcome misrepresentation of her statements in the faculty assembly and to participate democratically in that body. She pointed out the difficulties she faced in being taken seriously as both a female faculty member and the first woman chair of her department:

I think it was very difficult for me to be chair the first time I was chair. Six years ago, I was the first woman chair. . . . I think people inadvertently . . . it was difficult for them to take me as seriously as previous male chairs of the department. . . . It's hard to separate out being chair from the general situation of being a female faculty member when there just aren't that many on campus. And my experience of that is you have to be on every committee, but no one really cares what you say once you get there. You're not taken seriously when you make comments, for instance, in faculty assembly. I am frequently misquoted in the minutes of faculty assembly and have to kind of go back and say, "That's not what I said."

The female history chair noted that she was often the sole voice advocating for a particular course of action and could be outvoted by her department:

> I frequently found myself the only voice in the department advocating for a particular course of action, and of course, I was outvoted whether I am chair or not. I don't feel like it was deliberate; people don't look at gender and say, "You're a woman; I don't care what you think." It's not something that people are aware of doing, but I think when your opinion is different from everybody else's, it just doesn't weigh as much.

Given these observations of the roadblocks still faced by minority and female chairs within academe, ranging from dismissal of their views to outright exclusion, we now consider progressive approaches that both dominant and nondominant chairs in our study have undertaken to strengthen the day-to-day climate and interactions within their departments.

Building Inclusive Departmental Climates

Chairs in our study, on average, rated the climate for diversity in their departments as 4 on a scale of 5. Despite this generally favorable rating, the perspectives of our interview sample reflected a more nuanced and much more complex picture. Consider the perspective of a White female chair of computer science in a predominantly White midwestern university who identified the difficulty of building passion around diversity when individuals have not experienced discrimination directly themselves. Like other chairs in the study, she reported a kind of inertia around diversity issues that perpetuates the status quo. With the impact of workload pressures, faculty may have little time or energy to devote to diversity efforts and will fail to see diversity as their top priority. As the chair observed,

> Where philosophically, ethically, people may believe in diversity, they may see it as an important issue, they may want to be supportive. And then when the time pressures of what they have to do on a day-to-day basis come into play, then it can't be their job. . . .
>
> Just philosophically speaking, I think that people who have not themselves experienced discrimination can sometimes understand it intellectually but have a harder time building a significant passion around it because they have not experienced it. And until you have been put in a situation where you at least recognize that you could be discriminated against because you are a minority . . . sometimes it just becomes a stark reality: I'm in a different set of circumstances. I think it can be really hard to imagine what that feels like.

In response to this predominant departmental viewpoint, the chair actively pursues the creation of a *culture of conversation* in which all voices are both heard and included whether in discussion of routine business matters or in the formal processes of promotion and tenure review:

> What a department chair could do, if they wanted to take it seriously, I think it's just one of building a culture of conversation, making sure that as you conduct routine business, everybody's voice is heard equally. That doesn't mean that you single out that candidate and say, "You speak up now for the diverse people."
>
> You treat them the same as everybody else in the room when you are having discussions about research or funding or curriculum or whatever the issue is. You treat them as one of the larger group, and everybody is on equal footing. To me that is the ultimate goal: We're all equal. Giving people positives or negatives can sometimes work negatively in the long run. I think you have to establish that environment of everybody is valued and everybody's opinion is important and everybody is treated the same when it comes to promotion review, tenure review, those types of things. I'm not saying that's easy to do, but I think that has to be your goal.

Other department chairs in the study emphasized the importance of surfacing difficult diversity issues as part of their leadership role, despite the controversy this may entail. Take the forthright approach of a White female chair of higher education in a western public research university who actively counters faculty pushback against searching for diverse candidates in the hiring process with an insistence on responding to the demographics of the student population:

> The challenge is in working with faculty who have pretty traditional ideas, and I think the progress is just having those conversations. Just recently we were hiring for a temporary faculty position, and all the likely suspects were White males who were in the latter part of their careers. And I said, "All right that's great, but that's not the students we are trying to recruit, so why is it that we would only look at those faculty?" And then people write back, "Well they're the only people that are available." And [I was] trying to say, "Well what if I told you that we can't hire until we find someone? You will find somebody." Just trying to push the envelope a little bit.

A significant, covert barrier that chairs can face in building an inclusive climate is the existence of cliques of veteran faculty that can exert powerful influence over departmental direction. In chapter 4, we shared accounts of the intradepartmental tug-of-war that can occur between factions of senior faculty and newer faculty and the lack of leverage the chair may be able to exert to overcome these divisions. An African American male department chair of sociology in a private southern research university shared his strategy of creating social events that require faculty attendance and offer informal opportunities for faculty to mingle and learn more about each other on both a social level and a professional level. He noted the subtle ways in which exclusion can take place through party invitations and other social interactions:

> Those veterans . . . go to lunch together; they meet after work for cocktails, gossip. New people claim that they're never invited over to these peoples' home after work or on weekends; the kids have birthday parties . . . and their kids aren't invited; somebody might put a picture on their door of the party and you see all these people and you're not there; vegetable time, people have gardens, they leave bags of tomatoes or zucchini . . . on certain peoples' doors and not on other peoples' doors. You can't make people get along.

To counteract these subtle forms of exclusion, the chair created departmental social meetings off campus with attendance required of all faculty:

> So what I've done . . . is we have all department social meetings, off campus. It could be that you close shop early on a Monday afternoon or a Friday . . . and it's mandatory just like a department meeting, so people can't say, "Oh well, I can't make it, I have to take my dog to the salon" or whatever. It's similar to a department meeting; it's not for business, it's for a social hour. We've had it where we cordoned off a room, and new faculty would take 15 minutes to talk about their research so that people can't say, "I've been in the department 3 years, and I don't know what they do."

Furthermore, the department chair can set explicit and clear expectations for departmental civility that address the treatment of both faculty and staff. In this regard, a White male chair of economics in a southwestern public research university indicated that he made it clear that he expected civility in interactions within the department, despite the fact that people did not agree on all subjects. His efforts were also directed toward how the faculty interacted with staff and, in particular, with the tendency of male faculty to treat female staff with a lack of respect "as if they were personal assistants rather than professional personnel with job descriptions." As he observed,

> The women were expected to keep a fresh pot of coffee, keep the refrigerator stocked with water and soft drinks, run minor errands, etc. And several of the men were simply rude and arrogant when dealing with staff.

As a result, the economics chair held a number of "tense conversations" with faculty and also encouraged the staff to share any incidents of concern with him. He was willing to shoulder the burden of negative criticism and openly advocate the need for respect and civility in the day-to-day working environment.

The examples shared here reveal the decidedly activist approaches of department chairs in our study as they strive to create a culture of conversation that surfaces underlying assumptions about diversity, challenge behaviors that undermine inclusion, and instigate change in formal processes. From this perspective, the chair role offers people the opportunity to break the logjams of incivility and unequal opportunity. Chairs can seek to build a more representative critical mass of faculty within the department that will help offset regressive factions. Through the channel of social events and intergroup activities, the department chair can promote collegial interpersonal interactions that help offset the formation of cliques and promote an environment of cooperation and mutual professional respect. A White female chair of journalism in a western undergraduate university summed up the leadership role of the chair in setting the tone for the departmental culture:

> The chair has to lead and set the tone for what is important. . . . Your department has to decide what its culture is going to be like. If [the department] is not willing to embrace diversity or support recruitment for other [diverse] faculty, it's going to fail. If you don't have retention, it doesn't matter.

In support of this perspective, an African American chair of kinesiology, sport, and leisure studies in a historically Black southern university emphasized the importance of the chair's inclusive approach in framing the department's goals and what it is trying to achieve:

> It all depends on the administrator: What is the administrator's style? Is it charismatic, is it laissez-faire, is it autocratic, is it democratic, and is it inclusive? It helps to have a style that entails all of them, depending on what the situation is. One of the things I think that drives away faculty is to be firm and always autocratic. The more I sell what it is the department is about trying to become, the better the opportunity is for buy in on the part of the faculty.

Recruitment and Hiring: The Crucial Avenue to Diverse Faculty Representation

With several notable exceptions (see, e.g., Buller, 2012; Tucker, 1993), most departmental chair guides devote little attention to one of the most important and challenging roles of the department chair: recruiting and hiring a demographically diverse faculty. By contrast, our interviews revealed that hiring is at the forefront of chairs' consideration in terms of addressing the underrepresentation of women and minorities. Yet, as noted earlier, many chairs described situations of dwindling budgetary resources, lack of senior faculty turnover, and limited opportunities to recruit new faculty as the principal barriers to building a diverse faculty. Hiring opportunities are especially rare in small departments in liberal arts colleges, and departments can go for years without additional lines being added.

In addition, chairs cannot assume that the vacancy of a faculty member in their department means that they have the right to fill it, especially in eras of budget cutting or when the position is reallocated to a more favored department or one with a presumed greater need (Tucker, 1993). And if needed vacancies are not filled, departmental faculty may have to assume heavier teaching loads, and sections can be canceled (Tucker, 1993). As budgets tighten, adjunct or part-time faculty positions are usually the first to be cut.

Nineteen of our 98 survey participants (19.4%) indicated that their department does not use any resources to ensure a diverse applicant pool. This surprising response may be tied to a number of factors that include budgetary constraints, institutional recruitment practices, and the lack of new faculty lines. The majority of the survey participants indicated a reliance on multiple avenues for diversity recruitment that include disciplinary conferences, specialized websites, referrals, use of lists of recent minority doctoral recipients, ads mailed to doctoral departments, and recruitment from institutions with a high percentage of diverse graduates. Principal barriers to hiring diverse faculty identified by survey participants include the following:

- *No new faculty lines.* We noted in chapter 3 how constricting budgets have limited the ability of chairs to diversify their departments. Examples cited by chairs from public and private institutions in our study include not having new lines for the past 6 or 7 years. One department chair in a private university has been requesting a faculty line with a specialization that would draw diverse candidates for 6 years and was given only a postdoctoral line contingent on a retirement in another department. Other departments in public institutions have found it difficult to compete with more well-funded institutions in attracting diverse candidates.
- *Lack of qualified diverse candidates.* This barrier was cited by a number of survey participants in different disciplines in private and public institutions. Some of the fields cited were highly specialized, whereas other fields included the humanities (communication,

English literature, psychology, philosophy), education (educational leadership), business (management), and STEM (science, technology, engineering, and mathematics) fields (biological sciences, engineering, and pharmacy). Chairs of physicians' assistants and occupational therapy departments also cited difficulties in finding diverse candidates.

- *Administrative practices.* Several survey respondents identified barriers in their institution's administrative practices that including the timing of the release of the university/college budget late in the hiring cycle, limitations that prevent departments from running their own ads, insistence on boilerplate diversity language without allowing customization to departmental needs, and not permitting the use of specialized agencies or services with experience in diversity recruitment.
- *Compensation.* Faculty salaries were cited as one of the most significant obstacles to the hiring of diverse faculty in a wide variety of geographical locations, institutional types, and disciplines. High faculty workload was also cited as a deterrent. One chair described bidding wars at his selective public research university for qualified diverse candidates.
- *Need for recruiting resources.* A number of survey participants identified the lack of funding for recruiting and diverse outreach as a significant barrier to attracting and interviewing diverse faculty candidates.
- *Lack of collegial support and a supportive campus climate.* Factors of climate and the absence of collegial support were cited by a number of chairs from dominant and nondominant groups at different institutions. As a White male economics chair in a southwestern public research university observed, "Some (not all) senior faculty give only lip service to enhancing diversity." And a White female chair of education in a private western master's-level university noted, "The university has not committed to seeking out diverse candidates."
- *Geographic location.* This factor was seen as an obstacle by a number of participants in more rural and/or less diverse areas of the midwest, south, and west. By contrast, a chair from the Boston area noted that the diversity of the metropolis made it relatively easy to attract diverse candidates. Yet a White female chair of educational leadership in a western public research university commented, "I think the university sometimes falls back on the 'we can't hire people of color because of our location' argument too frequently."
- *Failure to see the difference between international diversity and domestic diversity.* Another factor raised was the failure to recognize the

importance of domestic diversity and the tendency to overemphasize international faculty as satisfying diversity requirements.

A number of respondents in different disciplines in both urban and rural settings indicated, in contrast to those factors cited as barriers in our survey sample, that they are not having difficulty in recruiting diverse candidates in disciplines that include the pharmaceutical sciences, cardiopulmonary sciences, mathematics, counseling and special education, graduate studies, and urban education.

Lack of Qualified Candidates: Myth or Reality?

How do we account for the variance between the reported difficulty of finding qualified, diverse candidates and the experiences of minority scholars who are unable to find faculty positions? Clearly, disciplinary factors may make a difference, particularly in more specialized fields that have fewer diverse doctoral recipients. Yet as Daryl Smith pointed out, many diverse candidates for faculty positions, as well as postdoctoral fellows and minority administrators, do not see themselves as subjects of bidding wars and, in fact, have trouble landing tenure-track positions (D. G. Smith, 2000; see D. G. Smith, Turner, Osei-Kofi, & Richards, 2004, for review). She noted this disjuncture of perception as a "schizoid condition" in the discourse of diversity, with each side supplying "competing anecdotes" (D. G. Smith, 2000, p. 48). In support of this perspective, a study of 299 recipients of prestigious Ford, Mellon, and Spencer fellowships conducted in 1996 revealed, for example, that only 11% of the minority scholars were recruited for a faculty post and encouraged to apply ((D. G. Smith, 2000; E. Smith, 1996).

As shown in Table 5.1, the question of the scarcity of diverse candidates finds only mixed support based on 2011–2012 doctoral graduation data. Minorities are well represented in certain fields such as education, with 15.4% Black or African American graduates, 6.5% Hispanic or Latino graduates, and 3.4% Asian graduates. In biological and biomedical sciences, Asian doctoral recipients represent 8.5% of doctorates, Hispanics or Latinos represent 4.1%, and Blacks or African Americans represent 3.5%. In business management, Asian Americans represent 6.3% of doctoral recipients, Blacks or African Americans represent 6.2%, and Hispanics or Latinos represent 2.8%. In English literature, Hispanic or Latino graduates represent 4.5% of doctoral recipients, followed by Blacks or African Americans at 4.1% and Asians at 2.9%.

Fields with smaller percentages of diverse candidates include economics, with 5.2% Asian doctoral recipients and only 1.2% Black or African

TABLE 5.1
Doctoral Recipients by Race (Percentages), 2011–2012

Field and Institution Type

Demographic	Business Management, Marketing, and Related Support Services			Biological and Biomedical Sciences			English Language and Literature/Letters			Education		
	Public (n = 907)	Private (n = 642)	Total (N = 1,549)	Public (n = 5,289)	Private (n = 2,635)	Total (N = 7,924)	Public (n = 1,084)	Private (n = 343)	Total (N = 1,427)	Public (n = 5,379)	Private (n = 2,911)	Total (N = 8,290)
American Indian or Alaska Native	0.6	0.3	0.5	0.5	0.3	0.4	0.7	0.6	0.7	0.9	0.3	0.7
Asian	6.5	6.1	6.3	7.3	11.0	8.5	2.9	3.2	2.9	3.3	3.5	3.4
Black or African American	3.0	10.7	6.2	2.9	4.6	3.5	4.0	4.4	4.1	14.8	16.6	15.4
Hispanic or Latino/a	2.3	3.6	2.8	4.0	4.3	4.1	4.7	3.8	4.5	5.8	7.9	6.5
White	37.7	43.6	40.2	49.8	49.4	49.7	70.2	63.8	68.7	62.4	57.2	60.6
Two or more races	0.4	0.6	0.5	0.6	1.1	0.7	0.5	1.2	0.6	0.5	1.1	0.7

Source. U.S. Department of Education, 2012, Washington, DC: National Center for Education Statistics, Integrated Postsecondary Education System. Analysis by authors.

American recipients and 1.3% Latino recipients, and chemistry, with 6.2% Asian American doctoral recipients followed by significantly smaller percentages of Hispanic or Latino graduates (2.6%) and Black or African American graduates (2.2%).

These statistics reveal that minority doctoral graduates typically represent a range of approximately 10% to 20% of doctoral recipients in many fields, with larger percentages in certain disciplines. Although attracting qualified minority applicants may require more creative and extensive search and outreach processes, the data suggest that diverse applicants are available.

The culture and practices associated with faculty hiring may be one of the principal reasons for the failure to diversify (Gordon, 2004). Because faculty hiring represents one of the most privileged processes governed by the faculty who demand the right to select their colleagues, the allegiances of faculty are to their discipline without necessarily considering the implications for life in the academy (Gordon, 2004). And given the negative correlation between rank and race/ethnicity, the predominance of White males on the search committee may make it difficult for a lone woman or minority member to advance a different perspective (Gordon, 2004). Because research suggests that how institutions handle hiring processes is more important than the pipeline issue, departments need to transform their search processes and substitute talk about diversity with substantive approaches to change (D. G. Smith, 2000).

Sixteen chairs in our sample identified search committee processes as a barrier to diversifying the department. For example, a Black chair of Hispanic ethnicity in a private southern research university noted that the "Black male chair faces challenges of hiring other non-White faculty; are they qualified?" Contrary to the principle of inclusive excellence, this question is often presented in an oppositional manner, as if diversity and quality are antithetical.

On the other hand, partnerships of the faculty hiring committee with the dean increase the likelihood of attaining diverse faculty representation (Gordon, 2004). A study of 689 searches from three large public research universities found that special-hiring interventions explained most hiring of underrepresented faculty of color at predominantly White institutions (D. G. Smith et al., 2004). Such institutional interventions were more likely to result in hiring of diverse faculty when the traditional search process was bypassed or enhanced (D. G. Smith et al., 2004). Underrepresented minority faculty were also more likely to be hired when a diversity indicator was included in the job description or when institutional resources allowed for special hires of talented individuals identified during the search (D. G. Smith et al., 2004).

As noted earlier, a number of institutions have developed recruitment programs that provide institutional incentives for diversity hiring. When the president and provost foreground faculty diversity as key objectives in the institutional and divisional strategic plans, such clear institutional direction can result in both allocation of resources and increased accountability at the department or school level. For example, a White male chair of political science at a private midwestern university described the impact of a new provost and president on diversity efforts:

> We need more resources to recruit candidates of color for faculty positions. There is new commitment to this by our provost and president who started at the university in the past year; the provost has developed short-term plans to increase faculty diversity. The president incorporated inclusion as one of four primary objectives in the new strategic plan.

Or take the Action Plan for Faculty Diversity and Excellence at the University of Pennsylvania, sponsored by President Amy Gutmann and Provost Vincent Price (*Penn's Action Plan for Faculty Diversity and Excellence*, 2011). This plan requires each school and all departments in larger schools to develop their own plans to increase faculty diversity, with allocation of substantial resources to support the plan (*Penn's Action Plan for Faculty Diversity and Excellence*, 2011). Because affirmative action reviews tend to take place too late in the hiring process to affect the applicant pool, in partnership with deans, the university has committed to developing more effective methods of assessing hiring patterns and holding colleagues accountable (*Penn's Action Plan for Faculty Diversity and Excellence*, 2011). Centralized bridge funding for faculty hires is also provided through a Faculty Opportunity Fund for up to 5 years until a retirement can free new resources (*Penn's Action Plan for Faculty Diversity and Excellence*, 2011).

Broader job descriptions are commonly cited as a strategy that will allow diverse candidates from different subspecialties within a discipline the opportunity to apply. Because of the underrepresentation of minorities in certain fields of study, a White male psychology chair in an urban research university asks his faculty to exercise intellectual flexibility in the field of specialization to allow the potential for consideration of underrepresented individuals. As he explained,

> One of the things that the research shows because minorities are, by definition, a smaller number, the odds just of finding a person who is underrepresented who studies exactly what you might set out to find statistically is just less because there are fewer people. So if we, for example . . . wanted to hire a cognitive psychology professor who studies reading . . . we might find plenty of individuals who study that, but the odds of finding an underrepresented minority who studies that particular topic are going to be less

statistically. You might find someone who studies not reading but psychology of language comprehension. So I would argue that's close enough to what we're interested in: We need to be flexible about the topics. So maybe we find someone who studies language comprehension but not necessarily in a reading setting.

Some faculty would make arguments like, "Well now we're changing what we want to hire just so we can hire a minority. We have someone who studies the psychology of reading, so that's what we should be hiring and not changing our goals just to accommodate this particular hire." I argue that's a lack of intellectual flexibility and that we need to take into account that just simply the odds of finding someone who is underrepresented is smaller. That's what underrepresented means. That's the kind of pushback I would get.

We also noted a troubling tendency to dismiss Asian American males as not representative of diversity, particularly in the STEM fields. This tendency arises from conflating foreign Asian scholars and students who have immigrated to the United States for graduate study with Asian Americans (U.S. citizens or permanent residents of Asian descent) (Goel, 2006). In contrast with recent Asian immigrants, Asian Americans have experienced growing up as a visibly distinct minority group in the United States and continue to face substantive racial discrimination (Goel, 2006). The model minority myth has reinforced the misconception of Asian Americans as a problem-free minority (Goel, 2006). And perpetuation of this myth has often resulted in the exclusion of Asian Americans from consideration in university diversity hiring initiatives.

Another barrier to hiring diverse faculty is the tendency to view graduates from prestigious universities as preferable to candidates from public research universities or state universities. Essentially, the Ivy League dominates the pinnacle of the pyramid of prestige, with eight private universities located in the Northeast: Brown, Columbia, Cornell, Dartmouth, Harvard, Princeton, the University of Pennsylvania, and Yale (Mullen, 2010). Graduates from the Ivy League are offered disparate rewards, including higher salaries, more prestigious occupations, high-status positions, and higher levels of life satisfaction (see Mullen, 2010, for review). And the student bodies at these highly selective institutions are heavily weighted toward the upper classes in terms of income, with lower percentages of Hispanic and African American students in comparison to the general population (Mullen, 2010). Because of a university's tendency to want to hire from the most selective institutions, minority PhDs from less prestigious institutions may have fewer opportunities for faculty positions, particularly in more highly ranked institutions.

The Road to Tenure

Department chairs play a critical role in assisting junior faculty in the process of attaining tenure. Not only do they hold a key vote on tenure committees on which they yield substantive influence, but they also can extend research opportunities, provide valuable mentoring support, and offer scholarly advice and professional encouragement. Chairs sometimes do not know their own power and need to recognize that junior faculty are fearful about asking for help, because chairs can make decisions that affect their careers (Ward & Wolf-Wendel, 2012). And they can play an instrumental role in helping diverse faculty learn the written and unwritten rules and practices that pertain to tenure and the benchmarks used to assess progress (Stanley, 2006). We share here some of the principal areas in which chairs in our study have assisted diverse faculty in the tenure process.

Mentoring. The importance of mentoring in the pretenure process has been emphasized throughout the research literature. Yet minorities and women in predominantly White institutions often experience difficulty in obtaining instrumental and social support in the workplace (see Ibarra, 1995; Stanley & Lincoln, 2005, for review). Because of the male-dominated nature of organizations, minorities are more likely to be in diversified mentoring relationships with individuals who reflect differing group membership associated with power differences (such as race, ethnicity, gender, sexual orientation) (see Ragins, 1997, for review). In such relationships, cross-race mentoring is an opportunity for majority faculty to serve as agents of change in building a more inclusive academic community (Stanley & Lincoln, 2005).

Consider the mentoring approaches offered by several chairs in the study who seek to offset political pressures and level the playing field for diverse faculty. A White female professor of special education in a western public research university described the creation of mentoring committees for pretenure faculty in her department. Each committee has three individuals on it, and one of them is the designated mentor for the junior faculty member. The committees are not intended to be advocacy systems but in place to help junior faculty navigate the institution and its requirements for tenure. The chair indicated that she wants individuals to serve as mentors who are helpful, realistic, and not patronizing. Recognizing that the process of teaching observations can be politicized, the chair tries to select "the right people" to ensure that junior faculty are evaluated in a fair way.

An Asian chair of periodontics in a midwestern public research university created a "junior faculty club" composed of tenure-track faculty who get together to review their progress and discuss topics of interest. The group has since "taken on a life of its own," yet as the originator of the group, the chair now serves as a consultant on an as-needed basis. The chair further described his role in overseeing the tenure-review committees in the three divisions he oversees. He outlined the specific steps that a chair needs to take to ensure that tenure review is not driven by personalities:

> I think (a) make sure that the faculty who are on the tenure track are aware of what the requirements are, and (b) during the annual review sessions, try to be as forthright as possible in setting goals for the year to come and review all the achievements of the year or the years past. Make sure the midterm review committee is informed and composed of people who have achieved obviously the status of being tenured but are also willing to be helpful. So the chair can control these committees that have been appointed to review progress. But the chair also reviews the progress of the pretenure faculty every year and tries to keep them informed. So I think the same steps apply for not only minority but any faculty. . . . Making sure that the faculty know what the expectations are for promotion and tenure, so that the process is followed, and it doesn't become a personality outcome if you will.

A White female chair of sociology in a public southwestern research university emphasized the relation of departmental climate to the way the tenure process is administered. She emphasized the need to hold all pretenure faculty to the same standard, hold frank discussions and demand accountability, and have discussions about the kind of advice to be offered to junior faculty.

Informal mentoring can also provide important psychosocial support and protection to diverse faculty. Consider the observations of a lesbian female department chair of kinesiology:

> Being gay has definitely impacted being able to offer resources to candidates. We have also had faculty who have gone up for promotion and tenure who felt like that might be an issue. I talked about my own experience with them, and that helped them.

A White male chair of internal medicine in a southwestern public research university described the active support he provided to an African American faculty member when she relayed experiences that might reflect discriminatory treatment in her clinical work in the community:

> She was a division chief, and I gave her a lot of freedom to make decisions and always tried to be as supportive as I could in every way possible. She did communicate sometimes reactions that she thought might be negative based on her race and/or sex. I did wonder at times if the treatment she

received could be partially due to our rural location and the very skewed demographics (predominantly White) of our region. We would meet and talk through the situation. "Do you think this was really the person's reaction, or could it be the fact that you asked them to do something that they really didn't want to do?" We tried to confront that. After she shared her experiences at least once, I met with the party that she had felt slighted by to discuss their responses. It was outside the university. Within the university we never had any problems. This division chief was an excellent leader and innovator and applied many of the concepts she brought back from attending the Executive Leaders in Academic Medicine (ELAM) course in her work in the community and in the university.

Student evaluations. A number of chairs in our study identified student evaluations as an instrument that can be used differentially to undermine a woman or minority faculty member in the tenure review process. The use of discretionary judgment that pertains to soft skills can result in differential and discriminatory impact on diverse faculty (Roscigno, 2007). Given the reliance on student evaluations as a tool for evaluating teaching, women and minorities must often contend with the subconscious biases of students that reflect role expectations often based on race and gender stereotypes (Lazos, 2012).

In a striking commentary, an African American chair of sociology in a private southern research university described the stereotypical student evaluations of women and minorities and explained how cherry-picking these evaluations can be used to run a faculty member out of the department:

> In terms of student evaluations . . . you get 30 evaluations in a class; 5 of them might say you are the dumbest person they ever met. Now 25 others are OK. What do they bring to the table? The 5. As a department chair, I resent student evaluations. First of all, they are never used to do anything. . . . My position was, and I had done some research on this, that women get certain types of evaluations and faculty of color get certain types of evaluations. Women if they're too short, they get this type, or if they're heavy, they get that type. . . . Faculty of color generally get an evaluation saying, "I can't understand them," "They don't speak English," or "They try to use big words." There are certain pieces on the evaluation that are the same. If it's a Likert scale, and it's one to five with three being average, you say, what do these things really mean? Are they even normed? Have they been pretested? . . . Chairs that don't have any statistical abilities whatsoever, they just find the ones where the students say . . . "I didn't like the book they chose for the course" or "I went to their office, and they weren't there." You say, "Were they supposed to be there? We have office hours, and they're not here every day."
>
> Faculty of color in the research on student evaluations really get slammed; women faculty really get slammed. And if you want to do a

faculty member in, you just drag out the evaluations. You can kill a faculty member with any one particular class evaluation. And if you have four or five classes over a year, you can cherry-pick the evaluations to say, "You know, the norm in this department, the score is 4, and you get a 3.6; you're under par." Under par for what? It's a game, it's a real bad game. . . . That's what I said about the turnstile: You can run somebody in for year one, year two, and run them out in year three, and the governance usually is, you don't have to have an explanation. Underperforming.

On the basis of her personal experience, a White female chair of urban education in a midwestern regional university described "the web of discrimination" she encountered in academe and described how student evaluations were used in a negative way against her in the tenure process:

But I have to say . . . as far as student reviews and hanging on to the one bad comment, those are things that I was up against also. I think that you can get lost in that battle, or you can stay in there and hold firm, and you gotta be a pretty strong person to do that. The first two women in our department that were successful were able to do that, but interestingly we both came from city management backgrounds and had been at the negotiation table before. Again we were never quite prepared for the complexity of the web of discrimination that comes about in academia.

A White male chair of sociology in a private midwestern liberal arts college indicated that student evaluations of faculty of color are likely to be lower and that minority faculty may be expected to "carry the torch" in various groups or activities that don't count for tenure or they may be viewed as unmotivated. He noted that such subtle differential treatment is more difficult to combat:

I think the student evaluations of faculty of color are certainly likely to be lower. Although no student or very few people will attribute it to that, it will be symbolic statements, like "lacks credibility," "is not forceful," or "is too forceful," or stuff like that.

Likewise, I think what I have observed is the new diverse faculty member is really expected to carry the torch for whatever their group is, in terms of student advising and programming and stuff like that, and if you don't do that, you are likely to be labeled as unmotivated or not active. But none of that stuff is going to count very much in terms of tenure. And therefore it becomes more difficult. . . . I think in my experience the frequent problem has been subtle and therefore more difficult to address or even combat.

The tax of service and devaluation of diversity-related scholarship. The tendency of minority faculty to be expected to devote time to serve as mentors and advisers to diverse students and serve on committees as a diversity representative has been well documented in the research literature. Although fulfilling, such work may be the least rewarded in the tenure process and can detract from the time needed to pursue scholarly research. In addition, the pursuit of diversity-related research has been discounted, discouraged, and devalued by some departments in the tenure process. In this regard, a White female chair of international programs in a private religiously affiliated western university has helped minority faculty say "no" to the many demands placed on them that do not contribute to tenure attainment so they will not be burned out:

> They are left to do a lot of work on campus that doesn't get kind of valued in the tenure process. Even though they may be very productive scholars, sometimes that kind of work is not valued in the same way. . . . One of the main ways that a faculty department chair has to help faculty of color is to help them to say "no." . . . I did that constantly with my faculty who wanted to do everything that they were asked to do. Just to help them realize that they are going to burn candle at both ends, and at some point they are going to be burned out, even if they make it through the tenure process.
>
> One of the things I have learned from my position in faculty development is that . . . tenured faculty can be the most disgruntled faculty, and once they've gone through that horrible process, they are just worn out: "Now I'm tenured, now what?" . . . I think helping people have a plan, a realistic plan, and to say "no" to a lot, and to realize that they don't have to do everything in the 6 years.

A White female chair of kinesiology in a southern public research university sees it as part of her role not only to have conversations about the value of the diversity-related research agenda with the promotion and tenure committee but also to promote the recognition such research has attained in professional associations and to discuss its contributions in her annual progress letter. She explained,

> There is just more of an appreciation for what they would call scientific research as opposed to social science research, first of all . . . as much as I have tried to have conversations about that. . . . And then just the valuing of the diversity research agenda, clearly it is not as valued. I think it comes down to method as much as anything, but that is a vicious circle. Because the way you study diversity is different than measuring your blood pressure. The certainty for scientists sometimes in basic science is a false certainty, but they don't perceive it at all in diversity-related research; there is not a valuing of it. So in the tenure process, I think the chair has to have a conversation about it.

The insightful strategies shared in this chapter highlight the chair's critical role in furthering the success of diverse faculty in formal processes and in navigating the informal complexities of institutional and departmental culture. Because tenure review processes directly affect the future of junior faculty, chairs have the ability to overcome tendencies toward politicization by exercising control over both the composition and the processes of tenure review committees. They can help ensure equity in the review of student evaluations and teaching observations and create a climate of mentorship that equips diverse faculty with the knowledge and psychosocial support that facilitates their advancement and inclusion.

The White female chair of international programs cited earlier summed it up by advising diverse faculty to build relationships broadly across the university, especially because the chair of the department may not be chair when he or she comes up for tenure:

> One of the things that is also important is to make them realize that whoever is chair now might not be the chair when they come up for tenure, so they have to make relationships more broadly in the department and across the college and not kind of hide away. I think it is really important for people to have allies, mentors across the college and even the university.

Recalling the political dynamics involved in her own tenure review, she urged pretenure faculty to be politically savvy in "playing the game" and not give others ammunition to use against them in the tenure process:

> I think that really helps me because there had been some really ugly stuff that happened in my department before I came up for tenure, which actually ended up helping me. Because two women left before I even came up for tenure, because the department was kind of seen as an old guys' network by the college rank and tenure committee . . . even though I was definitely tenurable and my file was great, it provided me with a buffer. . . . They didn't dare touch me at that point because their hands had been slapped once before. . . . So I think just helping faculty to be politically savvy is really important and to realize they can't do everything. . . . There is a certain level of playing the game. . . . It's really important that you're getting your ducks in a row and that you don't give people ammunition.

Concluding Perspectives: Strategies for Recruiting and Retaining Diverse Faculty

As we conclude this chapter, we offer a number of concrete strategies drawn from the observations of chairs in our study that will help facilitate the recruitment and retention of diverse faculty.

Keep the conversation going about diversity. Throughout the chapter, we have seen examples of chairs who are willing to challenge the status quo and to create a continuous culture of conversation around diversity. A White female chair of educational leadership in a public western research university observed,

> To truly advance diversity in American colleges and universities, we have to have really critical conversations about racism, sexism, and homophobia, and people don't want to have those conversations because they tend to refuse to believe that they are racist or sexist or homophobic. . . . The big thing as a chair is to keep the conversation going and bring it up over and over and over again.

An African American male chair of history in a midwestern religiously affiliated university emphasized the need for self-examination and for generating conversations about difference:

> An important thing for chairs, any chair, is to sit down and really look in the mirror and ask themselves, "What do you really know and what do you really believe about people who don't look like you?" And take it upon themselves to do some reading and have some conversations about race. They need to have some conversations about gender equality. They need to have some conversations with people about alternative lifestyles, because a chair can be a very influential position in an institution. And if you're chair and you're closed minded, ignorant, worst of all willfully ignorant on these kinds of issues, I think you can do a lot of damage.

Cast a wide net in faculty searches. A Black male chair of Hispanic ethnicity in an elite private research university commented on the need to cast a wide net in recruiting new faculty, because "otherwise White colleagues look at very few people as 'qualified' for the job." In addition, as recommended by many chairs in the study, pursue multiple avenues and include contacts with other institutions with diverse graduates, review minority doctoral recipient data banks, use referrals and community outreach, and consult with the offices of human resources, diversity, and affirmative action.

Expand recruiting beyond conventional networks to consider recent minority doctoral recipients at "less prestigious" institutions, including those that may have assumed temporary, visiting, part-time, and postdoctoral positions. Consider recently hired diverse faculty at less selective institutions with significant scholarly, research, and teaching potential.

Increase education regarding community resources that can be shared with diverse faculty in the interview process. A White female chair of kinesiology in a public southern research university emphasized the importance of sharing available community resources with diverse candidates in recruiting efforts:

> I don't think as a department or university we have been successful at saying, "What are the community resources?" We kind of walk on tiptoes a bit; we are afraid to say this may be available to you because that might be perceived as an assumption. So educating everybody about that. I feel comfortable, but I don't think that all faculty members do. . . . We have several White males in the department, and I don't [think] there is any ill intention. But I think there is a lack of education on presenting an array of resources versus those that they are familiar with. By resources [I mean] different churches, the LGBT community, etc. We have had a couple of candidates who have been interested in resources of that nature and have asked me directly about those resources. I know that we have faculty members that could assist me in giving more information. . . . What is it like to live here when you're African American? What is it like to live here when you're a gay or lesbian faculty member? Those kinds of conversations probably don't occur, and I think it hampers our recruiting efforts.

Look at curricular offerings and ask what courses would attract women and minority candidates. A White male chair of economics in a southwestern research university noted the general tendency of faculty to want to hire the best and brightest that will put the department on the map. By contrast, he emphasized the need to shift the conversation and ask questions about the kinds of courses that would attract diverse candidates.

When overcoming objections to hiring diverse candidates, focus on the value that diversity brings to group decision making. A White male psychology chair in a midwestern urban university has advanced consideration of diversity in recruitment by focusing on the value that diversity brings to group decision making. As he explained,

> In terms of hiring, a common approach that people adopt is to pursue the best scholar. And I was pushing us to consider the importance of diversity, and one of the things that I did was I actually gave our faculty research to show that groups that are diverse actually make more effective decisions than groups that are not diverse, to actually promote diversity as a positive attribute that's value added. It's not just diversity for diversity's sake. Making your faculty more diverse will improve the quality of faculty; it will improve the quality of decision making of the group.

Defeat the common myths about hiring and diversity such as "diversity means a compromise in quality" and "few qualified women or minority candidates are available."

Support the people you hire through a variety of means, including mentoring, pedagogical coaching, and "going to bat" for them. In the course of the chapter, we have seen how activist chairs have provided support in the tenure process in a range of areas from mentoring to student evaluations. In this regard, a White male chair of mathematics, physics, and computer science in an eastern private liberal arts college emphasized the importance of not only bringing in people of diverse backgrounds but also supporting the faculty that he hires. This responsibility, in his view, rests not only with the chair but also with the whole department. In his words, "Unless the whole department contributes, then the person will not feel included." For example, in his mentoring of international faculty, he works on pedagogical issues to suggest visual and graphical approaches that combat linguistic issues. He also sees it as his role to "go to bat" for faculty when student evaluations raise issues regarding language barriers and difficulty in communication.

References

Buller, J. L. (2012). *The essential department chair: A comprehensive desk reference*. San Francisco, CA: Jossey-Bass.

Chun, E., & Evans, A. (2012). *Diverse administrators in peril: The new indentured class in higher education*. Boulder, CO: Paradigm.

DiTomaso, N. (2013). *The American non-dilemma: Racial inequality without racism*. New York, NY: Russell Sage Foundation.

Feagin, J. R., & Feagin, C. B. R. (2012). *Racial and ethnic relations* (9th ed.). Upper Saddle River, NJ: Prentice Hall.

Goel, S. (2006). An invisible minority: Asian Americans in mathematics. *Notices of the American Mathematical Society, 53*(8), 878–882.

Gordon, M. (2004). Diversification of the faculty: Frank talk from the front line about what works. In F. W. Hale Jr. (Ed.), *What makes racial diversity work in higher education: Academic leaders present successful policies and strategies* (pp. 182–199). Sterling, VA: Stylus.

Hale, F. W. (2004). *What makes racial diversity work in higher education: Academic leaders present successful policies and strategies*. Sterling, VA: Stylus.

Ibarra, H. (1995). Race, opportunity, and diversity of social circles in managerial networks. *Academy of Management Journal, 38*(3), 673–704.

Kivel, P. (2004). The culture of power. In F. W. Hale Jr. (Ed.), *What makes racial diversity work in higher education: Academic leaders present successful policies and strategies* (pp. 24–31). Sterling, VA: Stylus.

Lazos, S. R. (2012). Are student teaching evaluations holding back women and minorities? The perils of "doing" gender and race in the classroom. In G. Gutiérrez y. Muhs, Y. F. Niemann, C. G. Gonzalez, & A. P. Harris (Eds.), *Presumed incompetent: The intersections of race and class for women in academia* (pp. 164–185). Boulder, CO: Utah State University Press.

Moreno, C., Jackson-Triche, M., Nash, G., Rice, C., & Suzuki, B. (2013). *Independent investigative report on acts of bias and discrimination involving faculty at the University of California, Los Angeles.* Retrieved November 2, 2013, from http://www.maildoc.ucla.edu/External_Review_Team_Report.pdf

Mullen, A. L. (2010). *Degrees of inequality: Culture, class, and gender in American higher education.* Baltimore, MD: Johns Hopkins University Press.

Ono, S. J. (2013, October 28). *Why so few Asians are college presidents.* Retrieved January 5, 2014, from http://chronicle.com/article/Why-So-Few-Asians-Are-College/142567/

Penn's action plan for faculty diversity and excellence. (2011). Retrieved January 5, 2014, from http://www.upenn.edu/almanac/volumes/v58/n01/pdf_n01/faculty%20diversity-action%20plan.pdf

Ragins, B. R. (1997). Diversified mentoring relationships in organizations: A power perspective. *The Academy of Management Review, 22*(2), 482–521.

Report of the trustee ad hoc committee on diversity. (2013). Retrieved from Princeton University Reports website: www.princeton.edu/reports/2013/diversity/report/

Roscigno, V. J. (2007). *The face of discrimination: How race and gender impact work and home lives.* Lanham, MD: Rowman & Littlefield.

Roscigno, V. J., Garcia, L. M., & Bobbitt-Zeher, D. (2007). Social closure and processes of race/sex employment discrimination. *Annals of the American Academy of Political and Social Science, 609*(1), 16–48.

Rosette, A. S., Leonardelli, G. J., & Phillips, K. W. (2008). The White standard: Racial bias in leader categorization. *Journal of Applied Psychology, 93*(4), 758–777.

Rowe, M. (2008). *Micro-affirmations and micro-inequities.* Retrieved January 5, 2013, from http://web.mit.edu/ombud/publications/micro-affirm-ineq.pdf

Smith, D. G. (2000). How to diversify the faculty. *Academe, 86*(5), 48–52.

Smith, D. G., Turner, C. S., Osei-Kofi, N., & Richards, S. (2004). Interrupting the usual: Successful strategies for hiring diverse faculty. *Journal of Higher Education, 75*(2), 133–160.

Smith, E. (1996). Leader or manager: The minority department chair of the majority department. *Journal of Leadership and Organizational Studies, 3*(1), 79–94.

Stanley, C. A. (2006). Coloring the academic landscape: Faculty of color breaking the silence in predominantly White colleges and universities. *American Educational Research Journal, 43*(4), 701–736.

Stanley, C. A., & Lincoln, Y. S. (2005). Cross-race faculty mentoring. *Change, 37*(2), 44–50.

Sue, D. W. (2010). *Microaggressions in everyday life: Race, gender, and sexual orientation.* Hoboken, NJ: John Wiley & Sons.

Tierney, W. G., & Bensimon, E. M. (1996). *Promotion and tenure: Community and socialization in academe.* Albany, NY: State University of New York Press.

Tucker, A. (1993). *Chairing the academic department: Leadership among peers.* Phoenix, AZ: Oryx.

U.S. Department of Education. (2012). Washington, DC: National Center for Education Statistics, Integrated Postsecondary Education System.

Ward, K., & Wolf-Wendel, L. (2012). *Academic motherhood: How faculty manage work and family.* New Brunswick, NJ: Rutgers University Press.

Young, S. (2003). *Micro-inequities: The power of small.* Retrieved January 5, 2014, from http://www.insighteducationsystems.com/PDF/WorkforceDiversity2003.pdf

6

BRIDGE BUILDING

The Chair's Role in Fostering Diversity Learning Outcomes and Student Identity Development

To create effective learning environments, we educators must begin by asking just what images are being reflected in the mirror of our institutions. Does that reflection affirm the identities of all our students or just a few? Every student should be able to see important parts of himself or herself reflected in some way. All should be able to find themselves in the faces of other students and among the faculty and staff. They should also see their images reflected in the curriculum as well as in cocurricular programming to avoid feelings of invisibility or marginality that can undermine student success.

—Beverly Daniel Tatum (1999, p. 550)

In this chapter, we consider the chair's role in student learning about diversity through what Beverly Tatum called "the mirror of our institutions" (Tatum, 1999, p. 550). How do academic departments create a learning environment for students that deepens their understanding of diversity, strengthens cultural competency and awareness, provides opportunities for interaction with diverse others, and affirms their identity? All these avenues represent critical pathways for students, leading toward greater self-understanding and ultimately preparing them with the knowledge and skills needed for careers in a culturally rich, global society.

Yet once again, few, if any, chair resources cover this important topic, and most of the existing literature focuses almost exclusively on the administrative aspects of the chair role. Perhaps the chair's role can be seen as bridgework for diversity that connects ideas, individuals, and institutions across both internal and external boundaries for the good of the students and for purposes of social justice (see Brooks, 2012, for review). And the concept of intentionality is critical to the creation of a departmental culture that nurtures and sustains diversity (Park, 2013). In this chapter, we share intentional practices that chairs have undertaken in the area of student diversity that communicate norms and ideals related to diversity and counteract spoken and unspoken behaviors that contradict these norms (Park, 2013).

Research identifies three strategic parameters in student diversity that are directly related to institutional mission: (a) structural diversity (access and success of diverse students), (b) curricular and cocurricular diversity (diversity within the curriculum and in service learning, internships, or other programs), and (c) interactional diversity (informal interactions including mentoring, advising, and informal student contact) (Denson & Chang, 2009; Milem, 2003; Williams, 2013). To these parameters, we add the fourth, critically important, factor of identity development. These four dimensions act in tandem, and the presence of the others is thought to impact each dimension (see Milem, 2003, for review). For example, even in the presence of structural diversity, if students do not have meaningful involvement in cross-racial contact, minority students were more likely to indicate less satisfaction with the college experience (see Milem, 2003, for review).

From an outcomes-based perspective, the four strategic parameters represent critical dimensions of diversity that yield both learning outcomes and democracy outcomes that will strengthen academic and intellectual skills (Gurin, Dey, Hurtado, & Gurin, 2002; Milem, 2003). In addition, process outcomes related to diversity include how students perceive diversity has enriched their college experiences through perceptions of campus climate and student satisfaction, for example (Milem, 2003). Process outcomes can have an effect on student persistence and achievement (Milem, 2003).

Empirical evidence of the impact of diverse learning environments on educational outcomes has been garnered through research studies over the past two decades. This evidence substantiates the role of diversity in enhancing students' critical thinking skills, intellectual engagement and motivation, understanding of difference, perspective taking, and ability to work with individuals from different backgrounds (see, e.g., Denson & Chang, 2009; Gurin et al., 2002; Milem, Chang, & Antonio, 2005). Racially diverse campuses that expose students to environments dissimilar to their home environments can provide student developmental gains that include openness to diversity, self-confidence, deeper thinking, and cognitive and identity growth (Denson & Chang, 2009).

A recent longitudinal study of 1,865 student responses representing 17 colleges and universities drawn from the Wabash National Study of Higher Education found that interactional diversity was the only dimension among typical high-impact college experiences that fostered four-year growth in critical-thinking skills among students (Pascarella & Blaich, 2013). And diversity was also the only dimension that had a significant impact on three standardized measures of cognitive development: critical-thinking skills, a positive attitude toward literacy activities, and the need for cognition (Pas-carella & Blaich, 2013). Most significant, White students and those who entered college least academically prepared seemed to benefit the most from diversity experiences (Pascarella & Blaich, 2013).

In particular, the first year of college is a formative period in terms of students' continuing engagement with diversity, with initial experiences lead-ing to increases in other diversity experiences in the senior year (Bowman, 2012). Furthermore, formal diversity course work is predictive of increases in students' informal interactions with difference (Bowman, 2012). Yet stu-dents' perceptions of the campus's level of commitment to diversity impact whether they can directly benefit from the diversity present in the environ-ment (Milem et al., 2005).

Although our study focuses primarily on curricular diversity and student identity development as integral aspects of the student experience of diversity in the academic department, these areas necessarily implicate institutional efforts to increase the structural diversity of both faculty and students and to develop cocurricular student programs that strengthen student experiences of diversity.

Interestingly, the majority of chairs (62%) in our online survey sam-ple indicated that they had not encountered any difficulty in incorporating diversity into their department's disciplinary offerings. The most prominent approach identified by chairs to strengthen diversity-related student learning outcomes is service learning (54%). Other approaches include international study, departmental scholarships and internships, and individual advising. Metrics used by chairs to gauge diversity-related learning outcomes include course-level metrics and comparison to national benchmarks. Chairs also noted the importance of faculty advising and mentoring, as well as admis-sions strategies in promoting the access, retention, and success of diverse students.

Only a small number of department chairs interviewed for the study identified formal or informal approaches designed to assist diverse students in the process of identity development. For the most part, they saw this responsibility as an institutional one or noted that they did not have train-ing in this area. These responses suggest that this crucial issue is not on most department chairs' agendas and is not typically viewed as an essential part of the departmental role. Nonetheless, diverse students often see the academic department and its faculty as a potential and even frontline resource when they are seeking clarity and assistance in the process of identity development.

Why are resources needed in the academic department to assist diverse students in building an affirming identity despite the marginalization and negative stereotypes these students may face? Consider the comments by the mother of an African American student at a predominantly White state university campus regarding the lack of a support system for minority students as compared to those offered at a historically Black college: "I don't think that the teachers or the professors are as interested or [that] they . . . give them the certain help that they need" (Feagin, Vera, & Imani, 1996, p. 182). The mother indicated that the university doesn't listen or care or take the time to guide or direct the students (Feagin et al., 1996). Consider also the comments of a Black student at a California university (Park, 2013, p. 119):

> I feel like a novelty. I feel like that toy in the toy store that everyone plays with. Being a black student on campus is lonely and tiring. It's tiring because I'm tired of waiting to feel like I belong. No one wants to be your friend because everyone assumes that you only want to be friends with your own ethnic group, because everyone wants to feel comfortable.

When students from nondominant groups encounter racism, sexism, and heterosexism on college campuses, these experiences of misrecognition or the failure to receive respect and recognition from White students, professors, police, advisers, and campus personnel communicate to the students their devalued position (Feagin et al., 1996). Because of the power differential between professors and students, few students possess the psychological or social resources to alter substantively the social position assigned to them by professors (Feagin et al., 1996).

The phenomenon of minority status stress indicates that the mental health of students from nondominant groups is likely to be affected negatively by additional stress that includes insensitive comments, questions of belonging on a campus, and discrimination that interferes with their adjustment to college (see Cokley, McClain, Enciso, & Martinez, 2013, for review). The fact that life is stressful for minority students on predominantly White campuses often comes as a surprise to White students and faculty, who frequently underestimate the powerful presence of both covert and overt forms of discrimination (Tatum, 1997). Whether it is minority students being singled out in class for the minority perspective of their particular group, being routinely overlooked as a lab partner in science courses, or suffering the pain of racial epithets, graffiti, or racist jokes sent in e-mail, such experiences constitute an affront to their personal identity (Tatum, 1997).

Given the urgent need for resources that address these salient issues, we now explore the reasons that student identity development has often eluded the attention of academic department chairs and share emerging practices of chairs in the development of approaches to assist diverse students in this iterative and unfolding process.

Identity Development for Diverse Students

The journey toward identity development for diverse students is a continuous and complex one in the face of negative stereotypes and perceptions they face on predominantly White campuses. As diverse students enter the college milieu and experience environments different from or discontinuous with their home environment, they may be challenged with how to define, internalize, reconcile, and embrace their own identity.

The commentary of a Black student on a predominantly White campus reveals the continual struggle faced by diverse students to move beyond stereotypes imposed by others: "You're always seen as a black person. And as a black woman. You're seen as a black person before you're seen as a woman" (Feagin et al., 1996, p. 93). She described the constant struggle involved in always having to assert her individuality and her personality. To attain recognition, she feels she has to go overboard to have others see her uniqueness in terms of her style and goals.

The work of psychologist Erik Erikson indicates that late adolescence and early adulthood represent the unique intervals when personal identity and social identity are formed (see Gurin et al., 2002, for review). As a result, the college experience represents a critical juncture in the process of identity formation. And identity is understood to be socially constructed in terms of the intersections of self and one's social group with the wider social context in which norms and expectations are typically directed by values of the dominant group (see Torres, Jones, & Renn, 2009, for review). The social construction of identity on campuses occurs in contexts that include institutional fit in terms of access and retention and the social identities of those in leadership such as faculty and department chairs (Torres et al., 2009). Our particular focus is on the experiences of diverse students on predominantly White campuses and the experiences these students may face when they encounter stereotypes relating to race, ethnicity, gender, sexual orientation, and disability.

A number of research studies underscore the formative role of the college experience in identity development for diverse students. For example, a study of 19 minority college seniors at a predominantly White public research-intensive university on the West Coast found that the students markedly increased their identification with their ethnicity during their college years within the context of a negative psychology climate for diversity and weak institutional commitment in terms of diversity initiatives (Maramba & Velasquez, 2012). In this context, students found alternative spaces on campus that contributed to their ethnic identity, including informal peer networks and ethnic student organizations (Maramba & Velasquez, 2012).

In another example, Vasti Torres's bicultural orientation model (BOM) presents a nuanced understanding of differences in identity formation based on an original study of 372 Latino students (Torres, 1999). This model identifies four alternatives or modalities for how Latino students navigate between two cultures: (a) bicultural (comfort with both cultures), (b) Latino/ Hispanic (orientation toward culture of family origin), (c) Anglo (strong connection with majority culture), and (d) marginal (discomfort with both cultures) (Torres, 1999). Torres later conducted a longitudinal study of 10 Latino undergraduates and found distinct differences depending on environment where they grew up, family influence and generational status, and self-perception of status in society (Torres, 2003). Students from diverse environments had a stronger sense of ethnicity, and students from areas where Latinos constitute a critical mass did not view themselves as minorities until they arrived on a predominantly White campus. First-generation college students struggled to balance the demands of schooling with parental expectations (Torres, 2003). Self-perceptions of ethnic identity relate to whether this identity is viewed as a source of privilege or nonprivilege and whether negative stereotypes are seen to pertain to the individual (Torres, 2003).

Sexual minority students also encounter substantial challenges due to how they are perceived based on sexual orientation, gender identity, and gender expression. A study of 14 campuses with a sample of 1,699 lesbian, gay, bisexual, and transgender (LGBT) individuals found that one third of LGBT students experienced harassment within the prior year (see Rankin, 2005, for review). And 41% of the respondents indicated that their institutions did not systematically address issues related to sexual orientation or gender identity (see Rankin, 2005, for review). In support of these findings, another study of 80 LGBT students, 126 faculty members, 41 student affairs staff members, 105 residence hall assistants, and 43 general students at a public midwestern research university concluded that LGBT students perceived their campus climate more negatively than did other members of the campus community (Brown, Clarke, Gortmaker, & Robinson-Keilig, 2004). Because student affairs staff members provided relatively stronger support than faculty members, the researchers suggested that opportunities for programmatic support and gaining allies may be stronger among student affairs staff than faculty members (Brown et al., 2004).

Beverly Tatum (1997) shed further light on the complex pathway of student identity development in her landmark work, *"Why Are All the Black Kids Sitting Together in the Cafeteria?": And Other Conversations About Race.* She described identity development as a circular process rather than a linear one, like moving up a spiral staircase, which is in some sense continuous and never complete (Tatum, 1997). Tatum drew on William Cross's five-stage theory of identity that (a) begins with pre-encounters with the beliefs and values of the dominant White culture, then (b) moves to a stage of encounter when racist acts draw attention to the significance of race and one's own devalued position, (c) immersion in the multiplicity of one's identity, (d) internalization of a positive identity that embraces one's own difference, and (e) internalized commitment to support the concerns of diverse others (Tatum, 1997).

Tatum's analysis illuminates the reasons why Black or other racial/ethnic minority students often segregate themselves in social settings such as the cafeteria or residence halls within academe. These students likely have encountered experiences of their own devalued position and are engaged in the process of internalizing their own identity.

The phenomenon of self-segregation by ethnic and minority group members also suggests that academic institutions are not addressing the issue of identity development. When institutions provide physical spaces for social interaction and support for student organizations and cocurricular programs that strengthen identity formation, such initiatives benefit not only the students involved but also the entire campus community. Sustained and systematic attention to the importance of identity development can facilitate the persistence, success, and satisfaction of diverse students in their college experience. Overall, such efforts promote the integrative functioning of the campus, improve race relations, enhance educational outcomes, and help create an inclusive campus climate.

Given the importance of the college experience for the identity development of diverse students, what accounts for the relative absence of the importance of identity development on the department chairs' radar screen? Several chairs identified the lack of formalized practices at their institutions, whereas others mentioned the greater involvement of student affairs in this area. Speaking candidly, a White male economics chair in a southwestern public research university explained that the identity development of diverse students had not been a priority in his department and had not even been discussed or thought about. Noting that his department had no African American graduate or undergraduate students, yet was heavily international, he indicated that little attention has been paid to this at the departmental level, although efforts have been made at the university level. Reinforcing this perspective, a White female chair of computer science in a private midwestern regional university identified the lack of faculty development focusing on student identity formation:

> In terms of how the faculty directly do that, I don't think there is a formal program that has taught us how to do that in any way. I do see there are student groups for Hispanic students and African American students, and

they have mentors in the faculty and staff who are advisers for those groups. I don't think there has been any formal training.

A White female chair of allied health in a private southern religiously affiliated university noted the lack of support for student identity development in universities she worked for previously:

> In some of the universities I have been in, I have been shocked at the lack of understanding, the lack of support by the university and by faculty for students of different backgrounds having these challenges. . . . I have been in some huge universities, and I am thinking of one in particular in the midwest, the African American students came from inner-city areas or towns that were 100% African American. . . . And on a campus that is predominantly White . . . the experiences can be really bad. Some of the biases of faculty who just don't know any better are unfortunate.

In contrast, departments more closely tied to issues of identity such as women's studies may be viewed by students as a more likely venue for individualized contact on issues of identity formation. In this regard, a White female chair of women's studies in a public midwestern college highlighted the somewhat disproportionate role of her office in mentoring diverse students because of the focus and diversity of the curriculum. She noted that the most "out" of the lesbian faculty members in the department often mentors lesbian and gay students and also indicated that underrepresented minority students frequently come to her department for advice and counseling. The chair emphasized, however, that these practices are informal and not institutionalized with a designated office or process:

> We get really positive feedback about [identity development]. Our faculty are not as diverse ethnically or racially as they could be. . . . We have one African American person who works for just women's studies, and among our affiliated faculty members, we have one African American woman and another Latino woman. We have a couple of women faculty who are identified as part of the LGBTQ community. So we have some diversity. And I know that their presence helps our students, because I know that probably the most "out" of the lesbian faculty members does do a lot of mentoring of students. And that a lot of our lesbian students come to her and possibly some of the gay male students come to her as well, that I am not sure about. But I know that she plays that role.
>
> But I also know that maybe because of the diversity of the curriculum that we teach . . . that we probably play a fairly disproportionate role in terms of mentoring students who are students of color and students who belong to other kinds of minority groups. So on campus, our director of

our disability resource unit has told me, and she can't tell me who belongs to what category . . . that we have a disproportionate number of students who have visible or invisible disabilities and/or mental illness. I think because we talk about the kinds of social problems that all of these students face, we do tend to attract a disproportionate number of students, at least to our classes, if not to our major and minor who are in those kinds of categories, and we do spend time a lot of time working with them one-on-one. None of that is institutionalized, and it is just a practice. So a lot of students do come to us for mentoring. This doesn't happen on an institutional level. We don't have an office for that or a formal process for that.

A White female chair in a western public research university also identified disciplinary focus as a key factor affecting intentionality about racial identity development:

I oversee two areas, so it's really different in each area. In one, since we have diverse faculty and students, I feel like there is intentionality about racial identity development, and it's on the table and discussed. In the other area, I'd say people are just traditional, and it's more like saying it's color-blind and it doesn't really matter. In those classes, people view the subject matter as being race neutral or diversity neutral, and it's the knowledge that is important. But we have recently revamped our research methods curriculum, and I have seen people change their minds on that. The short answer is it depends on the area, and in certain areas I feel like it's easier.

Chairs from nondominant groups may also be approached more frequently by students on these issues. A White male psychology chair in a private midwestern college acknowledged that despite a warm and supportive culture at his institution, "I don't think we White faculty really understood issues of privilege, and . . . Whiteness and maleness were still normalized." Or as an African American student on a predominantly White campus indicated, he would have loved to have more contact with Black professors in his courses: "If you just know somebody up there that went through struggles and tension and pain and he is actually teaching you" (Feagin et al., 1996, p. 106).

Although noting that his institution does not do enough in the area of student identity development, an African American male history chair in a private religiously affiliated midwestern university personally mentors as many students as he can and actively encourages his faculty to reach out to diverse students in their classes:

Unfortunately, I don't think we are doing enough. I am a faculty adviser for the Black student union. I try to mentor, and this is where it happens; I try to mentor as many students as can. I try to encourage our faculty to reach out particularly to Black and Latino students when they see them in their classes and take them under their wing not in terms of making the course easier but in terms of mentoring them. I don't see a whole lot of that going on, and maybe I just don't see it.

This chair also has observed a decline in the interest of minority students in an intense academic mentoring relationship that could be attributed to the diminished role of minority student activism on college campuses as students turn their attention to finding jobs in a difficult economy (see Altbach & Cohen, 1990, for review). As the chair explained,

> Years ago when I got here two decades ago, we had a huge racial crisis on this campus. . . . The silver lining in that crisis was that the students wanted an intense, real academic mentoring relationship. Not only did we do activism, not only did we do social awareness, not only did we do programming, not only did we have parties, but we read books together, we had discussion groups every week, we had lunch together every week on a particular topic. The students were driving this passion for learning more outside of the classroom.
>
> There were holes in the curriculum that they saw that weren't being met in terms of knowledge about people who looked like them. And that passion on the part of the students is not there right now. When I try to discuss the need for activism and more passionate mentoring, it has really kind of fallen on deaf ears. Maybe they think they know everything, maybe they are studying so hard that they don't have time. When I got here, the first course I offered in African American history had 22 Black students and 3 brave White females. Last semester, [when] I taught African American history, I had 18 students; 2 were African Americans.

A White female chair of education in a private western master's-level university located in a major urban area described her planned and purposeful efforts to hire minority adjunct faculty that will attract diverse students to the program and also serve as role models and mentors to these students:

> When I took over as chair in the department, all the faculty and adjuncts were White; predominantly the students were 100% White. I think what we know about those who are not White, if they have role models who look like they do or have experiences like theirs, then there is more of a likelihood that they will feel comfortable in this environment. . . .
>
> The faculty of color, one in particular, really has become a mentor to many of our students of color, and almost all our supervisors, our student teacher teachers are not White; it's a mix. I am doing that on purpose; it's · a purposeful plan. I talk to students about it. I ask students who, in the

community that you work with, would you like to see as part of our community? That's worked. I think that faculty understand that they have a responsibility to be mentors. It's a lot easier for an African American male to talk to an African American faculty member at least as an initial mentoring process. . . . We're lucky because we are in a major city.

Clearly, much work still needs to be done to develop both formal and informal programs devoted to student identity formation for diverse students on predominantly White campuses. Although some programming can and is being developed through student affairs, chairs can also foster a normative environment for diverse students that is hospitable and welcoming. As key institutional leaders, they can create spaces, programs, activities, and opportunities that promote inclusion and academic success. Mentoring activities and informal interactions with professors in the department are important avenues that permit diverse students to frame issues of identity and obtain psychosocial support and academic survival skills within the campus environment.

We now turn our attention to the chair's role in furthering diversity within the curriculum and chronicle the particular challenges and resistance they may face in their efforts.

Mirrors of Diversity in the Curriculum

As chairs consider how to bring greater diversity to the curriculum and learning process, this exploration includes an array of factors that include instructional strategies designed to address diverse learning styles, inclusive classroom approaches, curricular content, and normative faculty role models. A White male chair of educational leadership in a public western research university observantly framed the complex interaction among these components and their reciprocal influence on one another. He emphasized that diversity in its different forms prevents the "silver bullet" approach to education:

I think that one among many of the other factors we have to take in account when we talk about an education is also diversity of learning styles, of instructional strategies, and all of those kinds of different things that make schools and make education so complicated, and really make it a situation where you can't only focus on any one factor, because they all exert reciprocal influence on each other. If you start focusing on one thing, it sort of shifts dynamics in a different place. It keeps it all lively and exciting. But it also means that there is no kind of silver bullet approach to education. Diversity in the different forms that I am talking about and the ways that interact with each other is what sort of prevents the silver bullet school approach from having much of an impact.

Speaking of the isolated nature of teaching, the chair is planning a more critical approach to teaching in his department and initiating discussions about issues such as learning styles and pedagogical strategies at the department or program level. As a new department chair, he is implementing a plan of observing each faculty member's teaching as a means of enhancing the learning process:

> Like many new department chairs, I think I am starting off by doing several things that I have never seen a chair do before. But that I am trying to bring to this because I think it is something that chairs ought to do. I have been a professor for a total of 15 years now; I have never been observed once teaching. And so one thing I am doing is observing every professor over the course of the year and giving them some feedback and trying to get a conversation going at the department or at least the program level about teaching and learning, because I find the culture here is very isolating. . . . It's a challenge; it really is.
>
> The kind of isolating nature of university teaching makes it a little bit difficult to get those kinds of things going, but also because I am new, I'm also going to spend a lot of time going about it very carefully. Because I don't want to undermine our trust, and getting people to see that's what I am doing: giving feedback about teaching that is . . . fully honest, and it's intended so that we can all improve. I'm not out to get anybody.

Specific approaches to curricular diversity can include introduction of a new course that fills a curricular void and incorporation of content related to diversity in existing courses (Hurtado, Milem, Clayton-Pedersen, & Allen, 1999). Some universities have instituted a diversity course requirement in the general education curriculum. Yet initiating such curricular change can be a highly contentious process. An African American sociology department chair in a private southern research university described the intensity of the opposition he faced and the lobbying he had to undertake when introducing a diversity requirement in his university:

> I remember spending 2 or 3 years making so-called house calls with different faculty who were blocking the vote. Having breakfast meetings with faculty who are no different than you are, tenured, they've been on campus 8 to 10 years, having meetings with them to explain to them the value of the diversity requirement. . . . Nobody else has to do that. . . . The diversity thing is contentious, and if you have been in those meetings and seen it, it is unbelievably contentious.

He further elaborated on the differential obstacles that diversity courses encounter in the curricular review process, unlike any other standard course, and further observed that sponsorship of such courses can be risky for pre-tenure faculty:

> As the chair of a department, when your courses have to go through this curriculum committee, I mean you have to fight for it or set up a special offering course that can be taught two times before you come to committee. . . . You don't have a title; students don't know what the course is until they get there. You send out flyers; you have to go to the offices of diversity and different area studies to push the course. No standard types of courses have to do those types of things. And then the irony is, let's say you want a diverse faculty, in terms of how you provide it, and those people come to campus. . . . Then the first thing you know, you can't get the course through the curriculum, or they have five students and the rules are . . . you got to have 10 or 12 students. . . . So the next thing you know, they are teaching the 101 course in your discipline. And think about it: If those things happen to you in year one or two, by the time you get to year three, you have some marks on your CV.

And consider the challenges described by an African American male chair in history at a private, religiously affiliated midwestern university in the process of curricular reform. He encountered a powerful lobby seeking to maintain the dominant Eurocentric view of history. As he observed,

> One of the main challenges started about 15 years ago; we went through a curricular reform where we implemented a cultural heritage sequence. . . . The question of diversity was what constitutes the corpus of essential readings that we want all the students to read. And lo and behold . . . there was a very powerful lobby that wasn't buying what I and several of the historians were saying in the development of this curriculum, that we cannot have a completely Eurocentric data point of what constitutes the development of history over the last 5,000 years, and really over the last 500 years. And there was incredibly visceral disagreement to that position.

Our survey sample found significant variation in the extent to which chairs have identified ways to address diversity in the department's curricular offerings. Above all, disciplinary focus appears to be the driving factor that influences the degree to which diversity is operationalized in the curriculum. Chairs in the STEM fields expressed more difficulty and even skepticism in terms of the ability to create content-based connections with diversity. Take the observations of a White male chemistry chair in a midwestern teaching university:

Of course we try to cover topics in chemistry that reflect diverse think-ing. . . . Another thing that you could say is that when you are teaching the history of chemistry and we are talking about people who have made important advances . . . we don't have any formal program that tries to do that. We have Asian and Hispanic and Black professors, and they may or may not do that more than other people. I don't really know what you mean when you talk about diversity in the curriculum.

The chair also noted that although about 50% of chemistry graduates with a bachelor's degree are women, in the ranks of the professoriate, women are less well represented. At his institution, about one third of the chemistry faculty are women, but he has also noticed more departures among women faculty. As a result, he wonders if the university is accommodating the profes-sional needs of the women faculty as well as it does the men faculty.

Similarly, a White female chair of computer science in a midwestern research university identified the difficulty of incorporating curricular con-tent related to diversity:

That's a tough one in computer science, because in our discipline I don't think we think about social aspects like diversity in the curriculum all that much. . . . We don't think about it at all. But our classes are so techni-cally focused and almost not human focused, right? They are focused on machines and software and that type of thing.

Yet the computer science chair simultaneously identified two specific ave-nues to address diversity in the learning process: a focus on accessibility to diverse populations in the development of computer applications and the creation of inclusive classroom environments for the small minority of females in this field:

I think what we do try to do is be sensitive to the fact that what we may produce as software engineers is going to be used by a diverse audience. So we really look at diversity not so much in terms of the technical content that we do, but in other arenas. So if we are looking at graphical user inter-faces, for example, we might teach students about the fact that we might have visually impaired people and various types of disability where we have to be concerned about that. In terms of the other types of diversity, like gender and ethnic diversity, that's a lot harder to address in the context of computer science as far as I'm concerned. Maybe I just don't understand how to do it. But we have to worry about how we run the classes because we have only two females in them. It's not so much about the curriculum; it's the environment where it impacts us.

A White male chair of internal medicine in a southwestern public research university noted that although diversity is not formally addressed in the curriculum, resident medical students experience diversity through community interactions:

> I am not certain that [diversity] is addressed in our curriculum at all; I really am not aware if it is. . . . We do talk about cultural sensitivity and professionalism and respectfulness in people's beliefs and backgrounds. . . . That is definitely taught by our faculty to the residents. We are actually one of the 20 or so cities that receive refugees. . . . Our group is probably more attuned than most to the needs of those who are underserved otherwise. We also collaborate with the school of pharmacy and local physicians . . . and we set up free clinics for the poor in some of our poorer neighborhoods . . . and we have students come out and volunteer in those.

Chairs in disciplines that have a more obvious connection to diversity-related content such as sociology and foreign languages or to diverse constituencies such as journalism and education identified more substantive curricular approaches to diversity and cultural competency as a natural outgrowth of their disciplines. For example, a White female chair of special education in a western public research university described a course that future teachers take to understand how to teach students with disabilities, a course offering on diversity in schools and society, and the overall integration of diversity within many courses in her department.

Even when a particular disciplinary focus does not provide an obvious connection to diversity, chairs can encourage diversity in areas such as the use of data sets that represent diverse populations or inclusive research methodologies. Consider the approach taken by a White male chair of psychology in an urban midwestern research university. He explicitly required his faculty to develop a short statement of how diversity was incorporated in their course offerings. Although not forcing the issue, he also suggested ways that diversity could be incorporated within the context of research methods and data sets:

> One of the things I did as a chair . . . [was that] I asked our faculty to write a short description of how diversity was included in each of the courses that they taught. And for some courses, that was incredibly easy. For example, we had a course . . . called the Psychology of African Americans, so it was pretty easy. But then there were other courses such as research methods that might be much more difficult, but I wanted to know if people used examples about how to apply research methods to diverse groups. . . . In faculty meetings, we had a couple of discussions about the very broad ways that connections could be made. . . . But we encouraged people to try to think of ways that they could include issues related to diversity, broadly

defined, in their classes. And we did not force people to include issues of diversity in their class.

Another example of a class where it's difficult is statistics. . . . Perhaps examples or data sets could be used that represented diverse populations. Some people just said, "Well, statistics has nothing to do with diversity." And I would say, "That may be true, but the examples you use may represent diversity. . . ." The pushback, whenever I got it, was from a small number of people.

As we have seen from preceding examples, chairs can proactively initiate conversations with departmental faculty about diversity in multifaceted ways that include discussion of course content, pedagogical approaches, and learning styles. Furthermore, they can promote collaborative and cooperative learning experiences in the classroom that enhance student understanding of racial/ethnic and social issues affecting society as a whole (Hurtado et al., 1999). Research substantiates that direct contact with out groups reduces prejudice, and conscious efforts to establish racially mixed work groups tasked with significant goals can contribute to bias reduction (see Chun & Evans, 2009; Pettigrew & Tropp, 2006, for review). As a result, if faculty take tangible steps to design course activities that encourage students to engage in meaningful cross-race interactions on group projects, research assignments, and cooperative learning opportunities, these efforts can promote greater understanding and reduce bias through direct experiential interactions (Hurtado et al., 1999).

A White female chair of allied health in a private religiously affiliated southern university is cognizant of the challenges of racism that students may face in academic environments:

> Department chairs are going to deal with racism all the time . . . and they will see it happen to students. And it may happen to students by other students; it may happen to students by their instructors. . . . This is a huge issue . . . and will continue to be for some time.

She explained how her own background gives her a depth of understanding that assists diverse students in their exploration of identity:

> Coming into a very diverse community, I think my background and experience on three different continents . . . has made it easier for me to connect with those students who are from different backgrounds, especially those from developing countries. What I just mentioned has to do with retention and understanding differences between different educational systems and how that might impact students.

Summing up the importance of diversity in the learning environment, she concluded,

> Diversity must be clearly defined: It is a crucial part of what we do to create a learning environment that exposes students as part of their education to an international or global perspective and understanding of different people and different cultures. For our program and our university, it is not a big issue, but I think for many universities it is. Just exposing students to faculty of different nationalities, different ethnicities, different religions, different genders, all of that is important.

Although the chair realizes the challenges diverse students may face on predominantly White campuses, when attention is given to multifaceted approaches to diversity within the academic department, such consideration benefits all students and can serve as a vehicle for progressive and transformative diversity initiatives in the institution as a whole.

Concluding Perspectives: Strategies for Enhancing Diversity Learning Outcomes and Student Identity Development

The following strategies suggested by chairs in our study are designed to facilitate enhanced curricular and interactional diversity and promote guidance to students in identity formation.

Creation of formalized departmental mentoring programs. An Asian male chair of periodontics in a midwestern public research university has developed a mentoring program and vertical learning groups for dental students composed of students from all 4 years of residency. The chair explained how these innovative practices help students with survival skills and their successful academic progression:

> When my son was starting high school, he was assigned a mentor to help him survive the early phase of high school. And I was sitting there watching it. And I came back, and one of the things I created was both an internal and external mentor for each of my residents. The internal mentor is one of the faculty, and the external faculty mentor is one of the alumni. The idea was . . . to help them in formal and e-mail communication, e-portfolio, and work that they show to each other as well as the internal and external mentors . . . to help them feel comfortable.
>
> I created a couple of unique things for the school. One of them is what we call a vertical learning group, where we have first-year, second-year, third-year dental students who have been assigned to me as mentees in a group. We meet about once a month, and we go over cases and cover

survival skills in dental school, and it has changed the students, the residents, and the faculty.

Development of community-based internship programs. A White female chair of sociology in a public southwestern research university described how the department's internship program has helped students become involved with the community and provide unique service learning experiences that are also beneficial to the community.

Partnerships of departmental faculty with college or university-wide programs designed to attract and retain underrepresented undergraduate and graduate students. The sociology chair described a pilot mentoring program initiated by her university with professors who participate as advisers for incoming freshmen who are first-generation Hispanic students. She also highlighted the importance of a supportive administration and access to financial resources through undergraduate scholarships focused on first-generation college students and competitive graduate fellowships as critical factors in strengthening student diversity. As she explained,

> A very important aspect for the graduate student recruitment is that the university developed an emphasis on recruiting diversity, and we have . . . competitive fellowships . . . [that] have really helped us to recruit students. They're one of the primary sources of financial support for these students, so that has been invaluable . . . and we have supportive administrators, a supportive dean and department heads who emphasize diversity and the importance of it. And so the development of these norms and the access to resources are the crucial components.

Promoting faculty engagement in the curriculum revision process to include diversity. A White female chair of educational leadership in a western public research university actively encourages faculty to think about the curriculum revision process and how it relates to student needs. Leading that discussion in an open manner has encouraged faculty to speak up and participate in the process. As she observed,

> I just try to encourage people to think about what [curriculum revision] means. We recently had a small student uprising from students wanting more diversity in the curriculum. . . . We had that conversation about the curriculum. . . . The faculty think we are doing a good job, but the students don't. What does it mean to have diversity in the curriculum? Just having that conversation has done a lot. . . . I think people view me as a person who is willing to have the conversation. And that's been pretty significant in terms of people feeling free to speak up.

Linkage of professional standards and accreditation criteria to diversity-related curricular efforts. The tie between cultural diversity and the disciplinary standards of professional associations and the regional accreditation process can be an important level that strengthens the "business case" for diversity in the curriculum. Accreditation also can provoke conversations about diversity and what it means in terms of student learning outcomes, teaching styles, and classroom experiences.

References

Altbach, P. G., & Cohen, R. (1990). American student activism: The post-sixties transformation. *Journal of Higher Education, 61*(1), 32–49.

Bowman, N. A. (2012). Promoting sustained engagement with diversity: The reciprocal relationships between informal and formal college diversity experiences. *The Review of Higher Education, 36*(1), 1–24.

Brooks, J. S. (2012). *Black school White school: Racism and educational (mis)leadership.* New York, NY: Teachers College Press.

Brown, R. D., Clarke, B., Gortmaker, V., & Robinson-Keilig, R. (2004). Assessing the campus climate for gay, lesbian, bisexual, and transgender (GLBT) students using a multiple perspectives approach. *Journal of College Student Development, 45*(1), 8–26.

Chun, E., & Evans, A. (2009). *Bridging the diversity divide: Globalization and reciprocal empowerment in higher education* (ASHE-ERIC Higher Education Reports, Vol. 35, No. 1). San Francisco, CA: Jossey-Bass.

Cokley, K., McClain, S., Enciso, A., & Martinez, M. (2013). An examination of the impact of minority status stress and impostor feelings on the mental health of diverse ethnic minority college students. *Journal of Multicultural Counseling and Development, 41*(2), 82–95.

Denson, N., & Chang, M. J. (2009). Racial diversity matters: The impact of diversity-related student engagement and institutional context. *American Educational Research Journal, 46*(2), 322–353.

Feagin, J. R., Vera, H., & Imani, N. (1996). *The agony of education: Black students at White colleges and universities.* New York, NY: Routledge.

Gurin, P., Dey, E. L., Hurtado, S., & Gurin, G. (2002). Diversity and higher education: Theory and impact on educational outcomes. *Harvard Educational Review, 72*(3), 330–367.

Hurtado, S., Milem, J., Clayton-Pedersen, A., & Allen, W. (1999). *Enacting diverse learning environments: Improving the climate for racial/ethnic diversity in higher education* (ASHE-ERIC Higher Education Report, Vol. 26, No. 8). Washington, DC: Graduate School of Education and Human Development, George Washington University.

Maramba, D. C., & Velasquez, P. (2012). Influence of the campus experience on the ethnic identity development of students of color. *Education and Urban Society, 44*(3), 294–317.

Milem, J. F. (2003). The educational benefits of diversity: Evidence from multiple sectors. In M. Chang, D. Witt, J. Jones, & K. Hakuta (Eds.), *Compelling interest: Examining the evidence on racial dynamics in colleges and universities* (pp. 126–169). Stanford, CA: Stanford University Press.

Milem, J. F., Chang, M. J., & Antonio, A. L. (2005). *Making diversity work on campus: A research-based perspective.* Washington, DC: American Association of Colleges and Universities.

Park, J. J. (2013). *When diversity drops: Race, religion, and affirmative action in higher education.* New Brunswick, NJ: Rutgers University Press.

Pascarella, E. T., & Blaich, C. (2013). *Lessons from the Wabash national study of liberal arts education.* Retrieved February 8, 2014, from http://www.changemag.org/Archives/Back%20Issues/2013/March-April%202013/wabash_full.html

Pettigrew, T. F., & Tropp, L. R. (2006). A meta-analytic test of intergroup contact theory. *Journal of Personality and Social Psychology, 90*(5), 751–783.

Rankin, S. R. (2005). Campus climates for sexual minorities. *New Directions for Student Services, 111,* 17–23.

Tatum, B. D. (1997). *"Why are all the Black kids sitting together in the cafeteria?" and other conversations about race: A psychologist explains the development of racial identity.* New York, NY: Basic Books.

Tatum, B. D. (1999). Guest commentary: Which way do we go? Leading for diversity in the new frontier. *Journal of Negro Education, 68*(4), 550–554.

Torres, V. (1999). Validation of a bicultural orientation model for Hispanic college students. *Journal of College Student Development, 40*(3), 285–298.

Torres, V. (2003). Influences on ethnic identity development of Latino college students in the first two years of college. *Journal of College Student Development, 44*(4), 532–547.

Torres, V., Jones, S. R., & Renn, K. A. (2009). Identity development theories in student affairs: Origins, current status, and new approaches. *Journal of College Student Development, 50*(6), 577–596.

Williams, D. A. (2013). *Strategic diversity leadership: Activating change and transformation in higher education.* Sterling, VA: Stylus.

7

DEVELOPING A DEPARTMENTAL ACTION PLAN FOR DIVERSITY

A longtime mentor of mine once said that the greatest of all human inventions is the creative process, how we bring forth new realities.

—Peter Senge (2009, p. xi)

I f indeed department chairs represent transformative diversity leaders of progress in higher education, they will be engaged in bringing forth and sustaining new realities. Rather than producing a litany of traditional elements of strategic planning, they are called on to forge approaches that will shift mind-sets and culturally based assumptions within the department and also influence the deepened learning of students about diversity. Unlike other institutional planners, their particular emphasis is on teamwork within an environment of peer and intergroup leadership. Chairs epitomize the leadership of reflective practitioners, marshaling their research and analytical expertise in service of the practical process of reflection in action (Schon, 1983).

As reflective practitioners, chairs bring creativity and insight to the planning process to create the new realities needed. And the planning process involves a shift in what Otto Scharmer called "the social field" or the totality and types of interconnections through which participants in any given system converse, think, relate, and act (Scharmer, 2009, p. 4). Such a shift in the social field becomes easier to do after it is undertaken for the first time and leads to a clarified sense of direction and accomplishment, as well as heightened energy, awareness, and deepening of authenticity (Scharmer, 2009).

One of the primary problems for department chairs seeking to implement new diversity realities is to move beyond rhetoric to action. Consider the perspective of a recently appointed White male chair of educational leadership in a western public research university who described the difficulty of transcending buzzwords to engage faculty in substantive approaches to diversity:

> My perspective at the moment is that I keep seeing in the bylaws and the website there is a lot of talk about diversity, there is a lot of talk about multiculturalism, there is a lot of talk about social justice, and I don't see it at all. I see people using those things as buzzwords and not as a way of approaching work; I don't see people acting as advocates. . . . I see them sort of hiding from the policy discussions, especially when there are issues of equity and diversity that could be engaged or interrogated. And so I think we're a long way off as far as that goes. I don't think we're anywhere near where we need to be. . . .
>
> But I also feel a little bit conflicted about it in terms of how to move forward. It's going to take guts, it's going to take some people retiring, it's going to take some people finding their voice and their courage to stand up and say things. Like I said, I am still getting to know people. So I'm not sure who's going to be the person who can step up and actually be the social justice expert from that position and who is just talking the talk. There's a lot of talking, and I don't see much action of yet. But I just got here, and I am trying not to be judgmental.

A White female chair of international programs in a private religiously affiliated western university reflected her concern about the bifurcation between those who support the status quo and the women and minorities who are left to undertake the diversity work:

> But when it comes down to doing the diversity work, it's left up oftentimes to women and faculty of color and people who are themselves in that category. . . . Then it does end up supporting the status quo in terms of the old boys' network. So I think there are people with good intentions and then there are people who are almost antidiversity. And in some ways those people actually end up in positions of authority, because the work is left up to diverse faculty themselves.

A number of chairs in the study commented on the factionalization and pushback by members of the department who may be attached to the status quo for reasons of workload, other priorities, or even antidiversity sentiments. As the educational leadership chair noted, initiating the planning process will require courage and will benefit from the support of faculty allies who are willing to become advocates and speak up on behalf of diversity.

Then how can chairs begin? To attain breakthroughs, department chairs can call on the entire department as a panel of advisers (Buller, 2014). Chairs need to convey why change is necessary in the first place and then adopt a "strong sales mentality" that draws on faculty input to develop effective approaches and communicate priorities to the dean and provost (Buller, 2014, p. 4). Jeffrey Buller suggested an approach chairs can adopt in a faculty meeting to build support for the change initiative that we have modified in relation to diversity (Buller, 2014, p. 4):

> My first priority is to provide the support and resources you need to perform your work effectively. But as the university moves toward developing a diversity strategic plan, that emphasis is not sufficient. We know we need seed money for new faculty lines, for research, for curricular change. I need your help as we seek to convey our departmental needs to strengthen diversity to our dean and provost. Since some of you are better at conveying these priorities with impact and vision, let's work together in identifying the most effective means to moving from where we are today to where we need to be. Let's formulate strategies together and put these strategies within a concrete diversity action plan.

A White male chair of psychology in an urban midwestern university summed up this strengths-based approach to aligning departmental and university diversity goals:

> One of the goals of the department chair or head should be to try to make the department adapt or reflect the mission of the university. One of our clear missions is research related to diversity. This is kind of a win-win situation by helping the department emphasize diversity makes us fit the university mission better, which, in turn, is going to put us in a better position to get resources from the university. So you can think of that from the bad side as self-serving, or you can think of it from the good side as we are serving the university and trying to meet its mission. I try to use the university's and college's goals and mission to our advantage whenever possible. Fortunately, the department's mission very naturally aligns with the university's mission. . . . I can just emphasize our strengths in every possible way as a way of trying to get resources to help us improve our diversity.

Following initial discussion with the faculty, chairs can initiate a phase-based approach to the collaborative development of departmental diversity strategies that can include the following: (a) beginning the dialogue and overcoming departmental defensive routines, (b) identifying blind spots and levers for change, (c) visualizing the future, (d) conducting a gap assessment, and (e) building an agenda for action.

Begin the Dialogue and Overcome Departmental Defensive Routines

Chairs in our study emphasized the importance of breaking the silence about diversity through in-depth, searching, and critical conversations. As we have seen from the chair narratives, many subtle barriers to diversity and inclusion still exist below the surface of everyday experiences. Some chairs have spoken of internal conflicts or resistance to diversity, whereas others have described inertia resulting from demanding faculty workloads and other priorities.

Approaches that interrogate or bring to light organizational defensive routines can surface assumptions that hinder diversity progress. Organizational theorist Chris Argyris identified the discrepancy or mismatch between an individual's, or a group's, *theory-in-use* that represents the master program that guides the person's actions and his or her *espoused beliefs* or attitudes. The underlying theory-in-use is also governed by a set of values or beliefs. The phenomenon of aversive racism is a case in point. Aversive racism represents the mismatch or disconnect between the espoused egalitarian values of White Americans and the fundamental theory-in-use that involves underlying negative feelings and beliefs about Blacks (see Dovidio, Gaertner, & Bachman, 2001; Gaertner & Dovidio, 2000, for review).

When situations threaten to expose the negative attitudes of aversive racists, these individuals may amplify positive behavior and overreact in order to reconcile their underlying negative feelings with their espoused values and self-image (Gaertner & Dovidio, 2000). Put another way, individuals can engage in frontstage and backstage behavior related to issues of race (Picca & Feagin, 2007). They may present themselves as color-blind on the front stage, whereas backstage actions, commentary, and emotions reveal underlying racist, sexist, and heterosexist views (Picca & Feagin, 2007).

Individuals or groups may employ defensive routines when difficult diversity issues arise to prevent embarrassment or threat and to keep themselves unaware of the mismatch between the theory-in-use and the espoused beliefs (Argyris, 1995). Because individuals' sense of competence, self-esteem, and self-confidence is tied to theories-in-use and these theories have been internalized, strategies of bypass, avoidance, and cover-up can be consciously or unconsciously deployed to reinforce underlying theories-in-use (Argyris, 1995). As a result, the challenge is to help individuals work backward to transform espoused values (or the front stage) into theories-in-use (or the backstage) (Argyris, 1995; Picca & Feagin, 2007).

Producing sustained organizational learning around diversity is a change process that needs to overcome the inconsistencies between reasoning and the actions or lack of action undertaken (Argyris, 1996). Conversations that seek to unravel the governing theories-in-use and their accompanying values and then alter subsequent actions can generate what Argyris called "double-loop learning" (Argyris, 2002). By contrast, single-loop learning does not address the underlying theories-in-use. To the extent that dialogues about diversity can surface discrepancies and allow for changes in behaviors and actions, such dialogue will begin to erode the mental mind-sets and barriers that preclude the creation of new theories-in-use and governing values about diversity.

To assist in this process, departments may benefit from the guidance of an external facilitator such as a skilled organizational theorist. Organizational development interventions that employ a case study method approach can be used to provide insight into individuals' tacit causal theories through the medium of conversation and feedback (Argyris, 1995). Case studies allow participants to bring forward ideas and feelings that would not ordinarily be communicated and then to formulate alternative approaches to action (see Argyris, 1995, for review). The value of the case study approach is that it allows for indirection and distancing of participants from themselves without embarrassment, while simultaneously permitting self-evaluation of actions.

Identify Blind Spots and Levers

Moving to the next phase of building a departmental diversity action plan, we return to Scharmer's notion of shifting the social field to identify potential blind spots that represent invisible dimensions of everyday experiences of diversity (Scharmer, 2009). This process will enable chairs to probe for a strategic leverage point that will function as the Archimedean point that allows the social field to shift and evolve (Scharmer, 2009). Because such shifts deepen creativity beyond patterns of the past and occur spontaneously from small groups and networks of people, this leverage point creates communal connections that are permanent and stay on, even as people come and go from departments (Scharmer, 2009). This process will lead to a visualization of the future state of diversity that identifies the gains to be realized.

Consider the commentary of a White female chair of education on the challenges of developing evidence-based measures of diversity for accreditation:

> But more importantly, I don't even know how to evaluate it [diversity] in this era of evidence-based work. So we're about to go through accreditation at the institution. They want to know how I know my students have respect for diversity and how my faculty have respect for diversity. So what kind of diversity? Diversity of learning styles? . . . I think the politically

correct sense for that is that it's not just White folks sitting in the room who are middle class. But that's making assumptions about somebody who's a person of color, for example, has a particular point of view that is different from somebody who isn't, looking at notions of class as having power.

Given this chair's perspective on the complexity of measuring diversity progress, we now return to reconsider the framework provided in Exercise 1.1, the Chair Diversity Self-Assessment Profile in chapter 1. In Table 7.1, we include a sample domain of the profile and indicate representative blind spots that chairs have identified as barriers to diversity progress in each dimension. We then suggest specific levers to overcome the hurdles. Because blind spots are highly context specific, blank columns are provided for the chair's determination of the appropriate lever and the communal connections that will result from invoking the lever. The complete sample template can be found in Appendix B.

Visualize the Future

In visualizing the department's future and how it is to be built from networks or small groups of people, the metaphor of a *web of diversity* replaces a hierarchical frame (Kezar, Eckel, Contreras-McGavin, & Quaye, 2008). This metaphor is particularly apt in the departmental setting, because the academic department is, in essence, a network of peer-based rather than hierarchical interactions. As a result, in the formulation of each aspect of the department's diversity plan, the network model provides a way of articulating interconnections and interdependencies across organizational boundaries within the department, college, and university.

Bolman and Deal's four perspectives or frames of leadership provide insight into how leaders conceptualize reality: (a) the structural frame that emphasizes clear goals, roles, policies, and accountability; (b) the human resources (HR) frame that leads through facilitation and empowerment and defines problems in interpersonal and individual terms; (c) the political frame that views organizations as sites of conflict and competitions and emphasizes networks and coalitions; and (d) the symbolic frame that sees facts as interpretative rather than objective and sees meaning as a social creation (Bolman & Deal, 1991). Interviews with 27 college and university presidents conducted by Adrianna Kezar and colleagues revealed that strategies within the HR frame play a critical role in moving the diversity agenda forward (see Kezar et al., 2008, for review).

Six HR strategies identified by presidents in this study represent nodes on the web of leadership, as shown in Figure 7.1. The nodes on the web of

TABLE 7.1
Blind Spots and Levers

Domain	Dimension	Blind Spot	Lever	Chair's Perspective	Communal Connections
Classroom	Promoting inclusive pedagogies	Lack of review of teaching styles in the classroom	Initiate conversations about teaching systems; conduct developmental classroom observations		
	Providing support for marginalizing experiences of diverse faculty members	Lack of mentoring programs, including programs for promotion to full professor	Create peer mentoring program to strengthen interactional diversity		
	Assessing negative student evaluations in light of diversity issues	Acceptance of stereotypes as accurate	Hold workshop on stereotypes in student evaluation to strengthen organizational learning		

Figure 7.1. The web of leadership.

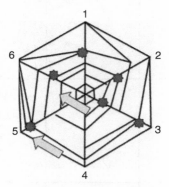

Source. From "Creating a Web of Support: An Important Leadership Strategy for Advancing Campus Diversity," by A. Kezar, P. Eckel, M. Contreras-McGavin, and S. J. Quaye, *Higher Education*, 55(1), p. 89.

leadership include (a) hiring the right individuals, (b) developing mentoring networks, (c) establishing partnerships with faculty to transform the teaching and learning environment, (d) supporting student affairs professionals and creating safe places for diverse individuals, (e) learning from and interacting with students, and (f) building external networks and support (Kezar et al., 2008). These strategies coincide in large part with the dimensions of the Chair Diversity Self-Assessment Profile.

With HR's emerging role as strategic partner in higher education, HR increasingly offers the capacity to enhance organizational capabilities through talent acquisition and talent management, organization development, diversity, and employee engagement practices (see Evans & Chun, 2012, for review). Although HR has been traditionally viewed as a function focused on staff rather than faculty, HR's contributions to the creation of a high-performance workforce include expertise in recruiting, hiring, diversity, organizational learning, compensation practices, work-life balance, employee engagement strategies, and employee assistance and mediation programs (Evans & Chun, 2012). As chairs consider resources available to them, HR strategies that link to the web of diversity on their campuses provide an important resource that is often overlooked or underutilized.

Conduct a Gap Analysis

Before chairs consider the structural components of a diversity plan, the next step is to conduct a gap analysis that will provide benchmarks for assessment, set goals, and provide qualitative and quantitative measures of progress. Gap analysis represents the research phase in the development of a departmental diversity plan. It facilitates deepened engagement by adopting a practitioner-as-researcher model that involves faculty and staff in the process of transformation through collaboration and self-reflection (Bensimon, Polkinghorne, Bauman, & Vallejo, 2004).

The scorecard approach in gap analysis provides a tool for taking an accurate snapshot of current conditions, reviewing formative progress, and summarizing expected outcomes (Williams, 2013). In developing a gap analysis, institutions can make comparisons with peer institutions to measure quantitative progress. The patterns that evolve from the data analysis will provide aspirational benchmarks in critical areas like hiring, attainment of tenure status, compensation, and retention.

The process of gap assessment also needs to address informal, behavioral barriers that inhibit inclusion. Most diversity plans address structural factors but do not attend to interactional factors such as differing expectations and lack of support in the workplace that can hamper the success of individuals from nondominant groups. By contrast, the *Report on the Initiative for Faculty Race and Diversity* (2010) at the Massachusetts Institute of Technology drew on qualitative interviews with underrepresented minority faculty (URM) and minority faculty forums with senior URM faculty to identify the accumulation of microinequities and stressors that include the following:

- Lack of peer recognition
- A perceived ceiling for higher level appointments
- Diversity fatigue deriving from past efforts to enhance diversity
- Accumulated microinequities

Throughout our study we have seen the underlying theme of unequal and asymmetrical power in a largely White male institutional hierarchy that can result in differential behavioral and process outcomes for members of nondominant groups. The sharing of power that occurs through the medium of reciprocal empowerment represents a significant counterbalance to patterns of marginalization and isolation. Reciprocal empowerment as a guiding philosophy is based on the concept of mutuality and the interdependence and interrelationship of organizational members. It consists of three primary principles: *self-determination,* or the power to define one's own identity; *distributive justice,* or the power to give oneself and others needed resources; and *democratic participation,* or the power to give oneself and others a voice (Prilleltensky & Gonick, 1994).

Attainment of reciprocal empowerment requires systematic attention to behavioral asymmetry that is reflected in prevailing stereotypes, persistent psychological biases, and even psychological abuse (Evans & Chun, 2007; Sidanius & Pratto, 1999). In Table 7.2 we share sample factors in the evaluation of faculty diversity that address both structural and behavioral components of diversity and lead to an environment characterized by reciprocal empowerment and the sharing of power (see Evans & Chun, 2007, for review). Factors that strengthen reciprocal empowerment include participation in decision making and elimination of stereotypes in attitudes and expected outcomes.

Gathering qualitative data related to behavioral barriers is much more difficult and requires a safe, confidential way to gather feedback. Because of the relatively smaller size of a department, the measures used at the university level such as focus groups or surveys of departmental climate may not be effective. Creating a forum for dialogue in a safe environment can provide a method of surfacing hidden tensions. McDermott (2010) suggested various modes of interaction for such dialogue, including Thomas Gordon's approach to noncombative problem solving that overcomes communication roadblocks arising from the following:

- Commanding or directing
- Threatening or warning
- Moralizing or preaching
- Advising or providing solutions
- Judging, blaming, or criticizing
- Buttering up or praising
- Being sarcastic

In addition, individual discussions and an informal survey mechanism that protects confidentiality can be considered as vehicles for gathering input.

Build an Agenda for Action

We now consider the development of an agenda for action as formalized in a departmental diversity strategic plan. Strategic diversity planning can occur at three levels: the university or college level, the college and professional school level, and the departmental level. Although university and school diversity strategic plans are already a well-established best practice, department-level diversity plans are less common but nonetheless quite highly developed at some institutions. Research indicates that less than 35% of institutions have decentralized diversity plans (Williams, 2013). The integration of university,

TABLE 7.2

Sample Gap Analysis of Structural and Behavioral Dimensions of Faculty Diversity

Barrier	Quantitative/Qualitative Measure	Sample Progress Indicator	Desired Outcome
Hiring	Affirmative action goals	Longitudinal hiring statistics; good faith efforts in outreach	Attainment of affirmative action goals; relative parity of faculty diversity with student diversity
Promotion and advancement	Tenure attainment and denial for minority and female faculty; promotion data for minority and female faculty; compensation analysis	Longitudinal improvements in tenure and promotion rates for women and minorities	Increased representation of minority and female faculty in tenured ranks and at senior levels; evaluation of equity in compensation
Lack of support	Tenure guidelines; invitations to attend faculty development opportunities; interdisciplinary research opportunities	Programs and workshops offered for pretenure faculty on tenure and promotion	Established guidelines for tenure advancement; participation in faculty development; grants for research
Failure to empower and include in decision making	Departmental minutes; participation in shared governance	Meeting and discussion opportunities	Channels for formal input into decision-making processes and communication of decisions
Differing expectations	Established criteria for review of student evaluations, teaching observations, and service	Protocols and guidelines for evaluative processes	Standardized evaluation processes; creation of cohort groups among junior faculty

(continues)

TABLE 7.2

Sample Gap Analysis of Structural and Behavioral Dimensions of Faculty Diversity (Continued)

Barrier	Quantitative/Qualitative Measure	Sample Progress Indicator	Desired Outcome
Stereotyping	Discussion in focus groups and climate studies	Conversations initiated at the departmental level	Workshops and discussions that discuss the impact of stereotyping on classroom management, performance expectations, and other interactions
Isolation	Statistics on underrepresentation of women and minorities	Qualitative feedback in one-on-one meetings	Attainment of critical mass of diverse faculty rather than a disproportionately small number of minority and female faculty
The revolving door	Evaluation of turnover of minority and female faculty	Exit interview data on climate; increased retention rates of female and minority faculty	Increase in retention rates of minority and female faculty

school, and departmental plans can be viewed as a continuum in building a web. Rather than cascading up to the university or school diversity plan, the departmental diversity plan can be conceptualized as building out the web of diversity.

Chairs are often seen as implementing the ideas of others rather than generating change—a role more traditionally reserved for the trustees and chief executive officers (Buller, 2014). As a result, in creating a diversity strategic plan, chairs need to explore how program objectives assist the institution in achieving its goals (Buller, 2014).

Naturally, departmental diversity plans will be highly context specific, varying in terms of institutional type, discipline, geographic location, and other factors. Three-year cycles are considered advantageous for decentralized diversity plans, with the preparation of the plan in year one, the implementation of the plan in year two, and an accountability review in year three (Williams, 2013).

Take, for example, the departmental diversity plans of the seven departments of the University of Minnesota's College of Food, Agricultural, and Natural Resources Sciences (CFANS) (*Departmental Diversity Plans*, 2013). Chairs prepare an annual review planning document that includes areas for programmatic development in teaching; incentive structure; training and professional development; recruiting, retaining, and graduating students of color; hiring; outreach; research; and professional climate. The departmental plans align with the overall college plan, which, in turn, has five diversity-related themes: innovation, curricular and pedagogical transformation, engagement, access and accountability, and academic and social culture issues. The broad themes of the college plan and its interrelation with the departmental plans provide a systemic approach to diversity transformation.

The Department of Agronomy and Plant Genetics' diversity plan depicts the overall alignment of its diversity plan with collegiate and institutional goals (*Cultural Diversity Enhancement Plan*, 2009). As depicted in Table 7.3, the plan takes the alignment process one step further by comparing departmental objectives with the framework for diversity provided by the Association of Public and Land-grant Universities (APLU; formerly known as the National Association of State Universities and Land-Grant Colleges).

Chairs in science, technology, engineering, and mathematics fields in our study expressed particular challenges in operationalizing diversity in systematic ways within their department's curricular offerings and planning. The chemistry department at Purdue University (n.d.) has developed a highly integrated diversity plan that can serve as a potential model in this regard. This departmental diversity plan aligns with the university's New Synergies strategic plan that centers on people, partnerships, and programs and speaks

TABLE 7.3
Cultural Diversity Enhancement Plan

Departmental	Collegiate	Institutional	APLU
Enhance cultural diversity of undergraduate student population and adjust curriculum toward more inclusive content	Teaching (inclusive content)	Historically underrepresented	Structural diversity Classroom diversity Interactional diversity Environmental diversity
Hire new faculty for newly developed positions	Hiring (historically underrepresented faculty)	Historically underrepresented	Structural diversity Classroom diversity
Strengthen programs and relationships with international partners	Inclusive outreach and research	International	Structural diversity Interactional diversity

Note. APLU = Association of Public and Land-grant Universities (formerly known as National Association of State Universities and Land-Grant Colleges).

to the "growth of human and intellectual diversity in the research enterprise with diverse and global perspectives." The New Synergies plan encourages the development of a "global mind-set" across the university and promotes cultural awareness, collegiality, and respect for diverse individuals and cultures.

Purdue's chemistry department diversity plan identifies "meeting global challenges" and "building diverse communities of excellence" as two of its four goals. It includes a metrics of progress that requires empirical evidence of (a) enhanced diversity among the faculty, staff, and student body; (b) increased retention rates of underrepresented groups; and (c) ratings of the climate as good or higher by faculty, staff, and students. Although recognizing that the chair's leadership role depends ultimately on collective faculty action and obtaining the buy in of members of the department, the chair can create opportunities for dialogue to crystallize departmental direction and to create synergies among faculty and staff that reinforce this direction.

When a department builds out the web of diversity, the size of the department plays a significant role in the extent to which such plans are formalized. Plans can be brief or more highly developed, depending on institutional type and department size. For larger departments, consider a more extensive plan that includes the following key components:

- Departmental vision
- Departmental mission
- Alignment with college and university diversity strategic plans
- Four or five key goals
- Quantitative and qualitative metrics
- Accountability measures
- Incentives
- Training and professional development
- Resource needs and availability
- University policies or protocols

Although our primary emphasis has been on the relation of department chairs to faculty and student diversity, staff diversity is also an integral component of the chair's responsibility and needs to be considered within the framework, strategies, goals, and projected outcomes of the diversity plan.

Concluding Perspectives: Strategies for Developing a Departmental Diversity Strategic Plan

Use the diversity action plan to evaluate structural and interactional aspects of diversity for faculty, staff, and students that relate to the department's mission.

Include evaluation of the department's efforts to assist diverse students in the process of identity development through mentoring, advising, service learning, internships, and related work.

Create planning discussions that promote genuine dialogue and create a safe environment for open and effective communication. Ask the group to collaboratively develop ground rules for these meetings (for sample ground rules, see Gerzon, 2009).

Develop coleadership for development of specific dimensions of the plan based on faculty interest and expertise.

Ensure that the plan has both "carrots" and "sticks" in terms of incentives for attaining desired goals.

Promote faculty participation in university-wide accreditation efforts related to diversity, as well as off-campus conferences with professional associations that discuss diversity issues.

Establish a regular mechanism and standard reporting format for progress on diversity goals to enhance a sense of common purpose and ensure accountability.

References

Argyris, C. (1995). Action science and organizational learning. *Journal of Managerial Psychology, 10*(6), 20–26.

Argyris, C. (1996). Unlocking defensive reasoning. *Across the Board, 33*(3), 18.

Argyris, C. (2002). Double-loop learning, teaching, and research. *Academy of Management Learning and Education, 1*(2), 206–218.

Bensimon, E. M., Polkinghorne, D. E., Bauman, G. L., & Vallejo, E. (2004). Doing research that makes a difference. *Journal of Higher Education, 75*(1), 104–126.

Bolman, L. G., & Deal, T. E. (1991). Leadership and management effectiveness: A multi-frame, multi-sector analysis. *Human Resource Management, 30*(4), 509–534.

Buller, J. L. (2014). Change leadership for chairs. *The Department Chair, 24*(3), 3–5. Retrieved September 6, 2014, from http://onlinelibrary.wiley.com/doi/10.1002/dch.20066/pdf

Cultural diversity enhancement plan: Department of entomology college of food, agricultural, and environmental sciences. (2009). Retrieved February 16, 2014, from http://www.cfans.umn.edu/diversity/web%20text/Ent%20Diversity%20Enhancement%20Plan%20final.pdf

Departmental diversity plans. (2013). Retrieved February 13, 2014, from University of Minnesota Departmental Plans website: http://www.cfans.umn.edu/diversity/Resources/departmental_plans.htm

Dovidio, J. F., Gaertner, S. L., & Bachman, B. A. (2001). Racial bias in organizations: The role of group processes in its causes and cures. In M. Turner (Ed.), *Groups at work: Theory and research* (pp. 415–444). Mahwah, NJ: Lawrence Erlbaum.

Evans, A., & Chun, E. B. (2007). *Are the walls really down? Behavioral and organizational barriers to faculty and staff diversity* (ASHE-ERIC Higher Education Reports, Vol. 33, No. 1). San Francisco, CA: Jossey-Bass.

Evans, A., & Chun, E. (2012). *Creating a tipping point: Strategic human resources in higher education.* San Francisco, CA: Jossey-Bass.

Gaertner, S. L., & Dovidio, J. F. (2000). The aversive form of racism. In C. Stangor (Ed.), *Stereotypes and prejudice: Essential readings* (pp. 289–304). Philadelphia, PA: Psychology Press.

Gerzon, M. (2009). Reaching across the aisle: Innovations for cross-party collaboration. In T. L. Pittinsky (Ed.), *Crossing the divide: Intergroup leadership in a world of difference* (pp. 203–218). Boston, MA: Harvard Business School.

Kezar, A., Eckel, P., Contreras-McGavin, M., & Quaye, S. J. (2008). Creating a web of support: An important leadership strategy for advancing campus diversity. *Higher Education, 55*(1), 69–92.

McDermott, J. C. (2010). *Models and frameworks for dialogue and deliberation: Strategies for effective civic engagement.* Retrieved February 16, 2014, from http://www.academia.edu/753801/Models_and_Frameworks_for_Dialogue_and_Deliberation

Overview of strategic plan goals. (2010). Retrieved February 13, 2014, from Purdue University Department of Chemistry website: http://www.chem.purdue.edu/aboutus/strategic_plan.asp

Picca, L. H., & Feagin, J. R. (2007). *Two-faced racism: Whites in the backstage and frontstage.* New York, NY: Routledge.

Prilleltensky, I., & Gonick, L. (1994). The discourse of oppression in the social sciences: Past, present, and future. In E. J. Trickett, R. J. Watts, & D. Birman (Eds.), *Human diversity: Perspectives on people in context* (pp. 145–177). San Francisco, CA: Jossey-Bass.

Purdue University. (n.d.). *New Synergies: Purdue University's strategic plan.* Retrieved February 13, 2014, from http://www.purdue.edu/strategic_plan/documents/StrategicPlanBrochure.pdf

Report on the initiative for faculty race and diversity. (2010). Retrieved February 16, 2014, from http://web.mit.edu/provost/raceinitiative/report.pdf

Scharmer, C. O. (2009). *Theory U: Leading from the future as it emerges.* San Francisco, CA: Berrett-Koehler.

Schon, D. A. (1983). *The reflective practitioner: How professionals think in action.* New York, NY: Basic Books.

Senge, P. (2009). Foreword. In C. O. Scharmer (Ed.), *Theory U: Leading from the future as it emerges* (pp. vii–xviii). San Francisco, CA: Berrett-Koehler.

Sidanius, J., & Pratto, F. (1999). *Social dominance: An intergroup theory of social hierarchy and oppression.* New York, NY: Cambridge University Press.

Williams, D. A. (2013). *Strategic diversity leadership: Activating change and transformation in higher education.* Sterling, VA: Stylus.

8

SUMMATION AND
RECOMMENDATIONS

We see that leadership is all about the way that this sense of shared sense of social identity is created, managed, maintained, and embedded.

—Michael J. Platow, Stephen D. Reicher, and S. Alexander Haslam (2009, p. 41)

Academic department chairs are in the vanguard of diversity transformation in colleges and universities. Although a great deal of attention has been given to the role of administrators in diversity progress, department chairs represent the real key to diversity change within institutions of higher education because of their direct impact on students and on the educational process. Operating at the core of the academic value proposition and working with faculty in their respective disciplines, chairs have the capacity to change the lives of students and affect their ability to serve as leaders in a diverse global society. Because of their direct tie to the institution's academic mission, chairs are change agents who are strategically positioned to affect not only the academic program itself but also the experiences of diverse students on college campuses.

Chairs are also positioned to develop collaborative intergroup leadership by creating positive relationships among distinct subgroups and developing a single, more inclusive superordinate group within their departments (see Dovidio, Gaertner, & Lamoreaux, 2009; Pittinsky, 2009, for review). When social identity is activated to reflect shared characteristics and goals, collective needs, standards, and objectives become primary (Dovidio et al., 2009). Through development of intergroup leadership, chairs can connect diverse students' identity development with their leadership capacity (Guthrie, Jones, Osteen, & Hu, 2013). This interconnectivity is the essence of boundary-spanning leadership.

Our interviews reveal a high degree of sophistication about diversity among many chairs, as well as a keen awareness of the challenges that accompany their efforts to strengthen diversity in their departments. Interviewees included White male and female chairs who are experts in the area of social justice and who seek to embody the principles in their work. For example, the statement of a White male psychology chair represents a clear call to action:

> If the chair is serious about this, it not sufficient just to avoid error: You have got to be proactive. I think it has to be more than a kind of political or ethical motivation. That's certainly there and ought to be there. I think that the chair also needs to believe and understand that the intellectual academic quality of the environment is going to be improved by a diverse faculty and a diverse student body. . . . Maybe we will get to a time where diversity or difference is diversity of philosophical opinion . . . but in the U.S. and in much of the world, social identity really does determine one's worldview, one's intellectual approach. So it's not enough to say that we want diversity in terms of different approaches to psychology in the psych department. It's got to be diversity around social identity to be genuinely intellectually rich.

Consider the insightful perspective of a White female chair of women's studies in a midwestern public undergraduate college who emphasized the "cloudiness" of issues surrounding diversity. Although her department actively tries to get at the root of such issues and talk about them immediately, the university culture does not necessarily encourage or support such efforts. As she explained,

> Now most of the time the kinds of issues that have emerged have been cloudy. In other words, it would be difficult to say, oh that issue that cropped up was an issue around including this group of faculty members, making them feel accepted and welcome and fully included. Most of the issues that have cropped up, they have come in the guise of something other than a diversity issue, right? So finding the diversity issue or finding the issue that has to do with inclusion beneath that cloudier issue is a challenge. . . .
>
> I think our department culture is such that we are able to talk about those things, but we are not embedded in a university culture where there is necessarily always an interest or willingness to look beyond whatever the apparent issue is. So, for example, we have had moments where this or that faculty member was supposedly not being collegial. So that's the sort of surface level, but there are some other issues behind that that many of us have felt have something to do with diversity and inclusion. It is very difficult to get beyond that cloudiness. We have tried to discuss those possibilities among ourselves and in meetings in order to try to do our best to make a more inclusive environment even in a context in which we are not necessarily being encouraged to do that.

We should also note that those chairs who were willing to be interviewed may represent a subset of individuals with a greater interest and commitment to diversity. The fact that two thirds of those participating in our online survey declined the follow-up interview indicates that diversity is still contested terrain in higher education. The concern for confidentiality expressed by chairs who participated in the interview process may reflect continuing divisions within their own departments.

The commentaries of White male chairs we interviewed demonstrate the importance of majority group members in actively leading diversity change. On the basis of lessons learned from the civil rights movement in which White leaders played instrumental roles in the success of the movement, the leadership of majority group members in the chair ranks will create a broader, more inclusive constituency supporting diversity progress (see Chun & Evans, 2009, for review). In fact, being White and male can be seen as positive attributes in advocating for change within a White male hierarchy. In this regard, a White male chair of educational leadership in a western public research university commented on his positionality and how it can afford him the ability to bring about positive change:

> I don't do the kind of research that they are used to seeing. I don't say the same kinds of things they are used to seeing. So being in that kind of ally/ advocate role that I play most of the time and . . . having the kind of background like I do is an interesting space to be in because you could get to be a part of conversations that often I find, anyway, some scholars of color are not privy to. The question is, however, what have I retained from those conversations and having the kind of resources that I do to make some positive changes.

White females also have the potential to dismantle the layers of gender and racial privilege from the vantage point of their own experiences of oppression as they assume more recent positions of power in the academy (Ropers-Huilman, 2008). As Becky Ropers-Huilman pointed out, "Privilege and oppression are two sides of the same coin, and both limit choices and modes of expression" (Ropers-Huilman, 2008). A number of female chairs shared examples of significant differential treatment they have experienced in their career trajectory. These experiences of subtle discrimination may have taken place when these women were pretenure faculty members or in their subsequent rise to department chair positions. Their experiences have heightened their sensitivity to the nature of discrimination and awareness of the ways in which covert discriminatory practices take shape in the academic workplace. Although women have made significant inroads in obtaining administrative roles, in the predominantly male academic hierarchy, they can still represent outsiders in what has been termed the "sacred grove" (Cooper & Stevens, 2002).

The seeds of change are clearly being sown by chairs who not only understand the barriers to diversity but also are developing intellectually nuanced strategies to address these obstacles. Some chairs expressed a significant degree of activism in the area of diversity and because of their tenured status and scholarly stature have been able to push the envelope and challenge the status quo.

Despite the high level of sophistication and commitment to social justice expressed by a number of chairs in our study, why are colleges and universities still struggling in their efforts to implement sustained diversity transformation?

Several reasons account for stalled diversity change. First, the major challenge faced by campuses is to implement a systems-based approach to diversity that transcends hit-or-miss, sporadic efforts. This strategic approach requires an orderly, phase-based evolution driven by unequivocal leadership purpose and accompanied by the appropriate metrics, accountability structures, and resources.

Second, strategic diversity transformation requires systematic and sustained organizational learning processes. These processes not only transmit the importance of diversity and unpack its many dimensions but also address the knowledge and skills that enable individuals to check their assumptions at the door and to work with and develop diverse people. In other words, organizational learning needs to address prevailing cultural assumptions, subtle biases, microaggressions, and microinequities and lead to the formation of new theories-in-use.

And third, the algorithm for diversity in our institutions of higher education may have been misunderstood and is often expressed in reverse. Given the goals of affirmative action, many faculty and administrators focus almost exclusively on representational diversity as an end in itself. This stance often causes substantial pushback among faculty and administrators, with allegations of reverse discrimination and even favoritism.

In actuality, the algorithm of inclusive excellence focuses intensively and exclusively on student intellectual and social development. The presence of diverse faculty in the classroom is an essential aspect of educational preparation for students in a demographically diverse global society. With an African American, Asian American, or Latino or Latina professor, students will not only have role models that represent mirrors of diverse identities but also be exposed to a broad array of viewpoints and experiential insights. The message of inclusive excellence is powerfully portrayed in the classroom by the presence of diverse and talented faculty leaders.

A major issue identified by chairs is the lack of formal chair training in specific issues that pertain to chair leadership. A case in point is the relative absence of mentoring programs at the departmental level that would assist diverse students in the process of identity development on predominantly White campuses. Although several chairs indicated their expectation that student affairs would be the main resource for student identity development, students often view faculty in the academic department as a frontline resource for psychosocial assistance, career guidance, and other concerns. The affirmation of identity that faculty can provide represents an unparalleled opportunity to have a lasting influence on students' future lives.

A finely tuned program of chair and faculty development will provide research-based approaches to diversity leadership, introduce pedagogical approaches that address different learning styles, model curricular change initiatives, and deepen diversity competencies. Such programs will, in turn, free faculty to practice their craft and will facilitate the transmission to students of the diversity expertise, knowledge, and cultural competencies needed for careers in a global society. Given the continued presence of behavioral asymmetry between dominant and subordinate groups, developmental programs also must delve below the surface to address behavioral barriers to diversity that include psychological abuse, mobbing, and bullying.

In this regard, a White female chair of education in a private western university highlighted the difficulty of recruiting faculty for this role due to the limited rewards and administrative work involved. She emphasized the need for training and interaction with other chairs at professional meetings:

> I think that chairs should be trained. I don't think we should just pass the job around. . . . I would love to have the opportunity to sit and talk with chairs and get other ideas about what they are doing, because as a chair we are so much immersed in the day-to-day stuff. I am a teaching chair: I teach, I advise, I manage the budget, I do the strategic planning. It's everything the dean does. . . . There are probably fabulous ideas people have about things that they have done and have been successful and things that I have done and could share with people, but we don't ever come together and talk. . . .
>
> I have said to John and Joe, "You should think about stepping in as chair." [They said,] "Oh no, no!" It's a lot of work. You get a couple of courses off, and I get a little tiny bit of a stipend. But they don't want to do the administrative work. How do we help faculty find . . . ways to do it that adds to their professional credibility instead of taking away from it? All this work I have been doing now for accreditation . . . I did not get one article done this year. . . . So I understand why people don't want to do it.

Issues, Resources, and Strategies

Throughout the study, we have discussed prominent barriers to diversity in the academic workplace and specific strategies and innovative practices that chairs have developed to address these barriers. On the basis of the survey and interviews, we offer a synopsis of the six most significant barriers identified by chairs, as well as approaches and resources to assist chairs in leveraging diversity change.

Faculty Recruitment Issues

Lack of funding to create new faculty lines that will enable diverse faculty to be hired is the most common barrier cited by department chairs. Once a line becomes vacant, chairs at public institutions indicated that they have difficulty competing with private institutions in terms of salary. In addition, limited funds are available for outreach and on-campus interviews.

Chairs in our sample also cited the difficulty of attracting a diverse candidate pool for faculty positions. Yet, as an African American male chair of sociology in a private southern university pointed out, the concept of hiring "the best person for the job" is often a fallacy and can lead to overlooking highly qualified, diverse candidates. He also emphasized the importance of considering American minorities who live, go to school, and work in the areas in which the university is located rather than focusing on foreign-born faculty with Ivy League degrees. As he explained,

> There's a lot of faculty who come through some of the highest level institutions out there, Harvard, Stanford, etc., and they come from other countries and they work here. And yet people who were born here who were educated, say, at the mid-level, they can't get jobs. So optimum-level diversity should look like the larger population of where we are. If I'm in the Southwest, and if the level of population is Chicano in the Southwest, I want to see Chicano faculty. If I'm out in the Pacific northwest, I want to see Native American faculty. . . . That's the easiest way to achieve diversity: This is where people live. This is where they go to school; this is where they choose to work; those are the folks who should also be given a shot at hiring. And yet the cliché is you want to hire the best person for the job. You can't tell me that the best person for the job . . . 80% to 85% of the time is [a] White male. I don't believe that. I absolutely don't believe that.

In the extensive discussion in chapter 5 of the perceived barrier of a lack of qualified diverse candidates, we offered specific suggestions to improve the culture and practices of hiring that will facilitate the attainment of diverse candidate pools.

Strategies. Develop innovative ways to establish new lines in partnership with the dean such as through making interdisciplinary hires, hiring more than one candidate for a vacancy, or converting adjunct lines. Consider creative outreach strategies that can be developed at virtually no cost or for a minimal investment such as networking at professional association conferences, obtaining referrals from colleagues, conducting outreach to feeder institutions, and using websites that include the university's online employment system, online academic sites that specialize in diversity, and social media. The university's or college's marketing office, human resources, and academic affairs can assist with marketing strategies and enhancement of websites. Initial interviews can be conducted using Skype at no cost.

Resources. A number of universities have developed excellent tool kits for recruiting diverse faculty, such as the University of California at Los Angeles' *Faculty Search Committee Toolkit* (UCLA Diversity and Faculty Development, 2013) and Stanford University's *Building on Excellence* (2008). In addition, institutions that were recipients of ADVANCE grants ("Increasing the Participation of Women in Science and Engineering") from the National Science Foundation have developed extensive search materials that are available on their websites. The ADVANCE portal also summarizes recruitment-related grants and projects (*Advance*, n.d.). Fine and Handelsman's *Searching for Excellence and Diversity: A Guide for Search Committees* was made possible by grants from the National Science Foundation (Fine & Handelsman, 2012). Consider also Lee's (2014) *Search Committees: A Comprehensive Guide to Successful Faculty, Staff, and Administrative Searches* that covers all aspects of the search process.

High Turnover Among Deans and Provosts

The frequency of turnover among deans and provosts can result in varied, uncertain, and sporadic support for diversity. Chairs operate with considerable autonomy but would benefit from greater resources and more significant authority to implement diversity initiatives. The tenured status of chairs does accord them the ability to weather the storms of administrative change. Yet even when the dean's support is present, resources may not be available to address outstanding needs.

Strategies. Participation in campus-wide diversity committees and governance activities related to diversity can help forge strong alliances that bring diversity issues to the forefront. In addition, campus-wide functions such as human resources, affirmative action, diversity and inclusion, student affairs, and the office of research may have explicit programs and funding to support diversity efforts. Partnerships with other advocates across the university can strengthen leverage and ensure the sustainability of initiatives.

Resources. A major resource for strengthening chair leadership capability even during times of administrative turnover is the American Council of Education's yearlong Leadership Academy for Department Chairs (*ACE Leadership Academy for Department Chairs*, 2014). Research by Walter Gmelch and colleagues provide insight into major sources of stress and strategies for coping with the stress that impacts chairs from multiple university levels (see, e.g., Gmelch & Burns, 1993, 1994; Gmelch & Miskin, 2011; Wolverton, Gmelch, Wolverton, & Sarros, 1999).

Factions or Cliques in the Department

A major barrier identified by chairs is the fractionalization around diversity issues, with lack of interest by tenured faculty and the isolation of one or two minority faculty members who are perceived to be the perennial diversity advocates.

Strategies. Use organizational learning interventions to begin to shift the social field, examine theories-in-use, and highlight the "business case" for diversity in terms of inclusive excellence. Break the silence about racism and reduce discomfort and fear around the topic by engaging in cross-racial dialogue (Tatum, 1997). Construct committee assignments that promote purposeful interaction among faculty members from nondominant and dominant groups. Showcase research and scholarly accomplishments through formal and informal events that promote the inclusion of all departmental members.

Resources. Key resources on organizational interventions and teamwork include Gmelch and Miskin's (2011) *Department Chair Leadership Skills* that provides a chapter with concrete guidance on managing conflict creatively and Edmondson's (2012) *Teaming: How Organizations Learn, Innovate, and Compete in the Knowledge Economy.* Some universities have created an ombudsperson that can assist with protracted or difficult conflicts within the department. The Massachusetts Institute of Technology under the leadership of Mary Rowe has developed extensive resources on subtle discrimination and microinequities in the workplace (*Ombuds Publications*, n.d.).

Difficulty of Including Diversity in Curricular Offerings

Barriers cited to diversity in the curriculum by chairs include the need to address core requirements in the curriculum allowing little time for students to take courses outside of the major or minor, lack of student interest, low enrollment, the complexity of approval processes, and faculty pushback. Chairs in science, technology, engineering, and mathematics (STEM) fields, in particular, expressed difficulty in finding ways to include diversity in the content of the curriculum and may view diversity as less relevant or even irrelevant to the discipline.

Strategies. Approaches that include diversity as a component or module of a core course or as a lens for examining issues within a given course such as through directed readings or projects are ways to incorporate issues of diversity into an established course structure. We shared earlier how a psychology chair requires his faculty to write a short description of how diversity is incorporated into each course that is offered in the department. Chapter 6 includes examples of approaches chairs have taken to introducing diversity-related curricular revisions.

For STEM fields, specific avenues to model diversity in the curriculum include focusing on inventions or contributions in the field by diverse scientists, linking discoveries with global changes that have enhanced the lives of diverse populations, sponsoring lectures by diverse thinkers in the discipline, and creating discussion groups that grapple with social issues related to the field. Mentoring diverse students is a critical part of the process of building a pipeline of STEM scholars.

Resources. A number of resources on diversity in the curriculum, inclusive excellence, and student engagement can be found on the website for the Association of American Colleges and Universities (*Diversity and Inclusive Excellence*, 2014). Professional associations also offer resources related to incorporating diversity into disciplinary offerings, such as the Association of American Geographers (*Diversity and Inclusion*, n.d.) and the American Association of Medical Colleges' cultural competence education resources for medical students (Association of American Medical Colleges, 2005).

Student Diversity Viewed as an Institutional Responsibility

For the most part, chairs in our study saw recruitment of diverse students as a university responsibility rather than a departmental one. For example, one humanities chair indicated that in nearly a quarter century at her institution, the department has never discussed attracting diverse students to the program, whereas another observed that in the past decade only three minority students have been majors in the program. In master's-level and doctoral research universities, the extent to which the department is involved in recruiting diverse students appears to vary considerably. In addition, in many departments, particularly those without an explicit tie to diversity in the curriculum, few resources or programs are available to address issues of student identity development.

Strategies. A prominent best practice was shared by a White female chair of sociology in a public southwestern research university, who stated that her department takes pride in the diverse graduate student population, with over half composed of individuals from underrepresented groups. She indicated that one of the most successful strategies has come from former students recruiting future students and letting them know that the department has a welcoming climate.

A wide variety of strategies are available, such as those cited in a study of 51 graduate directors, that include personal contact with diverse students, promotion of distinct programs, partnership agreements with feeder institutions, and ensuring that faculty and staff serve as mentors and role models (Quarterman, 2008).

Resources. Representative resources include the University of Washington's website on recruiting and retaining minority students (*Recruiting and Retaining Minority Students*, 2011) and the 2006 report developed by the Committee on Institutional Cooperation, *Graduate Recruitment for Diversity: Discipline-Based Recruitment and Retention Initiatives* (Zepeda, 2006) that highlights recruitment of underrepresented minorities to STEM disciplines.

In the area of mentoring, the University of Michigan's Rackham Graduate School has published a comprehensive guide, *How to Mentor Graduate Students: A Guide for Faculty* (2013), that includes discussion of mentoring in a diverse community and a list of support organizations. The Pathways to Advanced Degrees in Life Sciences program at the University of Minnesota at Duluth offers a multiyear mentoring program designed to increase the number of American Indians in biomedical sciences (*Bridges and Pathways*, n.d.). The role of the mentor is critical in navigating academic culture and facilitating the individual's science identity and career (Prunuske, Wilson, Walls, & Clarke, 2013).

Lack of Metrics to Gauge Diversity Progress

The overwhelming majority of department chairs responding to the online survey reported that they do not have a metric for gauging diversity progress. Some departments track retention and graduate rates for underrepresented students, as well as faculty demographics, as the principal indicator of progress. Others rely on university-wide metrics for evaluation of diversity efforts.

Strategies. Develop a baseline metric that transcends demographic data and includes measures of climate, student success, tenure attainment, and empowerment of faculty and staff.

Resources. The University of California at Los Angeles has developed an excellent self-assessment tool titled *Achieving a Culture of Inclusion* (2006) that provides a phase-based approach to six key factors leading to inclusion, including leadership, academic planning, accountability, faculty recruitment and retention, resource allocation and faculty rewards, and typical behaviors and beliefs (*Equity, Inclusion, and Diversity*, 2011). Although intended for use at the campus level, it provides a useful template for gauging the current phase of diversity development in the department.

Other examples of diversity metrics include the University of California, Berkeley's Strategic Plan for Equity, Inclusion, and Diversity (*Equity, Inclusion, and Diversity*, 2011), as well as the University of California's Appointment and Promotion Guidelines for Review and Appraisal Committees that address diversity contributions as related to faculty appointment, promotion, and appraisal (*Appointment and Promotion*, 2002).

Hubbard's *How to Calculate Diversity Return on Investment* (1999) offers insight into building comprehensive metrics to support the business case for diversity, although it is not specific to the higher education environment. The website of the University of Wisconsin at Madison's Women in Science and Engineering Leadership Institute (WISELI) offers a significant array of resources that include materials on enhancing departmental climate, exit interview protocols, and relevant research (*WISELI Reports and Publications*, 2009).

Institutional Recommendations

Overall, the findings of our study indicate that institutions of higher education still have some distance to travel in terms of defining and making the educational case for diversity in the curriculum, cocurricular programs, and extracurricular activities. In the absence of a clear rationale for diversity linked to educational mission, a college or university will be rowing upstream. Diversity must be viewed as an essential dimension of the academic process rather than seen as an extraneous element. For this reason, the chief diversity officer will be most effective when that individual is a tenured member of the faculty and can speak from that vantage point. Providing recognition for diversity in the tenure and promotion process is critical, because it provides incentives for faculty to participate in service learning, teaching, and research that support the infusion of diversity in the culture and curriculum of the institution.

As we have emphasized throughout the study, one of the critical aspects of the educational process for diverse students is identity development. When we continue to see racial polarization, separation, and gatherings of students without interracial contact on predominantly White campuses, we know that there is still work to be done to build inclusive campus communities. The struggles of students from nondominant groups on predominantly White campuses continue to require active academic sponsorship and mentorship. For these reasons, we offer the following institutional recommendations.

Include diversity components in the process of academic program review. The University of California, Berkeley includes a number of diversity-related components in the departmental self-study process for academic program review. These components not only include a review of success in hiring women and underrepresented minorities but also address how underrepresented faculty are mentored and retained and whether they are fully included in the intellectual life of the department and whether their chosen areas of research are appropriately appreciated and rewarded. The self-study also asks what courses fulfill the American cultures requirements and what other courses include topics related to racial, ethnic, cultural, or gender diversity (*UC Berkeley*, 2011).

Recognize chairs who have made outstanding contributions in the area of diversity. In chapter 4, we noted the recommendations of the Committee on Diversity and Cultural Competence of the university faculty senate of the 64 campuses of the State University of New York. In a position paper, *Making Diversity Count* (2013), the committee called for policy changes in the faculty reward system and suggested that a demonstrated commitment to diversity be included across the five criteria for faculty evaluation.

Provide funding allocations for recruitment and outreach through targets of opportunity and cluster hire funding to increase diverse faculty representation. The concept of "targets of opportunity" hiring is to accelerate the hiring of talented and diverse faculty and professional staff. Cluster hiring programs permit hiring in larger groups across a range of different areas to enable greater inclusion of individuals from diverse groups. Successful models include the University of Illinois at Urbana-Champaign's Targets of Opportunity Program (*Targets of Opportunity Program*, 2013), North Carolina State University's program for Target of Opportunity Hires (*Standard Operating Procedure for Target of Opportunity Hires*, 2012), and examples shared in MIT's *Report on the Initiative for Faculty Race and Diversity* (2010).

Appoint faculty equity advisers for each academic department. The vice chancellor for equity and inclusion at the University of California, Berkeley has established an infrastructure of equity advisers located in each academic unit. Advisers are active senate members at either the associate level or the full professor level and designated by the department chair or dean. Primary duties include assistance with faculty hiring and advancement and graduate recruitment and retention. Equity advisers also participate in strategic planning for the academic unit, to ensure that diversity is an active and meaningful part of the plan.

Create a nucleus of department chairs for participation in diversity planning at the institutional level. Too often chairs are not seen as active participants in diversity strategic planning or represented on key university-wide councils charged with bringing about diversity change. In actuality, a small group of chairs from different disciplines brought together to work collaboratively could recommend research-based approaches to enhance the link between inclusive excellence and educational mission through the retention and success of diverse students.

Provide a yearlong inclusive excellence chair leadership program that prepares chairs to assume greater university-wide or college-wide leadership roles in diversity. Such a program would provide chairs with the opportunity to work closely with university or college administration in an executive mentoring program and to attend seminars from leading national experts on curricular change, student identity development, pedagogical styles, classroom approaches, managing conflict, departmental climate, and related topics.

In this regard, an African American male chair of history in a private religiously affiliated midwestern university emphasized the importance of diversity-related professional development:

> I've been to a lot of these department chair workshops. And I have never been to one that ever had a session on what we are talking about. I think it is a big mistake. I think there is a perception that because we are in academia and because we are professors that we have had these conversations, and that's not true. Even if you may have a kind of enlightened position, there's a whole other realm of dealing with this institutionally as a chair, deans, provosts, and boards of trustees.

Work with shared governance entities and diversity committees to lead and actualize collaborative diversity change and address the chair's contributions to inclusive excellence. Shared governance offers the potential of "reclaiming the soul of campus collaboration" by proposing, initiating, and leading campus change through proactive and generative faculty efforts (Gallos, 2009, p. 138). In chapter 4, we discussed a cultural framework for shared governance that links governance with quality and underscores the role of shared governance in the university's or college's symbolic and communicative processes (Minor & Tierney, 2005).

Actively seek a greater representational balance of individuals from nondominant groups in the chair role. No more significant step could be taken by a college or school than to increase the representation of women, minority, and lesbian, gay, bisexual, and transgender (LGBT) faculty as department chairs. Until and unless universities obtain a critical mass of chairs from nondominant groups, academic leadership will fail to create a representative academic bureaucracy that is responsive to the needs of an increasingly diverse student population.

Address chair compensation through comparative benchmarking with peer institutions. Because of the limited compensation associated with chair appointments, highly productive faculty may be unwilling to forego their research in order to assume administrative roles. As a result, institutions need to reconsider the compensation process for chairs to ensure that these demanding roles are compensated competitively and appropriately.

Support participation in professional conferences and networks that address diversity, particularly for chairs in STEM fields. A wide range of conferences and networks such as those hosted by the Society of STEM Women of Color, Project Kaleidoscope of the Association of American Colleges and Universities and its Summer Leadership Institute, the National Institutes of Health Women of Color Research Network, the Association for the Study of Higher Education, and the National Conference on Race and Ethnicity, just to name a few, provide opportunities to explore current research and practices related to disciplinary diversity.

Support research and scholarship on strategies for diversifying the academic department. Because of the limited research on diversity within the academic department, studies that explore diversity issues relating to specific disciplines, institutional types, and curricular challenges would provide valuable data needed to enhance diversity practices.

Address varied microclimates within academic departments through institutional practices and policies that emphasize an inclusive and respectful workplace. To build a cohesive and consistent culture of diversity across departments, institutions can take the institutional pulse through focus groups, surveys, and turnover data that highlight areas of success, as well as areas of concern. The creation of policies, guidelines, and practices that support inclusive excellence across the academic disciplinary spectrum will strengthen the institution's collective efforts in the journey toward inclusive excellence.

In emphasizing the importance of institutional policy, the White female chair of women's studies in a midwestern public undergraduate college cited earlier noted the great difficulty of addressing individual issues of exclusion that may face faculty from nondominant groups. As a more effective institutional approach, she recommended the creation of policies and practices that address issues in a positive and preventive way before they arise. In her words,

> It's very difficult to argue on behalf of a single faculty member or even a series of faculty members who are perceived as being separate cases. Because each of those things is defined as individual, it is really hard to champion the causes of individuals as they pop up. But what is easier to do is to look at those things, try to find allies, and try to propose policies or

approaches . . . that can prevent those ahead of time. So when the problem emerges, it can be really hard to solve that problem. But what tends to work better is to come up with solutions to the problems and . . . take a positive approach. . . . But that argument doesn't always have to be "So and so was treated poorly." It can be something like, "This university and this university have this policy. . . . If we have this policy, we will be in line with so and so. . . ."

When you see a problem and point it out, that feels negative and sometimes there is nothing that you can do. You can try. But one of the things that does work pretty well or at least better (it's a lot of work, though) is to try to find policy solutions to the problems that you perceive and try and prevent them in the future.

Finally, much work still needs to be done to strengthen the pipeline for members of nondominant groups leading to the chair role and to support their professional development. Although undeniably this role can be taxing, detract from scholarly pursuits, and offer few financial rewards, it still represents an influential leadership position in the academic hierarchy.

We have highlighted the struggles of chairs from nondominant groups in largely White male departments and the difficulties they can encounter on a daily basis. Because minority, female, and LGBT chairs may encounter different realities in overseeing a department of majority group members, the support of the dean is critical to the success of chairs from nondominant groups. In essence, discrimination involves more than exclusion: It also involves differential treatment that results in status hierarchy maintenance (Roscigno, 2007). Diverse leaders may be subjected to different evaluative standards or encounter incongruity between expected male-female or majority-minority social roles (Chun & Evans, 2012). Minority supervisors, for example, can be seen as tyrannical, nasty, and controlling when they take actions that would be characterized as strong and effective when undertaken by White males (Chun & Evans, 2012). Similarly, minority females can be viewed as not aggressive enough or as too aggressive and trying too hard (Giscombe & Mattis, 2002).

We return to the perspective of an African American male chair of sociology in a private southern research university who emphasized the importance of the dean's support for chairs from nondominant groups in light of the continuing salience of gender, race, and ethnicity in the academy:

This is where the relationship with the dean comes in: You need support to make those things not happen or happen less. If your dean goes to the department and says, "Look, hold it. This is your chair. This is the person who I work with. The buck stops there. If there is a need to bring an issue to the dean, then I have confidence that the chair who I have appointed will do that."

The gender, race, ethnicity issue, I think we would be foolish if we thought those weren't important or paramount. I think women chairs can get slaughtered, walked over; the men more so than the women in the department just showing totally no respect whatsoever. If you are going to have an effective department, you can't have that kind of behavior. I think race, ethnicity, gender do play a role in leadership positions.

Because academic department chairs represent the lever for diversity change in institutions of higher education, their leadership will be truly realized when they receive support for their contributions, including efforts to embed diversity and inclusion in the curriculum, service learning, outreach, research, and student mentoring programs. The challenge remains for the entire educational community within individual institutions, throughout higher education, and in the standards of regional accreditation agencies to develop systematic and systemic approaches to respond to the educational imperative of diversity that will provide the competencies, expertise, and knowledge students need to be successful in an interconnected global society.

References

ACE leadership academy for department chairs. (2014). Retrieved March 9, 2014, from http://www.acenet.edu/leadership/programs/Pages/Leadership-Academy-for-Dept-Chairs.aspx

Achieving a culture of inclusion: A self-assessment tool. (2006). Retrieved March 9, 2014, from University of California website: http://www.ucop.edu/academic-personnel/_files/faculty-diversity-task-force/self-assessment-tool.pdf

Advance: Recruitment grants. (n.d.). Retrieved March 9, 2014, from http://www.portal.advance.vt.edu/index.php/tags/Recruitment-Grants

Appointment and promotion: Review and appraisal committees. (2002). Retrieved March 9, 2014, from http://www.ucop.edu/academic-personnel/_files/apm/apm-210.pdf

Association of American Medical Colleges. (2005). *Cultural competence education.* Retrieved March 9, 2014, from https://www.aamc.org/download/54338/data/culturalcomped.pdf

Bridges and pathways: RM. 297 medical school. (n.d.). Retrieved March 9, 2014, from University of Minnesota Duluth website: https://www.d.umn.edu/brpa/

Building on excellence: Guide to recruiting and retaining an excellent and diverse faculty at Stanford University. (2008). Retrieved March 8, 2014, from https://facultydevelopment.stanford.edu/sites/default/files/documents/Excellence.pdf

Chun, E., & Evans, A. (2009). *Bridging the diversity divide: Globalization and reciprocal empowerment in higher education* (ASHE-ERIC Higher Education Reports, Vol. 35, No. 1). San Francisco, CA: Jossey-Bass.

Chun, E., & Evans, A. (2012). *Diverse administrators in peril: The new indentured class in higher education.* Boulder, CO: Paradigm.

Cooper, J. E., & Stevens, D. D. (2002). The journey toward tenure. In J. E. Cooper & D. D. Stevens (Eds.), *Tenure in the sacred grove: Issues and strategies for women and minority faculty* (pp. 3–16). Albany, NY: State University of New York Press.

Diversity and inclusion. (n.d.). Retrieved March 9, 2014, from Association of American Geographers Projects and Programs website: http://www.aag.org/cs/diversity_and_inclusion

Diversity and inclusive excellence. (2014). Retrieved March 9, 2014, from Association of American Colleges and Universities website: http://www.aacu.org/resources/diversity/index.cfm

Dovidio, J. F., Gaertner, S. L., & Lamoreaux, M. J. (2009). Leadership across group divides: The challenges and potential of common group identity. In T. L. Pittinsky (Ed.), *Crossing the divide: Intergroup leadership in a world of difference* (pp. 3–16). Boston, MA: Harvard Business School.

Edmondson, A. C. (2012). *Teaming: How organizations learn, innovate, and compete in the knowledge economy.* San Francisco, CA: Jossey-Bass.

Equity, inclusion, and diversity. (2011). Retrieved March 9, 2014, from University of California, Berkeley website: http://diversity.berkeley.edu/strategic-plan-progress

Fine, E., & Handelsman, J. (2012). *Searching for excellence and diversity: A guide for search committees.* Retrieved February 24, 2014, from http://wiseli.engr.wisc.edu/docs/SearchBook_US.pdf

Gallos, J. V. (2009). Reframing shared governance: Rediscovering the soul of campus collaboration. *Journal of Management Inquiry, 18*(2), 136–138.

Giscombe, K., & Mattis, M. C. (2002). Leveling the playing field for women of color in corporate management: Is the business case enough? *Journal of Business Ethics, 37*(1), 103–119.

Gmelch, W. H., & Burns, J. S. (1993). The cost of academic leadership: Department chair stress. *Innovative Higher Education, 17*(4), 259–270.

Gmelch, W., & Burns, J. (1994). Sources of stress for academic chairpersons. *Journal of Educational Administration, 32*(1), 79–94.

Gmelch, W. H., & Miskin, V. D. (2011). *Department chair leadership skills* (2nd ed.). Madison, WI: Atwood.

Guthrie, K. L., Jones, T. B., Osteen, L. K., & Hu, S. (Eds.). (2013). *Cultivating leader identity and capacity in students from diverse backgrounds.* San Francisco, CA: Jossey-Bass.

How to mentor graduate students: A guide for faculty. (2013). Retrieved from Rackham Graduate School, University of Michigan website: https://www.rackham.umich.edu/downloads/publications/Fmentoring.pdf

Hubbard, E. E. (1999). *How to calculate diversity return on investment.* Petaluma, CA: Global Insights.

Lee, C. (2014). *Search committees: A comprehensive guide to successful faculty, staff, and administrative searches.* Sterling, VA: Stylus.

Making diversity count: A position paper by the Committee on Diversity and Cultural Competence University Faculty Senate. (2013). Retrieved February 23, 2014, from http://www.suny.edu/facultysenate/UFS-CDCC%20Position%20Paper%20 -%20May%202013.pdf

Minor, J. T., & Tierney, W. G. (2005). The danger of deference: A case of polite governance. *Teachers College Record, 107*(1), 137–156.

Ombuds publications. (n.d.). Retrieved March 9, 2014, from Massachusetts Institute of Technology Ombuds Office website: http://web.mit.edu/ombud/publications/

Pittinsky, T. L. (2009). Introduction: Intergroup leadership what it is, why it matters, and how it is done. In T. L. Pittinsky (Ed.), *Crossing the divide: Intergroup leadership in a world of difference* (pp. xi–xxvii). Boston, MA: Harvard Business School.

Platow, M. J., Reicher, S. D., & Haslam, S. A. (2009). On the social psychology of intergroup leadership. In T. L. Pittinsky (Ed.), *Crossing the divide: Intergroup leadership in a world of difference* (pp. 31–42). Boston, MA: Harvard Business School.

Prunuske, A. J., Wilson, J., Walls, M., & Clarke, B. (2013). Experiences of mentors training underrepresented undergraduates in the research laboratory. *CBE Life Sciences Education, 12,* 403–409.

Quarterman, J. (2008). An assessment of barriers and strategies for recruitment and retention of a diverse graduate student population. *College Student Journal, 42*(4), 947–967.

Recruiting and retaining minority students. (2011). Retrieved March 9, 2014, from University of Washington Graduate School website: http://www.grad.washington .edu/gomap/recruitment-retention/#page=introduction

Report on the initiative for faculty race and diversity. (2010). Retrieved February 16, 2014, from http://web.mit.edu/provost/raceinitiative/report.pdf

Ropers-Huilman, B. (2008). Women faculty and the dance of identities: Constructing self and privilege within community. In J. Glazer-Raymo (Ed.), *Unfinished agendas: New and continuing gender challenges in higher education* (pp. 35–51). Baltimore, MD: Johns Hopkins University Press.

Roscigno, V. J. (2007). *The face of discrimination: How race and gender impact work and home lives.* Lanham, MD: Rowman & Littlefield.

Standard operating procedure for target of opportunity hires. (2012). Retrieved from North Carolina State University website: http://www.provost.ncsu.edu/admin -resources/sops/sopTargetofOpportunityHires.php

Targets of opportunity program (TOP): Office of the Provost: Communication No. 7. (2013). Retrieved February 23, 2014, from University of Illinois Urbana-Champaign Office of the Provost website: http://www.provost.illinois.edu/ communication/07/2013/Communication_7-August_2013.pdf

Tatum, B. D. (1997). *"Why are all the Black kids sitting together in the cafeteria?" and other conversations about race: A psychologist explains the development of racial identity.* New York, NY: Basic Books.

UC Berkeley: Guide for the review of existing instructional programs. (2011). Retrieved March 10, 2014, from http://vpapf.chance.berkeley.edu/apr/GUIDE_May2011 .pdf

UCLA Diversity and Faculty Development. (2013). *Faculty search committee toolkit.* Retrieved March 7, 2014, from https://faculty.diversity.ucla.edu/resources-for/ search-committees/search-toolkit/FacultySearchToolkitPrintVersion12213.pdf

WISELI reports and publications. (2009). Retrieved March 10, 2014, from http:// wiseli.engr.wisc.edu/subject.php

Wolverton, M., Gmelch, W. H., Wolverton, M. L., & Sarros, J. C. (1999). Stress in academic leadership: U.S. and Australian department chairs/heads. *The Review of Higher Education, 22*(2), 165–185.

Zepeda, Y. (2006). *Graduate recruitment for diversity: Discipline-based recruitment and retention strategies.* Retrieved March 9, 2014, from http://www.cic.net/docs/ default-source/reports/gradrecruitreport4-13-06final.pdf?sfvrsn=0

APPENDIX A: DISTRIBUTION OF CHAIRS BY DISCIPLINE, REGION, AND INSTITUTIONAL TYPE

	n	*% of total*
Discipline		
Education	14	14.3%
Humanities	26	26.5%
Medical	12	12.2%
Professions and applied sciences	14	14.3%
Social sciences	20	20.4%
Science, technology, engineering, and mathematics	12	12.2%
Geographic Region		
East	9	9.2%
Midwest	32	32.7%
South	19	19.4%
Southwest	7	7.1%
West	31	31.6%
Institutional Type		
Public research university	26	26.5%
Public master's-level university	20	20.4%
Private research university	7	7.1%
Private master's-level university	24	24.5%
Public undergraduate college	9	9.2%
Private undergraduate college	12	12.2%

Note. Because of the proactive efforts of deans and administrators at several universities, the sample includes 9 chairs from a midwestern master's-level university, 5 chairs from a western private under-graduate university, and 4 chairs from a southern private research university. At each of these institutions, however, the chairs are from different disciplines.

N=98.

APPENDIX B: BLIND SPOTS AND LEVERS

Domain	Dimension	Blind Spot	Lever	Chair's Perspective
Classroom	Promoting inclusive pedagogies	Lack of review of teaching styles in the classroom	Initiate conversations about teaching systems; conduct developmental classroom observations	
	Providing support for marginalizing experiences of diverse faculty members	Lack of mentoring programs, including programs for promotion to full professor	Create peer mentoring program to strengthen interactional diversity	
	Assessing negative student evaluations in light of diversity issues	Accepting stereotypes as accurate	Hold workshop on stereotypes in student evaluation to strengthen organizational learning	
Curriculum	Initiating conversations about curricular revisions to include diversity perspectives, research methods, or other aspects of diversity	Difficulty of raising the issue in existing faculty culture	Demonstrate clear connections with student learning outcomes and model best disciplinary practices	
	Incorporating diversity in curricular offerings	Belief that the discipline has few, if any, connections with diversity	Create diversity modules and/or content within courses or diversity-related courses	

(continues)

Domain	Dimension	Blind Spot	Lever	Chair's Perspective
Research agenda	Encouraging research on diversity-related topics	Lack of valuing of diversity-related research; often not seen as mainstream	Have faculty share research progress in meetings; discuss qualitative research methods; promote interdisciplinary research	
	Providing support for diversity-related and cross-cultural research in the tenure process	Accepted cultural norms	Discuss with promotion and tenure committees, chief diversity officer, and dean or provost	
Departmental climate	Providing day-to-day support for an inclusive work environment	Existence of cliques of senior faculty	Create inclusive, informal social gatherings	
	Conducting inclusive faculty meetings	Overlooking suggestions by faculty from nondominant groups	Ensure minutes reflect different perspectives; brainstorm divergent perspectives; insist on civility	
	Ensuring inclusion of diverse faculty in departmental decision making	Lack of voice; isolation and lack of critical mass of diverse faculty	Ensure inclusion of perspectives of those who have been traditionally marginalized	
	Ensuring equitable resource distribution	Perception of favoritism in advocacy for diversity-related initiatives particularly by diverse department chairs	Draw on faculty allies who can make the business case for diversity and overcome inertia and resistance	
	Providing support for socialization and network formation for diverse faculty members	Lack of participation of some individuals in social events	Use community ties to expand social networks for the department	

(continues)

Domain	*Dimension*	*Blind Spot*	*Lever*	*Chair's Perspective*
Recruitment and hiring of diverse faculty	Forming diverse search committees	Overextension and unavailability of diverse faculty	Work with chief diversity officer to identify faculty in related disciplines willing to serve	
	Targeting outreach to diverse applicants	Lack of funding	Use low- or no-cost referrals, individualized outreach, and networking with possible feeder institutions	
	Providing concrete progress in remedying underrepresentation	Lack of creativity in formulating job descriptions and outreach strategies	Debunk myths about diversity, quality, and lack of pipeline; conduct effective outreach	
Retention of minority and female tenure-track faculty	Promoting faculty development that strengthens promotion and tenure attainment	Lack of clear communication on tenure progress and promotional criteria	Create clear guidelines that identify requirements and types of research and service needed	
	Providing informal and formal mentoring	Conflict of interest as reviewer in promotion and tenure	Utilize faculty centers and other institutional resources; develop peer mentoring	
	Providing supportive feedback on pre-tenure faculty evaluation	Lack of discussion of research requirements	Provide concrete suggestions in annual letter; develop clear guidelines	
	Assisting with research agendas of diverse faculty	Prevailing emphasis of department on certain foci, subject matters, and research methods	Initiate conversation in department on research methods, subject matter, etc.	

(continues)

Domain	Dimension	Blind Spot	Lever	Chair's Perspective
Student development	Offering educational and psychosocial support for diverse students	Perceived as an institutional and not a departmental responsibility	Develop informal mentoring approaches; provide training to faculty on cultural competency	
	Developing interest in departmental major through recruitment and outreach to diverse students	Lack of funding and institutional responsibility	Review demographics of current student population; conduct outreach	
Cocurricular activities	Providing inclusive cocurricular opportunities	Perceived as an institutional and not a departmental responsibility	Create service learning programs or community-based internships	
	Addressing diversity in symposia, forums, and learning communities	Lack of funding; lack of relation to discipline	Partner with chief diversity officer, human resources, or other institutional offices	

ABOUT THE AUTHORS

Edna Chun and **Alvin Evans** are award-winning authors and human resources (HR) and diversity leaders with extensive experience in complex, multicampus systems of higher education. Two of their books, *Are the Walls Really Down? Behavioral and Organizational Barriers to Faculty and Staff Diversity* (Jossey-Bass, 2007) and *Bridging the Diversity Divide: Globalization and Reciprocal Empowerment in Higher Education* (Jossey-Bass, 2009), are recipients of the prestigious Kathryn G. Hansen Publication Award by the national College and University Professional Association for Human Resources.

Recent publications include *Diverse Administrators in Peril: The New Indentured Class in Higher Education* (Paradigm, 2012), the first in-depth examination of the work experiences of minority, female, and lesbian, gay, bisexual, and transgender administrators in higher education, and *Creating a Tipping Point: Strategic Human Resources in Higher Education* (Jossey Bass, 2012), a research-based approach to the development of strategic HR talent management practices in higher education. Their most recent book, *The New Talent Acquisition Frontier: Integrating HR and Diversity Strategy in the Private and Public Sectors and Higher Education* (Stylus, 2013), received a silver medal in the 2014 Axiom Business Book Awards and is the first book to provide a concrete road map to the integration of HR and diversity strategy.

Evans and Chun have published a number of journal articles in leading HR and diversity journals on talent management and diversity strategies. Evans serves as associate vice president of HR for Kent State University, and Chun is associate vice chancellor for HR at the University of North Carolina at Greensboro.

the stresses of teaching controversial topics. The collection offers guidance that is particularly valuable for those just beginning to incorporate diversity in the classroom--and is pertinent to veteran teachers as well."

—*Diversity & Democracy (AAC&U)*

"All of the individual essays in this volume are quite useful and as a collection the volume is essential for faculty and administrators seeking to integrate diversity issues across the curriculum."

—*Teaching Theology and Religion*

Sty/us

22883 Quicksilver Drive
Sterling, VA 20166-2102

Subscribe to our e-mail alerts: www.Styluspub.com

to serve on them and for the candidates with whom those committee members will interact. Ensuring that new employees are a good fit within an academic institution is a tough job, and the market for highly skilled talent is extremely competitive. It's important that committees work quickly and diligently to ensure their institution will have the broadest candidate base from which to select. This book will help selection committees avoid the pitfalls that can slow their progress. Dr. Lee has done a fine job of making smart selection processes accessible to committee members and the employers who rely on the fruits of their work."

—Cheryl Crozier Garcia, Professor,
Human Resource Management and Program Chair, MAHRM Program,
Hawaii Pacific University

Faculty Mentoring
A Practical Manual for Mentors, Mentees, Administrators, and Faculty Developers
Susan L. Phillips and Susan T. Dennison
Foreword by Milton D. Cox

This book provides step-by-step guidelines for setting up, planning, and facilitating mentoring programs for new faculty members, whether one-on-one, or using a successful group model developed and refined over 25 years by the authors. While it offers detailed guidance on instituting such programs at the departmental level, it also makes the case for establishing school- or institutional-level programs, and delineates the considerable benefits and economies of scale these can achieve.

The authors provide guidance for mentors and mentees on developing group mentoring and individual mentor–protégé relationships (the corresponding chapters being available online for separate purchase), as well as detailed outlines and advice to department chairs, administrators, and facilitators on how to establish and conduct institution-wide group mentoring programs and apply or modify the material to meet their specific needs.

Getting Culture
Incorporating Diversity Across the Curriculum
Edited by Regan A. R. Gurung and Loreto R. Prieto

"This volume's editors have compiled a set of wide-ranging tools for teaching about diversity among diverse student populations. Articles cover an array of topics, including general approaches to diversity education, specific exercises within and across disciplines, and strategies for coping with

(Continued on preceding page)

Also available from Stylus

The New Talent Acquisition Frontier
Integrating HR and Diversity Strategy in the Private and Public Sectors and Higher Education
Edna Chun and Alvin Evans
Forewords by Andy Brantley and Dr. Benjamin D. Reese Jr.

"The demographic transformation of society compels leaders to adapt. This book makes the business case for integrated diversity and HR initiatives and shows how many sectors, whether public or private and including higher education, can learn from one another. This book is an excellent synthesis of research and original case studies that provides an excellent start for all of us. Those who would lead would be well served by reading this volume."

—Frank H. Wu,
Chancellor & Dean, University of California Hastings College of Law

Search Committees
A Comprehensive Guide to Successful Faculty, Staff, and Administrative Searches
Second Edition
Christopher D. Lee, PhD, SPHR
Foreword by Edna Chun

"Whether you are chairing your first search committee or your tenth, you will learn something important from this book. Emphasizing how to hire strategically and diversely, Dr. Christopher D. Lee gives detailed advice and proposes sound practices. Who knew, for instance, that the cost to hire a faculty member for 30 years comes to about $3 million, a fact that should give committees pause as they decide whether an applicant should be offered an interview? *Search Committees* will be of tremendous benefit to anyone involved in the academic search process, from board chairs to HR professionals and faculty members."

—Carol M. Bresnahan,
Vice President for Academic Affairs and Provost,
Rollins College

"The work of selecting new faculty, staff, and administrative colleagues is very challenging. Often, it is performed by committees made up of deeply concerned individuals for whom human capital issues are not part of their daily work. That's why this book is so important. Dr. Christopher Lee demystifies the work of selection committees—both for those who are asked

(Continued on preceding page)